GOURMET

L·I·G·H·T

"This book may well present one of the most innovative (and seemingly painless) ways yet to diet. Underwood bases her calorie-cutting system on 10 cooking techniques. . . . Underwood proves herself to be an imaginative cook whose recipes are well worth noting."
  —*Publishers Weekly*

"Her recipes for all courses of a meal are pretty and elegant, like a pale cauliflower soup garnished with a swirl of yellow pepper and basil puree."
  —*Library Journal*

"At last—a book that shows how to take a basic recipe and cut down its calories by reducing fattening ingredients without totally changing its taste."
  —*ALA Booklist*

Recipe with credit ran in "BerryGood" article
  —*Shape* magazine, July 1986

"Greer Underwood wrote **Gourmet Light** not as a weight-loss manual but as a collection of techniques and recipes aimed at *prevention* of weight gain for lovers of fine food."
  —*Woman's Day*

"A guide to cutting the calories without cutting the good taste. . . . The food is lighter, but definitely not short of taste."
  —*Richmond (VA) Times-Dispatch*

". . . For those who want to cut down rather than cut out."
  —The *Washington Post*

"(The recipes) call for French cooking techniques but are 'lightened' with special cooking methods that cut in half the calorie content of traditional gourmet meals."
  —*Tufts University Diet & Nutrition Letter*

"For lots more tips and recipes on cooking leaner, we like Greer Underwood's *Gourmet Light*."
  —*Mademoiselle*

"Offers a ten-step plan for improving your diet, and gives nouvelle-style recipes and complete menus for a variety of occasions."
  —Bruce Jenner's *Better Health & Living* magazine

GOURMET
L·I·G·H·T

Simple and Sophisticated Recipes
for the Calorie-Conscious Cook

by GREER UNDERWOOD

Illustrated by Frank Westerberg

The Globe Pequot Press

CHESTER, CONNECTICUT

Nutritional Analysis
by Frances Stern Nutrition Center

Library of Congress Cataloging in Publication Data

Underwood, Greer.
Gourmet light.

Includes index.
1. Low-calorie diet — Recipes. I. Title.
RM222.2.U54 1985   641.5'635   85-9986
ISBN 0-87106-872-9

Manufactured in the United States of America
Cover and book design by Barbara Marks
Cover photography by Georgiana Silk
First Edition/4th Printing

Shown on front cover:
Veal Chops with Red Pepper Butter, page 136
Asparagus Mimosa, page 232
Pea Pod and Water Chestnut Salad
with Sherry Ginger Dressing, page 113
Candied Oranges with Melba Sauce, page 289

Acknowledgments

❖

This book is hardly the work of a single person despite the credit on the cover. The know-how of a lot of people is bound between these covers; were it not for them it would never be done. Thanks to all, and to Cary Hull for her enthusiastic guidance. And for their contributions of another sort, thanks to my three guys.

Contents

❖

Introduction:

The Calorie-Conscious Cook

❖

These are exercise-crazed yet food-happy times. Never have so many Americans panted and pumped their way to visions of physical perfection. And never have so many been interested in food and its paraphernalia—an irony peculiar to this running-shoe era. The culinary consciousness of the last decade, like the national devotion to exercise, has grown more rapidly than a croissant can rise. The challenge of the times is to enjoy the one without compromising the other.

Fitness is more than physical, it's a healthy psyche as well as a strong body. It's a vitality of body and spirit that can't be nurtured on an inadequate diet. One too rich in calories or too poor in nutrients defeats all that hard work. As eaters one and all, we have our homework to do. The basics of nutrition are as foreign to most of us as the intricacies of a silicon chip. While we wouldn't try to build a computer without knowing how one works, we often try to build our bodies on a similar lack of knowledge. Of the three classifications of food, proteins, carbohydrates, and fats, which do you think nutritionists recommend should make up the bulk of our daily diet? And the second? Most experts agree carbohydrates should account for slightly more than half (53 percent), fats for a bit more than a third (35 percent), and the proteins the remaining 22 percent.

You may think your daily fat intake is decidely below that 35 percent figure. Yet in this century, according to the Food and Nutrition Board of the National Academy of Sciences, fat intake has risen from 32 percent to 42 percent of our daily intake, probably due to the excessive use of fats, oils, and to some degree, meat. We have one of the highest fat content diets in the world. It lurks in most everything we eat, from avocados to zwieback, making a 100 percent fat-free diet as impossible as it is unhealthful. With our burgeoning culinary curiosity and fat intake, it makes sense to cut calorie corners where we can—without diluting our pleasure or endangering our health.

Voicing a concern about calories or vitamins was once the province of health food faddists, the type who would forage for wild nuts and berries rather than eat anything a machine had touched. Today, the cook who is unconcerned with overprocessed foodstuffs, nutritionally empty foods, and calories is the rarity. We're learning about the foods we eat even as we begin to hanker for pâté instead of meat loaf. Many are finding it difficult to indulge their love of fine food and maintain a healthy respect for the body. This book will point the way.

Thinking Thin

Is your life a revolving cycle of Spartan restraint followed by hedonistic indulgence? Do you diet successfully for a week or two, denying all pleasures, then binge on goodies? Is a hot fudge sundae your idea of a reward for losing weight?

If you answered yes to all of the above, you're probably still looking for a way to lose weight. The most successful dieters are those who don't. Don't binge diet, that is. They enjoy good food, in moderation, every day. They are aware of calorie counts in common foods. They know that there is no such thing as a skinny food, that only water is calorie-free. And they are active people, not necessarily marathon runners, but people who stand when they can sit, walk instead of ride, climb stairs, and shun elevators. Successful dieters know, at least intuitively, that taking fat off via exercise and semi-starvation is much harder than not eating to begin with.

Consider this: A 120-pound person running an eight-minute mile expends about 82 calories per mile; a 160 pounder will use about 110 calories. That's the calorie equivalent of an apple for the lighter runner, or a glass of low-fat milk for the heavier one. Nutritionists estimate that a pound of fat represents about 3,500 calories your body didn't use. Assuming you can exercise off 100 calories for every mile run, it would take 11 or 12 days to lose a pound of fat running 3 miles every day. Disheartening, isn't it? In light of these figures (and your own), thinking thin is more than a state of mind, it must be a mode of life.

What Gourmet Light is

To be a winner at the weight-loss game means educating yourself about the basics of metabolism and nutrition. It means learning how to eat to satisfy your hunger and learning how to cook to satisfy your appetite. This is a cookbook, an everyday guide to good, healthful eating habits. Many of you don't need to lose a pound, but you are looking for ways to eat well and maintain your happy weight state.

Gourmet Light is for those who enjoy fine food, but keep a calorie-conscious eye peeled. This is a cookbook for people who exercise not only for the sport of it but because it feels good also. This is also a cookbook for people who plan to exercise but can never quite fit it in, people looking for viable ways to trim extra calories from their daily meals. This is for those who like to keep abreast of food trends, from sun-dried tomatoes to shitake mushrooms, and for people who relish a meal not only for what it is, but also for what it is not.

Herein the reader will find information on nutrition, metabolism, the role of fats, proteins, and carbohydrates and, of course, good reduced-calorie recipes. You'll find out what pot to buy for which task, how to store foods, and sources for hard-to-come-by ingredients. There are short soliloquies on everything from how to peel an artichoke to the virtues of extra-virgin olive oil. Because not everyone is a seasoned cook, the recipes are thorough and detailed. If you already know your way around the kitchen, this book will teach you how to reduce calories in many of the dishes you now prepare, as well as give you some new and delicious ideas. When the ten techniques of *Gourmet Light* cooking become as natural to you as boiling water, you'll be able to pare calories from many of your favorite dishes.

This is not meant to be the only cookbook you'll ever need, for there are decidedly occasions when a no-stops, full-calorie-ahead, four-star dinner is in order. This is a way of cooking for everyday sort of use that you can live with happily, for a lifetime. Learn to pare a few superfluous calories from your daily "bread" and those strident days of diet may become a thing of the past.

What it is not

This is not a diet manual. No promise here of pounds lost in two easy weeks, no ersatz ingredients, no forbidden food lists. Avoidance, yes, but you won't have to take the pledge with *Gourmet Light* cooking. Wine, spirits, butter, and beef are all used, but in moderation.

It's tempting when writing a reduced-calorie cookbook to imply that all manner of foods can be prepared in such a way as to render them skinny. Not so. You'll find a Mimosa Sherbet but not ice creams. You'll enjoy Duck Breast with Zinfandel Sauce, but neither the accompanying wild rice, nor the sauce itself, is aswim in butter. Many dishes can be rewritten to remove excessive calories; those that can not simply aren't here. The aim was not to make do but to do well, and if that couldn't be done the recipe wasn't included. There is a place for plenty of fresh unsalted butter, for swirls of whipped cream, and well-marbled beef, but it is not here. Instead, indulge in Sole and Crab Peppers, Chilled Tomato Soup with Tarragon Ice, Turkey Cutlet with Cranberried Apple Sauce, and finish with a smooth Mango Mousse. Here are the techniques of good cooking without excessive use of highly fatty, cholesterol-choked foods.

How it came to be

Internationally, the French have always been acclaimed for turning out the world's best chefs, and it is to them we have turned for decades to decree what's new. When they threw away the flour bin, reaching instead for the stockpot and mounds of butter, we followed (or at least au courant restaurants did). When they threw the vegetables into the food processor creating smooth purees, we did too. When they started undercooking not only beef, but also lamb and fish, we at least agreed the beef should be very rare, and many started enjoying lamb that way, too. If they said "Pirouette!" we obliged like good students. They taught us haute cuisine, they brought us nouvelle cuisine, and they introduced cuisine minceur, the "skinny" cooking of Michel Guerard. One hears little of cuisine minceur these days, mostly because it is time-consuming and expensive to duplicate in the average kitchen, but I would be amiss not to mention what was a large inspiration for this book. I had long believed that good food didn't have to be fattening and that thin food didn't have to be boring, and had worked on ideas to that effect. But it was the international interest in Guerard's cuisine minceur that led me to believe others were looking for good, but not fattening, food. Guerard's cuisine minceur is not for the single-person kitchen or even for the American kitchen, calling for such delicacies as squab and spiny lobster. But it is a volume to which I still go to browse.

Food today in France and the United States has been strongly influenced by nouvelle cuisine as outlined by Guerard, Paul Bocuse, and other French chefs. There are fewer red meats; fish and poultry predominate. There is a greater emphasis on vegetables and how food looks. Sauces are lighter, not to be confused with thinner, for they're enriched with oodles of butter and cream rather than flour. Portions are smaller. The grill is in. Precious and often hard-to-find ingredients such as radicchio, yellow and eggplant-hued peppers, and bonsai (miniaturized) vegetables reign.

In the United States there is a newfound pride in our native foods and chefs, less dependence on the grand masters—a surge of independence. Everyone is talking about the new American cuisine, its dedication to simplicity, homegrown ingredients, and the home-town talent responsible for it. Although when one sees a recipe that typifies the new cuisine such as Chèvre-Stuffed Chicken Breast with Wild Mushroom Sauce I sometimes wonder just who redefined simplicity. Perhaps the crux of the matter is best explained by the French gastronome and cook, Raymond Oliver, who wrote, "To innovate in cooking it is more difficult to attack a boiled egg than a pheasant mousse." Cooks have long known it is easier to elaborate than delineate, easier to pile luxury on excess than improve on the ordinary. Nevertheless, the new American cuisine remains true to its indigenous roots—namely plain food, in the sense of native products such as corn, grits, buckwheat, and maple syrup are coming into their own again. Our chefs are becoming the trendsetters in a field heretofore dominated by Europeans.

Gourmet Light cooking includes a bit of all these trends, for it is a product of our times. Its soul lies in French techniques, lightened in the spirit of the day and using the very freshest and best our native seas and lands have to offer—but always with an eye on the scale. So, enjoy!

RECOMMENDED DAILY DIETARY ALLOWANCES OF SOME NUTRIENTS

Age	Weight	Height	Calories per day	Protein, g	Vit. A, IU**	Vit. C, mg	Thiamin, mg	Vit. B$_6$	Riboflavin, mg	Calcium, mg*	Phosphorus, mg	Iron, mg	Zinc
Females													
19-22	120	64 in.	2100	44	4,000	60	1.1	2.0	1.3	800	800	18	15
23-50			2000	44	4,000	60	1.0	2.0	1.2	800	800	18	15
51+			1800	44	4,000	60	1.0	2.0	1.2	800	800	10	15
Males													
19-22	154	70 in.	2900	56	5,000	60	1.5	2.2	1.7	800	800	10	15
23-50			2700	56	5,000	60	1.4	2.2	1.6	800	800	10	15
51+			2400	56	5,000	60	1.2	2.2	1.4	800	800	10	15

Carbohydrates and fats: Recommended dietary allowance for carbohydrates and fats has not been established. It is recommended that 30 to 35 percent of the day's total calories come from fats, and 50 to 55 percent from carbohydrates.

Cholesterol: The American Heart Association recommends limiting cholesterol to 300 mg/day.

Sodium: There is no recommended dietary allowance for sodium. An individual's need depends on physical activity and exposure to high temperatures. The estimated safe and adequate intake is between 1.1 to 3.3 grams/day for adults.

*The Food and Nutrition Board may raise this recommendation.
**IU = International Unit

Food & Nutrition Board
National Academy of Sciences, Revised, 1980

About the Recipes

❖

1. For better flavor and to keep the sodium level of a recipe low, I recommend you use unsalted butter whenever butter is called for. Our nutritional analysis of these recipes was based on unsalted butter.
2. To further reduce sodium, use homemade stocks made without salt instead of canned products.
3. Skim milk has 60 percent fewer calories than whole milk. Take advantage of this in your cooking.
4. You can save on calories by using aerosol cooking sprays, but to avoid a possible fire, never spray them near a heat source.
5. Carefully read each recipe before beginning to cook to avoid the disappointment of lacking a necessary ingredient or piece of equipment. If you envision each step as you read it, the actual preparation will be greatly simplified. If you're new to cooking and making more than one recipe at a time, make yourself a brief timetable. I remember one enthusiastic student breezing into cooking class with the proud announcement that he had cooked the previous week's menu for his appreciative wife. "How was it?" we all wanted to know. "Great," he beamed, "the only problem was the flaming bananas were done before the steak, and the potatoes were done after both of them!" Timing is one of the most difficult things for a budding cook to get the hang of. But planning and practice bring results.
6. When possible, instructions have been given for what may be done ahead, and what needs last-minute doing. Freezing information is also given, where feasible.
7. Saute sometimes appears as "saute" for the cook is actually boiling the food in a small amount of liquid rather than frying it in fat.

Chapter 1
THE PRIMER

The Primer

***

The Primer is perhaps the most important chapter in this book, for here are the ten techniques of *Gourmet Light* cooking. Once you've mastered them, paring calories from most any recipe will become automatic. Nothing here is tricky or requires culinary expertise; anyone who can separate an egg can cook—deliciously—the thin way. Success rests on your resolve to think thin, always looking for ways to cheat a dish of excessive calories but not at the expense of flavor.

This Primer will teach you how to cut down on the overuse of butter, fats, oils, and calorie-heavy flour thickenings. You'll discover how some readily available and inexpensive kitchen equipment can make you a winner at the calorie game. And you can have some fun testing your calorie IQ.

So hone up those knives, and fill your kitchen with appetizing aromas fat only with flavor and happy cooking!

Getting Started

***

Not convinced? Think the only way to watch your weight is to go on a celery and water regime for a few days? Perhaps the following tallies will give you pause. The same meal, one prepared the traditional way and one the *Gourmet Light* way. Both are good, but which would you choose?

The Traditional Meal

Gazpacho, made with oil and croutons	157 calories/cup
Sauteed sole (6 oz) with Hollandaise	425 calories
Asparagus Mimosa (1 cup)	115 calories
Mixed-Green Salad with Vinaigrette	135 calories
Apple Pie	404 calories
	TOTAL 1236 calories

The Gourmet Light Meal

Gazpacho (limited oil, no croutons)	90 calories/cup
Steamed sole (6 oz), Reduced-Calorie Hollandaise	229 calories
Asparagus Mimosa (1 cup)	65 calories
Mixed-Green Salad with Herbed French Vinaigrette	50 calories
Hot Apple Tart	145 calories
	TOTAL 579 calories

Cooking the *Gourmet Light* way is no more difficult than any other. It takes only the resolve to want to change a few habits, the knowledge of what to change, and a nodding acquaintance with calorie counts. Why not test your Calorie IQ right now with the quiz below? And then on to the stove! (Or do you have to exercise first?)

Check Your Calorie IQ

You can't play the game until you know how to score. Calorie awareness is the key to weight control. While it's not necessary to carry a pocket calorie guide, it is sensible to have a working knowledge of some basic calorie facts. Check your calorie IQ here.

TRUE or FALSE
1. A glass of soda water and a glass of tonic water have about the same number of calories
2. A handful of Pepperidge Farm Goldfish have roughly the same number of calories as an equal amount of peanuts.
3. Low-fat milk has about half the calories of whole milk.

4. A banana, a half-cup of dried lima beans, and a baked potato have about the same number of calories.
5. A 4-ounce serving of poached salmon has fewer calories than a 4-ounce serving of lean broiled steak.
6. An apple has more calories than a cup of popcorn.
7. A tablespoon of honey has more nutrients and is lower in calories than a tablespoon of sugar.

CIRCLE THE FOOD LOWER IN CALORIES
8. A 5-ounce piece of steamed haddock seasoned with parsley, dill, and lemon or 1 deviled egg.
9. A tablespoon of vegetable oil, margarine, or butter.
10. A cup of cottage cheese or a chocolate-coated ice cream bar.
11. A McDonald's Fillet o'Fish sandwich or a McDonald's hamburger.
12. A veal chop or a piece of pizza.
13. A half-cup serving of chocolate pudding, a cup of New England—style clam chowder, or 1 cup of fruited yogurt.

THE ANSWERS
1. False. Tonic water, which is sweetened, contains about 70 calories in an 8-ounce glass; soda water contains none.
2. False. A half-ounce of Pepperidge Farm Goldfish contains about 59 calories; a half-ounce of oil-roasted peanuts contains about 90 calories.
3. False. One percent low-fat milk contains about 100 calories a cup; whole milk contains about 160. Low-fat milk with 2 percent fat has as much as 145 calories a cup. Skim milk contains about 90 calories per cup.
4. False. The potato and the banana each have about 90 calories; dried lima beans, a half-cup serving, contain as much as 131 calories.
5. True. But the difference is much smaller than you might think. The salmon, a relatively fatty fish, has about 246 calories for 4 ounces; the beef, with visible fat removed, about 272.
6. True. An apple contains about 80 calories; the popcorn, 23 calories, salted but unbuttered.

7. False. A tablespoon of honey has 61 calories; a tablespoon of sugar has 46. Honey does supply a very small amount of potassium.
8. The haddock has about 112 calories in 5 ounces; the egg, made with 1 tablespoon of mayonnaise, has 180 calories.
9. All the same, approximately 100 calories per tablespoon.
10. A 2½-ounce bar of chocolate-coated ice cream has 147; the cottage cheese has 240 calories a cup.
11. The McDonald's burger has 257 calories; the fish sandwich, 407. Although the fish is lower in calories than the beef, the frying and the mayonnaise used in the sandwich make up the extra 150 calories.
12. One-eighth of a 14-inch size, home recipe of a sausage pizza has about 176 calories; a veal chop about 300.
13. The New England–style chowder has 157 calories, the pudding 192, the fruited yogurt about 260.

11–13 correct	highest honors
8-10 correct	honor roll
5-7 correct	passing grade
0-4 correct	it's study time

This is not to suggest that those interested in losing pounds or maintaining their weight should opt for a chocolate-coated ice cream bar instead of cottage cheese, or pizza instead of a veal chop. Its intent is to point out some commonly held misconceptions and myths; fish is *not* automatically low in calories, how it's prepared is essential. There are several vegetables more fattening than potatoes, and butter is not more fattening than margarine. A paperback calorie guide is good reading for anyone interested in weight control.

Here are the ten techniques of *Gourmet Light* cooking. Digest them and say good-by to diets forever.

The Ten Techniques
of Gourmet Light Cooking

❖

1. "Saute" in stocks, broths, and wine instead of fats and oils

When a recipe calls for butter and/or oil for the sauteing of onions, garlic, shallots, and so on, substitute stock, broth, or wine or a combination for calorie-free cooking. Add enough liquid to cover the bottom of the pan by about one-eighth inch, bring to a boil, add food to be "sauteed," cover, and reduce heat to medium. Stir frequently, adding more liquid should it evaporate before the food is cooked.

2. Replace heavy cream with skim or low fat milk

The importance of using milk, either whole, low fat, or skim, is best stressed by the figures (pun intended):

Skim milk made from dry solids	80 calories/cup
Skim milk	90 to 100 calories/cup
Low fat milk with 2 percent nonfat milk solids	130 calories/cup
Whole milk	150 calories/cup
Half-and-half	300 calories/cup
Light cream	480 calories/cup
Heavy cream	800 calories/cup

How many calories you want to save will determine which of these dairy products you use. My recipes specify milk; whether you choose whole, skim, low-fat, or reconstituted from dry solids is your decision. Should you opt for the latter, remember this: Dry milk doesn't have to be chilled for cooking purposes, but reduce cooking temperatures somewhat, for this product scorches more easily than whole milk. A nutritional aside: Cooking with skim or whole milk supplies almost twice the amount of protein found in cream.

3. Reducing and replacing oil in salad dressings

When a skinny bowl of greens is lavished with 2 tablespoons of regular dressing, the result is a caloric avalanche of at least 200 calories. If you eat but 5 salads a week, it will only take 3 1/2 weeks for that dressing to be a pound of fat. Why not reduce or even eliminate much of the oil used in dressings with a skinny alternative? The unlikely but excellent surrogate is chicken stock (the kind you make yourself) or canned beef consomme. Why homemade? Why the consomme and not just canned broth? Both the canned consomme and your own homemade stock contain enough gelatin—one occurring naturally as the collagen in the bones melts, the other added—to somewhat duplicate the natural viscosity of oil. Another very acceptable alternative is enriched commercial broth; instructions may be found on page 18. Stock-based salad dressings are light, flavorful, and nutritious.

4. Thickening with cornstarch and arrowroot instead of flour

Although the current culinary trend, popularized by nouvelle cuisine, is to thicken sauces by reduction (that is, boiling down), it is occasionally necessary to thicken a soup, stew, or classic sauce such as a mornay by means of a starch—either flour, arrowroot, or cornstarch. Note these measures for the *same* thickening ability:

3 teaspoons flour (1 tablespoon)	50 calories
2 teaspoons cornstarch	20 calories
1 teaspoon arrowroot	15 calories

Arrowroot and cornstarch (you may also use potato starch) give a shiny, translucent quality to a sauce, flour gives a more opaque look. Both arrowroot and cornstarch must be dissolved in a little cold liquid before using, and if heated too long or brought to a boil, a sauce thickened with arrowroot or cornstarch may liquefy, a process called hydrolizing. Always keep foods with these starches added to them on moderate heat to avoid this.

5. The magic of crème blanc

Sometime in my early twenties I became aware of the omnipotent presence of the calorie god. Now every morsel I ate and drank seemed to get counted whereas before it had gone unnoticed. As a child, I yearned for the independence of adulthood, only to find it came harnessed with responsibility. Mother didn't make me finish eating liver anymore, but that didn't mean I was free to eat potato chips for dinner either. To escape the calorie god's ever watchful eye, I became a constant calorie counter, being careful not to overindulge. To avoid the boredom of diet foods, I experimented in the kitchen a great deal, developing the cooking style you find here. One wonderful way I found to cheat the calorie god at his own game was crème blanc, a mixture of cottage cheese and yogurt used in place of sour cream and sometimes butter, which adds a touch of finesse and variety. You'll find out how to make it on page 37.

6. Retaining the natural moisture in foods

It may seem redundant to stress the importance of buying fresh foods in a day when processed foods are as "in" as a beehive hairdo, but natural flavors are so vital to the success of *Gourmet Light* cooking that it can't be stressed enough. Second only to buying the best is to select the cooking method that most retains the natural moisture in foods, reducing, even eliminating, the need for fats, oils, and rich sauces. Here are suggestions in no particular order of importance.

a. *Parchment paper, aluminum foil, and wax paper*—By encasing the food in an envelope, evaporation is greatly reduced and the food stews in its own juices, creating a natural sauce. Lettuce, cabbage leaves, and cornhusks may also be used.

b. *Salt-encased cooking*—This very old method of cooking is excellent for roasting large pieces of meat, fish, or poultry to juicy perfection. The food is encased in a paste of coarse salt and water, forming an inedible crust that is cracked open and discarded after roasting. Oddly the salt doesn't permeate the food; because of the salt, the moisture in the food isn't lost.

c. *Poaching*—The term means to immerse a food in a simmering liquid. Poaching is generally reserved for poultry, but lamb and even beef can be deliciously poached. For oven poaching the food is placed in a film of liquid, covered with aluminum foil or wax paper, and roasted; it's excellent for chicken breasts.

d. *Steaming*—Using either a cake rack, Chinese bamboo steamer, or metal basket with folding sides, the steaming of fish, poultry, and vegetables is much used in *Gourmet Light* cooking.

e. *Grilling*—This watchword of the new American cooking is ideal for our purposes, for foods pick up the added flavor of the smoke and cook with a minimum of added fats.

7. Pureeing vegetables

This darling of nouvelle cuisine, which like so many trends is really a revival more than a discovery, is an excellent way to add variety and create a richly satisfying dish without butter. Pureeing vegetables, either alone or in creative combinations, is best accomplished in a food processor, but it can be done using a food mill or ricer.

8. Desserts

Because *Gourmet Light* cooking doesn't use saccharin or other ersatz substitutions, most of the desserts in this book rely on the natural sweetness of fruits. You will find recipes for them poached in wine, iced, or pureed. There are also recipes that use reduced amounts of sugar. But taste was always the deciding factor: If a reduced-sugar recipe tasted like something was missing, it wasn't included here.

9. Presentation

Presentation is important because I've always felt cooking is a little bit of art; its visual appeal is nearly as important to me as its sapidity. But spending precious time carving radish roses and lemon baskets is best left to well-staffed kitchens. Mine, as I suspect yours is, is most often a one-person show. So presentation for me has come to mean simple garnishes, minced fresh parsley, twisted lemon slices, a grating of carrot, or a snippet of chive. It means taking care to wipe away a dribble of sauce and arranging the food on the plate or platter with an eye toward color and order. Nor is presentation an afterthought. It rightly belongs up-front during menu planning when you consider not just what tastes good together, but what looks good together as well. And while considering color contrasts, don't overlook texture, what I call "toothsomeness." Pair something hard with something soft, something crisp with something creamy. The art of cooking doesn't stop at the stove, it is part of both the conception and the presentation, and all the workings in between. Cooking is a pragmatic art, a personal expression that brings pleasure and satisfaction. Do with these recipes as *you* will, your creative input will make them work for you.

10. Equipment for reduced-calorie cooking

The cook who wants to incorporate the *Gourmet Light* way into his or her cooking style may like to investigate the following:

a. *Cooking sprays*—There are a few aerosol sprays on the market that grease a pan while adding only minimal calories. You could probably accomplish the same by dipping a pastry brush or paper towel in oil and rubbing it on the pan surface. Naturally, you won't achieve perfect browning, but foods won't stick if cooked at moderate heat.

b. *Teflon- and Silverstone-coated pans*—Although it is difficult to brown foods in these pots and pans, they do allow high heat searing and cooking without sticking. I recommend owning at least an 8-inch skillet.

c. *Degreaser*—Looking like a measuring cup with the spout coming off the bottom, degreasers have become widely available of late. They are excellent for separating fats from soups, broths, and sauces.

d. *Ice cream maker*—A luxury item useful for creating fruit ices and sherbets.

e. *Parchment paper*—Covered in Technique 6, parchment and wax papers allow food to cook without losing precious juices to evaporation.

f. *Chinese bamboo steamer*—Also covered in Technique 6, this inexpensive and useful contraption allows you to cook a whole meal in one pot.

g. *Immersion blenders*—Immersion blenders are like mechanically powered whisks. They make it possible to whip milk and are advantageous for persons with arthritis.

h. *Grill*—Also listed under Technique 6, indoor or outdoor grills allow for fat-free cooking with maximum flavor.

Chapter 2

THE FOUNDATIONS: STOCKS AND SAUCES

The Foundations

❖

We've covered the ten techniques that can help you to lose or maintain weight loss without depriving yourself the enjoyment of good food. The following are the foundations upon which this cooking style is built: the stocks, or enriched commercial products, reduced-calorie egg sauces—Hollandaise, Béarnaise, and mayonnaise—wine sauce, cheese sauce, basil-walnut sauce, and more.

Taking Stock

❖

Because stocks and broths are used extensively in *Gourmet Light* cooking, you might like to make your own in quantity, freezing this indispensable ingredient in plastic containers for future use. Although making stock is a lengthy process (four hours for chicken, eight hours minimum for beef), it is not time spent entirely over a hot stove. The preparation time is about 20 minutes, cleanup time about the same. Canned broths may be used or enriched with additional bones and/or vegetables if added flavor or thickness is desired. Commercially prepared consomme is an excellent alternative, because the added gelatin nicely equates the natural thickness of a homemade stock.

If you decide to make your own stock, you'll need at least a 12-quart stockpot; making any less is a waste of time in my opinion.

Although a heavy pot is preferable as it will prevent vegetables from scorching on the bottom and ruining the stock, a thin pot is considerably less expensive and fine for a trial run; a lobster steamer is ideal. It's also good to have some old, thin kitchen towels for straining or you'll need to purchase cheesecloth at a hardware store or in the cleaning department of the grocery store.

Because of the high concentration of proteins, homemade stock should be frozen if not used within 48 hours. Fish stock must be frozen if not used within 24 hours of preparation. Always boil stock a minute or so before using, too. Freeze stock in plastic containers, so you can defrost quickly by placing the container in simmering water or under hot water. When the block is loosened, slip it into a saucepan, cover, and turn heat to medium high. Frozen stock will keep without flavor loss for up to one year. If you use a variety of sizes of freezer containers, you can just reach for the size you need, rather than have to thaw more than necessary.

Although the clarity of a stock is simply a matter of aesthetics and won't affect the flavor of a finished dish, here are some tips for producing jewel-clear stocks:

- scrape the scum that rises to the surface in the first hour of cooking
- once the boiling point is reached, reduce the heat so stock just simmers
- don't stir, this makes the stock cloudy (if you are using a thin pot, disregard this advice, better a cloudy stock than a burned one)
- if you add wine to the stock, don't use an aluminum pot or the stock will appear gray
- don't add starchy vegetables such as potatoes or cooked leftovers
  Here are some general hints about stocks:
- tomatoes added to a stock cause it to sour more readily, mushrooms darken it (handy for beef stock), and members of the cabbage family such as parsnips and turnips lend an unpleasant flavor
- keep uncooked beef and chicken bones in plastic bags in the freezer until you have enough to make the stock
- don't treat the stockpot like the garbage disposal, it is not a catchall for leftovers
- add no salt, this is done when seasoning the completed dish

Beef Stock

❖

8 pounds uncooked beef bones, marrow bones
   highly recommended
3 carrots, sliced (no need to peel)
3 small to medium onions, sliced (no need to peel,
   the skins add color)
3 celery stalks, sliced
7 quarts water
1 cup red wine (optional)
a small handful fresh parsley stems, chopped
freshly ground pepper to taste
1 bay leaf
1 garlic clove, halved

1. Put the bones in a large roasting pan with the carrots, onions, and celery, and roast about 40–50 minutes in a 400-degree oven, or until the bones and vegetables are beginning to brown.
2. Strain away and discard the fat. Put the bones and vegetables in a 12-quart stockpot, cover with the water, add the wine, and bring to a full boil.
3. Reduce heat to a simmer and scrape the scum that rises to the surface with a slotted spoon. Repeat scrapings two or three times until most of the scum is removed.
4. Add parsley, pepper, bay leaf, and garlic. Half cover the pan and simmer about 8 hours, adding more water if the volume falls more than a quart below the original.
5. Wring out an old kitchen towel or a piece of cheesecloth in cold water and line a strainer with it. Pour or ladle the stock through the strainer.
6. If using the stock immediately, pour what you need into a degreaser to complete the defatting, or refrigerate the stock. A pan-

cake of fat will form that is easily scraped off. Freeze stock in plastic containers of various sizes.

Yield: 3½ to 4 quarts
Calories per cup: 18
Protein per cup: 1g

Fat per cup: 0
Carbohydrates per cup: 4g
Sodium per cup: 20mg

Meat Glaze (Glacé de Viande)

Like an expensive perfume, meat glaze is used sparingly — a little goes a long way. Half a teaspoon stirred into sauces or soups boosts the flavor without making its presence known. It is truly a chef's secret. A commercial alternative is meat extract or concentrated beef-flavored broth, usually available in the gourmet section of the supermarket or at specialty food shops. Use half the amount of the commercial as you would the homemade; it tends to be salty.

Simply boil 3 quarts of homemade or bone-enriched commercial beef stock down to 1½ cups of iridescent, deep brown syrup. It should be thick enough to coat a metal spoon.

Meat glaze will keep in the refrigerator in a sterile glass container for about two weeks. After that a harmless mold may form that can be scraped away. Or freeze the glaze in ice cube trays and pop them into plastic bags when frozen. Thaw the cubes in a small, covered saucepan with a tablespoon of water.

Yield: 1½ cups
Calories per tablespoon: 9
Protein per tablespoon: 0

Fat per tablespoon: 0
Carbohydrates per tablespoon: 2g
Sodium per tablespoon: 10mg

Veal Stock

Veal stock is made as beef stock is, simply using veal bones for beef bones. However, it is so difficult for the home cook to obtain veal bones that I don't call for it in this book. Should you have a ready supply of veal bones, you'll find it works wonderfully whenever beef or chicken stock is called for.

Chicken Stock

> 5–6 *pounds uncooked chicken bones (saved from boning breasts, or buy wings and backs)*
> 2–3 *carrots, sliced (no need to peel)*
> 2 *medium onions, sliced*
> 2 *celery stalks, sliced*
> 4 *quarts water*
> 1 *cup dry white wine (optional)*
> *a small handful fresh parsley stems, chopped*
> *freshly ground pepper to taste*
> 1 *bay leaf*
> 1 *garlic clove, halved*

1. A rich, brown chicken stock is made like the beef stock (see page 14), by browning the bones and vegetables in a 400-degree oven for about 40–50 minutes. Strain away and discard the fat. Place the browned bones and vegetables in a stockpot, cover with water, add the wine, and bring to a boil. Continue at Step 3.
2. A "white" stock is made by putting *un*roasted bones and vegeta-

bles in a 12-quart stockpot, cover with the water, and add the wine. Bring to a boil.

3. Reduce heat to a simmer and scrape the scum that rises to the surface with a slotted spoon. Repeat scrapings two or three times until most of the scum is removed.

4. Add the parsley, pepper, bay leaf, and garlic. Half cover the pan and simmer about 4 hours, adding more water if the volume falls more than a quart below the original.

5. Wring out an old kitchen towel or a piece of cheesecloth in water and line a strainer with it. Pour or ladle the stock through the strainer.

6. If using the stock immediately, pour what you need into a degreaser to complete the defatting, or refrigerate until a pancake of fat forms. Scrape off the fat and freeze the stock in plastic containers of varying sizes.

Yield: About 3 quarts
Calories per cup: 21
Protein per cup: 1g

Fat per cup: 0
Carbohydrates per cup: 4g
Sodium per cup: 20mg

❖ ICE CUBE STOCK ❖

Freeze homemade stock in ice cube trays and pop the frozen cubes into a plastic bag. Use when a few tablespoons of broth are called for to "saute" an ingredient.

Enriched Quick Commercial Beef or Chicken Broth

❖

½ pound uncooked beef or chicken bones
3 unpeeled carrots, sliced
1 onion, chopped
1 tablespoon oil (optional)
1 quart canned beef or chicken broth
½ cup red or white wine (optional)
1 bay leaf
1 clove garlic, halved
freshly ground pepper to taste
a small handful fresh parsley stems, chopped

1. If dark color is desired, brown the bones and vegetables in the oil in a covered skillet over high heat for about 6 minutes. Deglaze the skillet with 2 tablespoons wine (from the ½ cup).
2. For a "white" stock simply put all the ingredients in a 2½-quart saucepan, half cover, and simmer 30 minutes.
3. It may be used immediately after straining and discarding bones, vegetables, and herbs.

Yield: 3½ cups
Calories per cup: 126
Protein per cup: 7g

Fat per cup: 6g
Carbohydrates per cup: 12g
Sodium per cup: 923mg

Fish Stock

❖

This delicate stock must be frozen if not used within 24 hours.

> 1 fish rack (skeleton) weighing about 1 1/2 pounds
>   from a white-fleshed, nonoily fish such as
>   haddock or cod, innards removed and rack rinsed
> 6 cups water
> 2 cups dry white wine (optional)
> 1 small onion, chopped
> 1 small carrot, chopped
> 1 bay leaf

1. Put the fish rack (don't shy away from using the head, as it contains lots of collagen, which melts into gelatin) in a heavy pot, preferably nonaluminum if using the wine, and add the water and wine.
2. Bring to a boil, reduce heat so liquid just simmers, and scrape the scum away with a slotted spoon. When most of the scum is removed, add the remaining ingredients and half cover pot. Simmer 40 minutes.
3. Rinse out an old kitchen towel or a piece of cheesecloth in water, line a strainer with it, and pour or ladle stock through. Store in the refrigerator or freezer if not used within 24 hours.

Note: Bottled clam juice is a very acceptable substitute in recipes calling for fish stock. Dilute the bottled product with 1/4 cup dry white wine or vermouth to 8 ounces clam juice, and omit salt from the recipe.

Yield: Approximately 1 quart
Calories per cup: 33
Protein per cup: 1g

Fat per cup: 0
Carbohydrates per cup: 8g
Sodium per cup: 10mg

The Trademarks of Classic Cooking—Sauces

❖

The cynosures of fine cooking are frequently the sauces: lemony Hollandaise ribboning asparagus, rich and pungent Béarnaise complementing a flavorfully steamed fish, the cool richness of crème blanc offsetting a steamy bowl of beet soup. *Gourmet Light* cooking doesn't deny the lover of good food the pleasures of the table. Here, follow the reduced-calorie versions of such classic recipes.

Egg-Based Sauces

Egg-based sauces owe their creamy richness to the emulsion that forms when egg yolks poach in butter and an acid such as lemon juice (Hollandaise), vinegar (Béarnaise), or wine. My thin versions of these classic sauces use chicken stock for the majority of the butter, but are otherwise the same. You'll find them packed with flavor that belies their lightness, and you'll be happy to note that they may be prepared ahead and gently reheated with little danger of curdling or separating.

The *Gourmet Light* version of the classic Hollandaise is a great favorite in my kitchen, because it is much less fattening (34 calories per tablespoon compared to 80 calories for the traditional recipe), tastes lighter, holds better than the traditional sauce, and may even be gently reheated. It is wonderful on eggs, poultry, fish, and vegetables, and with the addition of a bit of mustard, terrific with lamb as well. Note the range of uses with a slight variation in ingredients.

Regardless of the method you choose, direct heat or blender, remember Hollandaise and its cousin Béarnaise were never meant to be served hot, just warmed. Should you accidentally heat the sauce beyond 140 degrees, causing it to separate or break, put a teaspoon of acid (lemon for Hollandaise, vinegar for Béarnaise) in a food processor or blender and slowly dribble in the sauce. It will form the emulsion again.

Hollandaise Sauce
DIRECT-HEAT METHOD

I prefer this method for it makes a thicker sauce more quickly. Choose a 1-quart heavy-bottomed saucepan; enamel over cast iron, lined copper, or anodized aluminum all are excellent pans.

> 4 tablespoons lemon juice
> ¾ cup chicken stock or canned broth
> 5 large egg yolks (whites may be frozen for another use)
> 2 tablespoons butter, melted
> ¼ teaspoon salt (optional)
> dash of cayenne pepper (optional)

1. In a small pan, combine the lemon juice and stock. Boil until reduced to ¾ cup. Cool slightly.
2. Beat the egg yolks with a whisk until foamy in the heavy-bottomed saucepan. Place on low heat and dribble in the chicken stock, whisking vigorously until the sauce thickens, about 2–3 minutes. Remove the saucepan from heat and whisk in the melted butter. Season with salt and cayenne, if desired. The sauce will thicken more on standing.

Yield: 1 cup
Calories per tablespoon: 34
Protein per tablespoon: 1g

Fat per tablespoon: 3g
Carbohydrates per tablespoon: 1g
Sodium per tablespoon: 5mg

Hollandaise Sauce
BLENDER OR FOOD PROCESSOR METHOD

❖

5 large egg yolks
5 tablespoons lemon juice
¾ cup chicken stock or canned broth
2 tablespoons butter, melted
½ teaspoon salt (optional)
dash of cayenne pepper (optional)

1. Place egg yolks and 1 tablespoon of the lemon juice in the bowl of the food processor or in the blender. Process 45 seconds.
2. Meanwhile, boil the remaining lemon juice and stock until reduced to ⅔ cup.
3. With the machine on high, dribble in broth and lemon juice.
4. Pour sauce into a heavy-bottomed 1-quart saucepan and whisk over low heat until sauce thickens, about 2–3 minutes. Whisk in the butter. Season with salt and cayenne pepper, if desired. The sauce will thicken more on standing.

Yield: 1 cup
Calories per tablespoon: 34
Protein per tablespoon: 1g

Fat per tablespoon: 3g
Carbohydrates per tablespoon: 1g
Sodium per tablespoon: 5mg

Hollandaise Variations

❖

1. Maltaise Sauce is a classic accompaniment for asparagus. Using the Hollandaise recipe, substitute orange juice for the lemon juice, adding 1 teaspoon lemon juice and a bit of grated orange rind to the finished sauce. (Or refer to the recipe for Asparagus Maltaise, page 233.)
2. A fabulous sauce for fish, cauliflower, asparagus, and broccoli, a classic Mousseline Sauce is made by folding ¼ cup heavy cream, which has already been whipped, into a finished Hollandaise. If you have an immersion blender, you can whip skim milk and fold it into our thin version of Hollandaise for a cloudlike sauce just this side of heaven.

❖ **THINKING THIN TIP** ❖

If you tire of lemon juice on vegetables, try the juice of an orange next time.

Béarnaise Sauce
DIRECT-HEAT METHOD

❖

Béarnaise is the classic sauce for grilled steaks and roasted tenderloins. It is equally good with grilled fish, chicken, and vegetables, too.

> 2 tablespoons red wine vinegar
> 1 tablespoon finely minced shallot
> 1 tablespoon fresh tarragon or 1 teaspoon dried
>   tarragon
> 4 large egg yolks
> 4 tablespoons chicken stock or broth
> 1–2 tablespoons butter, melted
> ¼ teaspoon salt (optional)
> freshly ground pepper to taste

1. In a 1-quart heavy-bottomed saucepan, combine the vinegar, shallot, and tarragon. Boil until reduced by half.
2. Put the egg yolks in a heavy-bottomed 1-quart saucepan and whisk until foamy over medium heat.
3. Dribble the reduced vinegar-shallot mixture into the egg yolks, whisking over low heat until foamy and slightly thickened. Remove from heat.
4. Heat the chicken stock until almost boiling.
5. Dribble chicken stock into egg-vinegar mixture over low heat. Whisk it until thickened. Whisk in butter. Season with salt and pepper. The sauce will thicken more on standing.

Yield: 1 cup
Calories per tablespoon: 21
Protein per tablespoon: 1g

Fat per tablespoon: 2g
Carbohydrates per tablespoon: 0
Sodium per tablespoon: 0

Béarnaise Sauce
FOOD PROCESSOR OR BLENDER METHOD

❖

2 tablespoons red wine vinegar
1 tablespoon finely minced shallot
1 tablespoon fresh tarragon or 1 teaspoon dried
    tarragon
4 large egg yolks
4 tablespoons chicken stock or canned chicken broth
1–2 tablespoons butter, melted
1/4 teaspoon salt (optional)
freshly ground pepper to taste

1. In a small saucepan, boil until reduced by half the vinegar, shallot, and tarragon.
2. Meanwhile, process the egg yolks in the blender or food processor until foamy.
3. Dribble the vinegar-tarragon mixture into the egg yolks, with the machine on high.
4. While the machine processes the yolks and vinegar, heat the chicken stock in the now-empty pan just to the boiling point.
5. Dribble the stock into the yolks while the machine is running.
6. Pour the sauce into the empty stock pan and whisk over medium-low heat until the sauce thickens. Whisk in butter. Adjust seasoning with salt and pepper. Sauce will be frothy and light, it will thicken on standing.

Yield: 1 1/4 cups
Calories per tablespoon: 21
Protein per tablespoon: 1g

Fat per tablespoon: 2g
Carbohydrates per tablespoon: 0
Sodium per tablespoon: 0

Béarnaise Variations

❖

1. Add 1 tablespoon tomato paste to the finished Béarnaise to make Sauce Robert. This is an excellent sauce with meats.
2. Horseradish Béarnaise is delicious as a spread for cold roast beef. Add 2 teaspoons prepared horseradish to the finished Béarnaise.

Mayonnaise I
HEAT METHOD

❖

Probably the most used sauce in America, mayonnaise is readily available on supermarket shelves in regular and low-calorie renditions. Once you try either of these recipes, I doubt you'll often opt for the store-bought version. Either will keep in the refrigerator for a little more than a week and may be frozen. This first version is the thinner of the two and must be cooked for a couple of minutes to thicken; the second, using more oil, is necessarily weightier but needs no cooking. I prefer a light oil when making mayonnaise; a nearly tasteless vegetable oil such as corn oil produces a light-tasting sauce, but many prefer the stronger taste of an olive oil.

> 4 large egg yolks
> 1/4 teaspoon salt
> 1 tablespoon lemon juice
> 1/2 teaspoon prepared mustard
> 1/2 cup oil of your choice
> 1/2 cup chicken broth, boiling hot
> dash cayenne pepper

1. Place egg yolks and salt in a food processor or blender and process until yolks are pale yellow, about 1 minute.
2. Add lemon juice and mustard and process 30 seconds more.
3. Using only a few drops at a time to start, dribble in the oil. The success of your sauce depends on adding this very slowly.
4. Dribble in the hot broth in a slightly thicker stream. Transfer the sauce to a 1-quart heavy-bottomed saucepan.
5. Whisk the sauce constantly on medium-high heat until it thickens, about 2 minutes.
6. Use sauce as is or vary the flavor with one of the additions (see below). Sauce may be served hot or cold.

Yield: Approximately 1¼ cups   Fat per tablespoon: 7g
Calories per tablespoon: 61   Carbohydrates per tablespoon: 0
Protein per tablespoon: 1g   Sodium per tablespoon: 30mg

Mayonnaise II

❖

4 *large egg yolks*
¼ *teaspoon salt*
1 *tablespoon lemon juice*
½ *teaspoon prepared mustard*
¾ *cup oil*
¼ *cup chicken broth, boiling hot, reduced to 2 tablespoons*
dash cayenne pepper

1. Make the sauce as described for Mayonnaise I, steps 1—4. The sauce will not have to be cooked.

Yield: Approximately 1¼ cups   Fat per tablespoon: 9g
Calories per tablespoon: 85   Carbohydrates per tablespoon: 0
Protein per tablespoon: 1g   Sodium per tablespoon: 30mg

Mayonnaise Variations

❖

To 1 ¼ cups mayonnaise add any of the following:

2 tablespoons chopped fresh dill for use with fish salads.

2 tablespoons chopped fresh basil for use with tomatoes (or use 1 teaspoon dried basil).

1 tablespoon chopped dill pickles, 1 tablespoon capers, 1 tablespoon fresh tarragon (or 1 teaspoon dried), and 1 tablespoon chopped chives for a Gribiche Sauce for steamed or poached fish.

1 tablespoon horseradish and 1 tablespoon minced fresh parsley for use with cold roast beef.

3 tablespoons tomato paste, 3 tablespoons minced green pepper, and 1 teaspoon snipped chives for use with hamburgers or as a dip for raw vegetables.

Flour-Based Sauces

Flour-based sauces, what Mother called white sauce and the French term Béchamel (made with milk) or Velouté (made with milk and stock), have fallen out of favor with the advent of nouvelle cuisine. Instead of being thickened with flour, sauces are now thickened with reduced cream, mounds of butter, or by reducing naturally gelatinous homemade stocks to a syrupy stage and then enriching them with butter. Naturally, with the exception of the reduced stock, none of these are appropriate for reduced-calorie cooking. Therefore for the rare, but nonetheless real occasion when a dish would benefit from a "cream" sauce, here is a recipe for *Gourmet Light* Velouté, with less than half the calories of a traditional Velouté, as well as a reduced-calorie Cheese Sauce.

Cheese Sauce

❖

Again, cheese sauces have fallen from de rigueur to déclassé, but to enliven a pallid cauliflower I offer the following. The sauce may be made ahead and reheated.

> *½ cup chicken stock*
> *½ cup milk*
> *1 ½ tablespoons cornstarch or arrowroot dissolved in*
> *   2 tablespoons of stock*
> *1 tablespoon butter, at room temperature*
> *freshly ground pepper to taste*
> *freshly grated nutmeg*
> *a few shakes paprika*
> *1 tablespoon sherry*
> *½ to ¾ cup grated cheese such as cheddar (about*
> *   1 ⅛ to 2 ounces)*

1. In a saucepan, heat the stock and milk until small bubbles appear at the edge of the pan.
2. Gradually whisk in the cornstarch over a low heat. Cook, stirring, for 1 minute. Whisk in the butter.
3. Add the pepper, nutmeg, paprika, and sherry. Stir in the cheese.
4. Cook over low heat, stirring constantly until smooth and thick, about 5 minutes.

Yield: Approximately 1 ¼ cups   Fat per tablespoon: 1.5g
Calories per tablespoon: 22   Carbohydrates per tablespoon: 1g
Protein per tablespoon: 1g   Sodium per tablespoon: 24mg

Velouté Sauce

❖

2 cups stock, use whatever will complement the dish:
    fish, beef, or chicken
1 tablespoon grated onion
2 teaspoons cornstarch or arrowroot dissolved in
    2 tablespoons milk or half-and-half
1 ½ tablespoons butter
¼ teaspoon salt
a dash of white pepper to taste
a few gratings fresh nutmeg

1. Combine the stock and onion in a saucepan and bring to a boil.
2. Reduce the heat to medium, whisk in the cornstarch or arrowroot, and cook, stirring, about 5 minutes or until the sauce is
   smooth and thick.
3. Cut the butter into 3 pieces, whisk each in after the previous one
   melts. Taste and season with salt, pepper, and a bit of nutmeg.

Yield: Approximately 2 cups
Calories per tablespoon: 8
Protein per tablespoon: trace

Fat per tablespoon: .5g
Carbohydrates per tablespoon: .5g
Sodium per tablespoon: 20mg

Herb-Based Sauces

Fresh herbs combined with stock, a hint of oil, and nuts or cheese make wonderful sauces for pasta, salads, and poached chicken or fish. They are a snap to make with the aid of a food processor and keep up to a week when refrigerated.

Lemon Parsley Sauce

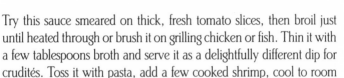

Try this sauce smeared on thick, fresh tomato slices, then broil just until heated through or brush it on grilling chicken or fish. Thin it with a few tablespoons broth and serve it as a delightfully different dip for crudités. Toss it with pasta, add a few cooked shrimp, cool to room temperature, and serve as a hot-weather meal.

> 1/2 cup fresh parsley, snipped
> 1/2 cup fresh watercress, snipped
> 3 tablespoons dried bread crumbs
> 1/2 teaspoon prepared mustard
> juice of half a lemon
> 1 tablespoon oil
> 1 egg yolk
> 1 tablespoon chicken broth or consomme
> freshly ground pepper to taste
> 1 teaspoon sugar

1. Combine all the ingredients in a food processor or blender. Use as described above.

Yield: 2/3 cup
Calories per tablespoon: 22
Protein per tablespoon: 0

Fat per tablespoon: 2g
Carbohydrates per tablespoon: 1g
Sodium per tablespoon: 10mg

Basil-Walnut Sauce

❖

This Basil-Walnut Sauce is reminiscent of the ever-popular pesto minus most of the oil and with the added sparkle of balsamic vinegar. It has one-fourth the calories of a traditional pesto sauce. Its uses go far beyond a simple and delicious toss with pastas (a wonderful hot-weather dinner). Brush it on grilling chicken or fish the last few minutes of cooking, dab it on sun-warmed tomatoes, or stir it into a cool bowl of fresh Tomato Soup (page 74).

> *1/2 cup fresh parsley, snipped and loosely packed*
> *1/2 cup fresh basil, snipped and loosely packed*
> *1 tablespoon extra-virgin olive oil*
> *1 tablespoon balsamic or malt vinegar*
> *2 tablespoons grated Parmesan cheese*
> *1 teaspoon sugar*
> *2 tablespoons chicken broth, more if a thinner sauce*
> *is desired*
> *1 clove garlic, minced*
> *3 tablespoons finely chopped walnuts*
> *freshly ground pepper to taste*

1. Combine and process all the ingredients in a food processor or blender. Use as described above.

Yield: ¾ cup
Calories per tablespoon: 30
Protein per tablespoon: 1g

Fat per tablespoon: 3g
Carbohydrates per tablespoon: 1g
Sodium per tablespoon: 10mg

Acid-Based Sauces

The most popular sauces in today's au courant restaurants are those made by emulsifying (blending) large amounts of butter in small amounts of acid, such as lemon juice or wine. Since no magician's wand can render 8 tablespoons of butter calorie-free, *Gourmet Light* cooking will forgo any attempt to produce a beurre blanc. However, here are two acid-based sauces, one based on wine and another on lemon, which will fend off the boredom associated with reduced-calorie cooking.

Lemon Butter Sauce

When you've eaten all the dry green beans you can, try this. Simple and delicious.

> 1 ½ tablespoons butter
> 2–3 tablespoons freshly squeezed lemon juice
> ½ teaspoon salt
> freshly ground pepper to taste
> 1 clove garlic, minced
> 1 teaspoon minced fresh parsley
> ½ teaspoon minced shallot or scallion

1. Combine all the ingredients in a small skillet or saucepan and heat until butter melts. Pour over cooked, drained vegetables.

Yield: 4 servings
Calories: 44
Protein: 1g

Fat: 4g
Carbohydrates: 1g
Sodium: 270mg

Wine Sauce

❖

A very good, hearty sauce that belies its modest ingredients and ease of preparation. Serve this with beef, such as the Paupiette on page 128. This will keep a week in the refrigerator or up to six months without flavor loss in the freezer.

2 teaspoons oil or noncaloric cooking spray
2 large carrots, scrubbed and chopped
2 medium onions, chopped
2 cups beef stock or broth
1/2 teaspoon meat glaze (see page 15) or 1/8
    teaspoon commercial meat extract
1 cup red wine such as a Burgundy
2 or 3 sprigs fresh parsley
1/2 teaspoon salt
freshly ground black pepper to taste

1. Heat the oil in a medium skillet. Add the carrots and onions and saute, covered, until lightly browned, about 5 minutes. When browned, reduce heat to medium low and continue cooking, covered, about 8 minutes, or until vegetables are soft.
2. Add the stock, meat glaze, wine, parsley, salt, and pepper, and simmer, covered, for 1 hour.
3. Remove cover, turn heat to high, and boil until the sauce is reduced to about 1 1/4 cups (about 10 minutes).
4. Puree the sauce in a food processor or blender.

Note: If sauce is too thin, thicken it by stirring in a slurry made by dissolving 1 teaspoon potato starch, arrowroot, or cornstarch in a tablespoon of wine. Sauce may be strained if you prefer a smooth texture.

Yield: Approximately 1 ½ cups   Fat per tablespoon: 0
Calories per tablespoon: 14   Carbohydrates per tablespoon: 2g
Protein per tablespoon: 0   Sodium per tablespoon: 52mg

❖ DISCOLORED SAUCES ❖

Although aluminum is one of the best, meaning fastest conductors of heat, an unlined aluminum pot may discolor a sauce if there is acid present, such as tomato, wine, vinegar, or lemon juice. The discoloration is caused by a reaction of the acid with the stain. Unlined aluminum pans become stained when washed with a high-alkali cleanser or are used for cooking high-alkali foods such as potatoes. The acid in the sauce removes some of that stain, transferring it to the sauce, causing a grayish tint that is unappetizing but fortunately, not a health hazard.

Tomato Sauce

❖

Tomato-based sauces are used extensively in *Gourmet Light* cooking, for they score on flavor not matched by their calorie tally. Although many will opt to purchase tomato puree to make the sauce recipes called for in this book, here is a homemade version for those with gardens and/or the inclination to prepare their own.

> 2 pounds tomatoes, roughly chopped or 44 ounces canned tomatoes (2 large cans)
> 1 small onion, chopped
> 1 clove garlic, minced
> 1 tablespoon tomato paste
> 2 cups chicken stock (1 cup if using canned tomatoes)
> 4 leaves fresh basil, snipped, or 1 teaspoon dried basil
> 2/3 teaspoon sugar
> 1/2 teaspoon salt if using fresh tomatoes (omit if using canned)

1. Combine all the ingredients in a medium-size saucepan and boil, uncovered, until reduced by half.
2. Puree the mixture in a food processor or blender, and strain to remove the seeds and skins if desired.

Yield: Approximately 3 cups
Calories per cup: 96
Protein per cup: 4g

Fat per cup: 1g
Carbohydrates per cup: 21g
Sodium per cup: 380mg

Crème Blanc

❖

This simple mixture of cottage cheese and yogurt is to this book what butter, sour cream, and heavy cream are to others. It is a flavor enhancer, while contributing to good nutrition as well. Cookbook readers will note its similarity to fromage blanc. It will keep in the refrigerator for up to one week, and its flavor and texture will improve after being made.

4 ounces low-fat cottage cheese
4 tablespoons plain low-fat yogurt
2 tablespoons milk

1. Combine the ingredients in a food processor or blender, and mix until perfectly smooth. The sauce will thicken after being chilled about 6 hours.

Note: Two teaspoons of cornstarch (20 calories) added to this mixture will prevent it from separating during high heat cooking. You may then disregard my notes to cook crème blanc over low heat.

Yield: Approximately 1 cup
Calories per tablespoon: 11
Protein per tablespoon: 2g

Fat per tablespoon: 0
Carbohydrates per tablespoon: 1g
Sodium per tablespoon: 40mg

Chapter 3
SAVORY LITTLE SOMETHINGS

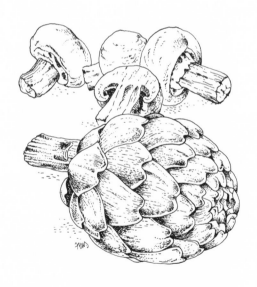

Savory Little Somethings

❖

By any name—smorgasbord, *tapas*, antipasto, *zakuska*, or hors d'oeuvres—appetizers are often pound packers. A 2-inch square of cheddar cheese, a mere ¼-inch thick (about ½ ounce), atop a cracker is an astounding 75 calories. Typical cocktail fare is generally high in fat, such as cheese, or fried in fat, such as chips, so that a few bites can really wreak havoc with the day's total calorie intake. Just 10 potato chips will bulk you up with 114 calories; an ounce of peanuts contains 160, and a tablespoon of cream cheese dip for a little celery stick has at least 50 calories.

In a cookbook dedicated to slimming meals, the emphasis on appetizers is understandably minimal; the chief ingredients are on the slender side, with vegetables and seafood predominating. But even on elaborate occasions, two or three offerings at most are sufficient. An array of appetizers makes for a very nice party or a fine dinner, but both are not needed on the same evening. If you offer your guests the sort of trim but tempting foods found here, they'll still be able to appreciate and enjoy your dinner.

There is a new trend evident at even the toniest restaurants. Customers are ordering lighter meals, often eschewing an entree in favor of, say, a side order of asparagus, followed by a salad of grilled duck breast. Saving money is not the object, banking calories is.

Most of the nibbles that follow are small tasty bites. Some, such as the Chèvre-Stuffed Artichokes, would make a lovely first course if nestled on a tangle of mixed greens dressed with a light mustard vinaigrette. Others would do well in the light supper or lunch slot, such as the Fresh Mozzarella and Tomato Pizza.

Presentation is particularly important when serving appetizers.

The mind must feast while the stomach yet waits. Mushroom caps on a white cloth napkin on a dark tray, crudités arranged attractively in baskets, chicken and pork skewers circled in spoke fashion with a tomato rose at the center—this attention to detail is key. Cooking without garnishing, no matter how simple, is like dressing in polka dots and stripes.

Chèvre-Stuffed Artichokes

This recipe may be prepared with either frozen artichoke hearts or fresh baby artichokes, an easy size for cocktail fare. For larger servings, suitable for a salad, prepare the bottoms from fresh artichokes. The larger cheese-stuffed artichoke bottoms make a delicious salad or appetizer when placed in a tangle of greens and dressed with a mustardy *Gourmet Light* vinaigrette. The recipe may be made through Step 6 as much as a day before serving.

For Artichokes

1 *package frozen artichoke hearts, thawed, or 6 baby*
   artichokes or 4 large artichokes
4 *tablespoons lemon juice*
4 *tablepoons flour*
1/2 *cup cold water*

For Marinade

4 *tablespoons chicken broth*
2 *tablespoons red wine vinegar*
1 *tablespoon lemon juice*
1 *tablespoon oil*
a *few sprigs fresh thyme or* 1/4 *teaspoon dried thyme*
freshly ground black pepper to taste

For Stuffing

2 ounces chèvre (goat cheese), such as Montrachet,
  or a spiced cream cheese
2 tablespoons milk
1 tablespoon butter
½ clove garlic, minced
1 tablespoon dried bread crumbs

To prepare the artichoke bottoms

1. Lay an artichoke on its side and slice off the top third with a stainless-steel knife. With scissors cut the spiny tips off the leaves. Cut away the tough outer leaves with the knife as if peeling an orange. You'll now have an inner core of pale green leaves. Slice this off, leaving the bottom. Trim it to remove tough green fibers. As you finish each one, cut into thirds, and drop the pieces into a bowl of water with 2 tablespoons of the lemon juice added to help keep the artichoke from turning brown.

    To prepare baby artichokes, follow the preceding instructions until you get to the inner core of pale leaves. Cut the artichoke in half the long way, and scrape away the fuzzy center.

To cook

1. Make a paste with about 4 tablespoons flour in a half cup of cold water. Stir this into a quart of water with the 2 remaining tablespoons lemon juice. Bring to a simmer, stirring occasionally. Add the artichoke bottoms and simmer until tender, about 10 minutes for the larger bottoms and 6 minutes for the baby ones. Drain, and when cool enough to handle, scrape away the fuzzy center.
2. Marinate the bottoms or thawed artichoke hearts in the chicken broth, vinegar, lemon juice, oil, thyme, and pepper at least 4 hours or overnight.
3. Preheat oven to 350 degrees. Drain and discard the marinade.
4. Mix the goat cheese with the milk until smooth and creamy. Fill a pastry bag with the mixture or spoon the mixture on the artichoke hearts or bottoms.

5. Spray a baking sheet with cooking spray. Arrange filled hearts on it.
6. Melt the butter in an 8-inch skillet. When foamy, cook the garlic over medium-low heat 1 minute. Add the bread crumbs and stir until lightly browned.
7. Divide the bread crumb mixture over the cheese. Bake 10 minutes in the preheated 350-degree oven until heated through.

Yield: 12 artichoke hearts
Calories per heart: 46
Protein per heart: 1g

Fat per heart: 4g
Carbohydrates per heart: 1g
Sodium per heart: 20mg

❖ CHÈVRE ❖

Goat cheeses, collectively known as chèvres, have long been popular in Europe. In America they have recently become the darling of the upbeat food world and the star in many a recipe. Creatively turned out in various guises from stuffing for pasta to souffles, the import and local manufacture of these distinctive handmade cheeses have grown greatly.

The flavor of chèvre is best described as a clear, tangy, and fresh, not the sort of cheese to eat by itself, but in combination with other flavors. Banon (wrapped in chestnut or grape leaves) is the mildest; Crotin de Chazignol is the sharpest; and Bucheron and Montrachet perhaps the best known.

Beef with Broccoli

❖

These tasty roll ups are a snap to fix, particularly if you have some reduced-calorie mayonnaise (page 26) on hand or a bit of leftover Béarnaise (24) or Hollandaise (21). Make these as much as 8 hours ahead and chill. Cover the dish with plastic wrap until serving time. Delicatessen roast beef is very good for this recipe.

> $\frac{1}{3}$ to $\frac{1}{2}$ head broccoli, about $\frac{3}{4}$ pound
> 5 thinly sliced pieces roast beef, about $\frac{1}{3}$ pound
> 3 tablespoons Béarnaise, Hollandaise, or mayonnaise
> a few shakes salt
> 4 tablespoons extra sauce for dipping

1. Discard the leaves from the broccoli. Peel the stalks with a vegetable peeler. Cut each spear into thin strips.
2. Bring a 2-quart saucepan $\frac{3}{4}$ full of water to a boil. Add the broccoli, cover, remove from heat, and let it rest 7 minutes. Drain.
3. Cut the flowerets from the stalks, cut the stalks into 1 $\frac{1}{2}$-inch long, very thin pieces.
4. Trim any visible fat from the meat. Cut each slice in half the long way.
5. Place the meat on a counter so its long side is parallel to the counter's edge. Spread the 3 tablespoons sauce over the meat. Place a broccoli floweret perpendicular to the meat on the far left side of the meat strip so the broccoli stem rests on the meat and the bud shows over the top. Place 2 thin stalk pieces on either side of the floweret stem. Season with salt. Roll up tightly so stem and stalk don't show and broccoli bud does.

6. Arrange the rolls in spoke fashion on a platter, with extra sauce in a scalloped lemon half in the center.

VARIATION: Add a bit of horseradish to the Hollandaise or mayonnaise for a bit more bite.

Yield: 10 rolls
Calories per roll: 51
Protein per roll: 6g

Fat per roll: 2g
Carbohydrates per roll: 2g
Sodium per roll: 70mg

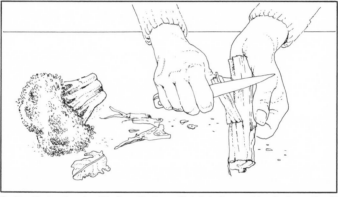

Peeling the tough outer skin from the broccoli stalk before cooking the broccoli will make the whole stalk more tender to eat.

Clam and Sausage Appetizers

❖

These clam and sausage-stuffed shells make a delicious hot cocktail nibble. The recipe may be prepared through Step 9 early in the day, and cooked at the last minute. The appetizers reheat nicely when covered with foil.

> ½ small onion, chopped
> 1 clove garlic, minced
> ½ cup chicken broth
> ¾ cup dry white wine
> 12 hard-shell (littleneck) clams (about 2 pounds), well scrubbed
> 2 teaspoons cornstarch
> 3 ounces fully cooked sausage such as kielbasa
> 3 tablespoons dried bread crumbs
> 1 tablespoon minced fresh parsley

1. "Saute" the onion and garlic in the chicken broth in a covered 2-quart saucepan until the vegetables are limp and almost transparent.
2. Add the wine (reserving 1 tablespoon for Step 3) and clams, cover pan, and steam over high heat until clams open, about 8 minutes.
3. Dissolve the cornstarch in the reserved tablespoon of wine.
4. Skin the sausage and chop it.
5. Lift opened clams from the broth with a slotted spoon. Line a sieve with a piece of cheesecloth or a heavy paper towel wrung out in water, and pour the broth through the sieve.
6. Pour 6 tablespoons strained broth back into the now-empty saucepan. Add dissolved cornstarch and cook, whisking, over medium heat until thickened. Set aside.
7. Pull clams from their shells, discard one half of shell. Chop clams roughly.

8. Combine chopped clams, sausage, and thickened broth.
9. Spoon mixture into shells. Sprinkle ½ teaspoon bread crumbs on each stuffed shell.
10. Clams may now be baked in a 425-degree oven until bubbly and browned (about 12–14 minutes) or held, chilled, for baking later in the day. Broil briefly if the crumbs don't brown in the oven. Garnish the stuffed, baked clams with parsley.

Yield: 14
Calories in each: 59
Protein in each: 5g

Fat in each: 3g
Carbohydrates in each: 4g
Sodium in each: 120mg

Chicken and Pork Skewers

❖

This tasty combination of chicken and pork is for those who like it hot. If you prefer a milder flavor, reduce or omit the chili paste with garlic. Marinate the chicken and pork as much as two days before preparing. Soaking the wooden skewers 45 minutes before grilling will keep them from scorching.

1 *whole chicken breast, boned and skinned*
5 *ounces boneless pork from chops or tenderloin, fat trimmed*
6 *tablespoons soy sauce*
1 *tablespoon sesame oil, available at Chinese or specialty food shops*
2 *tablespoons chicken broth*
1 *scallion (white part only), chopped*
a *1-inch piece of ginger root, peeled and minced*
2 *teaspoons chili paste with garlic, available at Chinese or specialty food shops*

1. Put the pork in the freezer for 2 hours, place the chicken in the freezer about 10 minutes.
2. Slice the chicken in long, thin strips, slanting the knife slightly. Cut the pork so the strips are wide as well as long by placing what was the bone end flat on the cutting surface and slicing down.
3. Place the chicken and pork in a plastic or a glass bowl with the soy sauce, sesame oil, chicken broth, scallion, and ginger root. Marinate in refrigerator 2–4 hours.
4. Drain poultry and meat, reserving marinade. Thread the chicken and pork alternately on skewers. You may refrigerate assembled skewers up to 12 hours before cooking.
5. Mix the marinade with the chili paste. Grill or broil chicken skewers, brushing with chili paste marinade, 12–16 minutes or until done. The meat and poultry should be juicy, not overdone.

Note: Sodium-reduced soy sauce is available in many markets for those wishing to restrict the amount of sodium.

Yield: 15 skewers
Calories per skewer: 49
Protein per skewer: 5g

Fat per skewer: 3g
Carbohydrates per skewer: 0g
Sodium per skewer: 270mg

❖ **THINKING THIN TIP** ❖

A good way to become aware of calorie counts in foods you commonly eat is to keep a diary of *everything* you consume for a few days, then tally the calories with the help of a calorie listing.

Crudités and Skinny Dips

❖

Raw vegetables cut into bite-size pieces (crudités) have been a popular nibble for years. Obviously, they're just right for *Gourmet Light* cooking too, if the accompanying dip is on the slender side.

When choosing vegetables for a crudité basket, keep color and texture in mind. Mushrooms, a soft vegetable, need the crunch of a celery stick, for example, and radishes can be offset with cherry tomatoes. Choose any vegetable that can be eaten raw. Happily, most vegetables can be prepared in advance and held as long as two days in ice water, which keeps them crisp. Those that resemble a flower bud, such as cauliflower and broccoli, are great timesavers, requiring no more preparation than the snap of a stalk.

Because most baskets are too deep for the vegetables to look attractive in, a false bottom will create the illusion of bounty. Layer crumpled-up wax paper in the bottom, and cover with a cloth napkin. Position the dip, in a bowl or one made from a vegetable, in the center and arrange prepared vegetables around it.

Another pretty presentation is to choose a rectangular tray. Arrange the vegetables in "ribbons" that run diagonally, a mirror image on either end of the tray, with small bowls of different dips (also on the diagonal) in the center.

Sauce Verte

❖

A fresh herb dip, also nice on sun-warmed, ripe tomatoes.

> ½ cup crème blanc (page 37) or 2 ounces cottage
> cheese and 2½ ounces plain yogurt
> 2 tablespoons farmers cheese
> 1 tablespoon cream cheese or Neufchâtel cheese
> 5 fresh basil leaves, snipped, or ½ teaspoon dried
> basil
> 1 tablespoon minced fresh parsley
> 1 clove garlic, minced
> a few shakes salt
> freshly ground pepper to taste

1. Combine all the ingredients in a food processor or blender and mix
   well.

Yield: ½ cup
Calories per tablespoon: 23
Protein per tablespoon: 2g

Fat per tablespoon: 1g
Carbohydrates per tablespoon: 1g
Sodium per tablespoon: 70mg

Sun Spread

❖

This mix of dried fruits and nuts in a "cream" base is a delicious spread on crackers, as well as a good dip for raw vegetables. Its light, clean taste is a pleasant change.

2 tablespoons cottage cheese
3 tablespoons farmers cheese
1 tablespoon cream cheese
2 dried apricots, minced and soaked 20 minutes in
  1 tablespoon sherry
1 tablespoon sherry
1 tablespoon golden raisins
1 teaspoon chutney
1 tablespoon walnuts, roughly chopped

1. Combine the cottage, farmer, and cream cheeses in a food processor or blender until smooth.
2. Stir in the apricots and sherry, golden raisins, chutney, and walnuts. Refrigerate up to a day before serving.

Yield: ⅔ cup
Calories per tablespoon: 27
Protein per tablespoon: 2g

Fat per tablespoon: 2g
Carbohydrates per tablespoon: 2g
Sodium per tablespoon: 40mg

Roquefort Skinny Dip

If any of this is left over, it will make a romaine lettuce salad a great partner.

> 2 ounces Roquefort or blue cheese
> ½ cup crème blanc (page 37) or 2 ounces cottage
>   cheese and 2 ½ ounces plain yogurt
> 2 tablespoons farmers cheese
> ¼ teaspoon paprika
> ½ teaspoon sugar
> freshly ground pepper to taste

1. Combine all the ingredients in a food processor or blender and mix well.

Yield: 1 cup
Calories per tablespoon: 21
Protein per tablespoon: 2g

Fat per tablespoon: 1g
Carbohydrates per tablespoon: 1g
Sodium per tablespoon 80mg

Duxelle Melba

A delicious way to use up aging mushrooms, these cocktail toasts may be made when the spirit strikes and then frozen.

> 1 tablespoon butter, melted
> 4 slices thin-sliced white bread
> 6 ounces mushrooms

2 tablespoons shallots, minced
2 tablespoons chicken broth
1 ounce semisoft mild cheese, such as Havarti or
   Muenster, grated
1 tablespoon minced fresh parsley
1 tablespoon pine nuts or almonds, chopped
1/8 teaspoon salt
freshly ground black pepper to taste

1. Preheat the oven to 325 degrees while melting butter in an 8-inch skillet. Spray a baking sheet with cooking spray.
2. Place the bread slices in a stack and slice twice on the diagonal, making 16 triangles. Arrange on the baking sheet.
3. Dab each *croustade* (bread triangle) with melted butter on one side. Bake 12 minutes or until slightly crisp, in the preheated oven.
4. Wipe the mushrooms clean and mince them by hand or in a food processor. Scrape onto a kitchen towel, gather into a ball, twist ends of towel, and squeeze the mushrooms over the sink, extracting as much water as you can.
5. "Saute" the shallots in the chicken broth in the now-empty skillet. When liquid is evaporated and shallots are softened, spray the skillet with cooking spray, add the mushrooms, and cook at medium-low heat, gradually increasing the heat, about 5 minutes.
6. Remove mushrooms from heat, stir in the grated cheese, parsley, and pine nuts making a duxelle. Season with salt, pepper, and nutmeg.
7. Divide *duxelle* over the *croustades*, being certain to cover the bread points or they will burn. The hors d'oeuvres may be broiled now until browned, about 2–3 minutes or baked at 325 degrees until browned, about 12 minutes. You also may freeze them, uncooked, for future use.

Yield: 16   Fat in each: 2g
Calories in each: 30   Carbohydrates in each: 3g
Protein in each: 1g   Sodium in each: 50mg

Mushrooms à la Grecque

❖

The phrase "à la Grecque" means to blanch vegetables (though only mushrooms have been used here) in a pickling brine of oil, wine, and herbs (a court bouillon) and then to macerate and finally serve them in the cooking liquid. It's a pleasing change from crudités and needs no further dressing. Serve the mushrooms at room temperature or only slightly chilled for best flavor. Mushrooms and vegetables prepared this way will keep up to 4 days chilled.

> 8 ounces mushrooms, caps and stems or just caps (as you please)
> 1 cup water
> 1 cup chicken broth
> ½ cup dry white wine
> ½ teaspoon salt
> 2 tablespoons oil
> 1 tablespoon balsamic or red wine vinegar
> juice of half a lemon
> 1 teaspoon fresh tarragon leaves or ½ teaspoon dried tarragon
> 1 tablespoon minced fresh parsley
> 1 clove garlic, sliced in 3 pieces
> a few sprigs fresh thyme or ¼ teaspoon dried thyme
> ¼ teaspoon oregano

1. Wipe the mushrooms clean with a towel and set aside for use in Step 3.
2. In a nonaluminum saucepan, combine the water, broth, wine, salt, oil, vinegar, and lemon juice to make a court bouillon. Make a bouquet garni of the tarragon, parsley, garlic, thyme, and oregano by placing the herbs on a double-thick 3-inch square of cheesecloth. Roll the cloth in jelly-roll fashion, bring the ends

together, and tie in a knot. Add this herb bundle to the liquid and bring to a boil for 1 minute.
3. Add the cleaned mushrooms, boil 3 minutes. Lift vegetables with a slotted spoon to a nonmetal bowl or glass jar.
4. Boil the court bouillon over high heat until only 1 cup remains. Remove and discard bouquet garni. Pour liquid over mushrooms, and chill 2—4 hours or up to 4 days. Serve at room temperature, or slightly chilled.

Yield: 8 servings
Calories per serving: 44
Protein per serving: 1g

Fat per serving: 3g
Carbohydrates per serving: 3g
Sodium per serving: 140mg

❖ GARLIC ❖

Romans fed garlic to their slaves to make them strong, and to their warriors to make them brave, and then forbade anyone having just eaten it to enter the temple of the Goddess of Nature. Perhaps the Romans didn't know that if the garlic had been simmered, long and slow, it wouldn't have been so offensive. Pureed garlic on French bread and Chicken with 40 Cloves of Garlic are popular dishes with many, the pungency of the bulb subdued thanks to long, slow cooking.

To mince garlic, cut the clove (one of the tissue paper –like wrapped crescents in the bulb) in half the long way. There's no need to peel it. Cut off the tiny brown nub at the tip. Place the garlic, flat side down, on the cutting surface, position the flat side of the knife over the clove, and smash down (carefully, on the broad side of the knife) with the heel of your hand. The garlic skin will lift off easily and the clove may be minced. Sprinkling the garlic with a little salt may help soften it to speed mincing. Lemon juice will help remove the garlic scent from your fingers.

Mussels
in Remoulade Sauce

❖

Although mussels have long been popular in Europe, until recently they've been disregarded here. Now in greater demand, mussels are being cultivated, bringing a cleaner bivalve to the market. That means less scrubbing for the cook! Poach the mussels and make the sauce the day before, assemble them as much as two hours before serving this cold hors d'oeuvre.

1 *pound mussels, about 15–20*
3 *tablespoons cornmeal*
2 *cups dry white wine*
1 *whole clove garlic*
1 *tablespoon minced fresh parsley*
1 *bay leaf*

The Sauce

1 *egg*
1 *egg yolk*
5 *drops lemon juice*
1/8 *teaspoon salt*
1/3 *cup corn oil*
1/3 *cup reserved, strained mussel broth, boiling hot*
1/2 *teaspoon Dijon-style mustard*
1/2 *teaspoon capers*
a pinch cayenne pepper
1/2 *tablespoon minced fresh parlsey*
sprig of parsley for garnish (optional)

To Prepare the Shellfish

1. Discard any mussels that don't close when you poke the inside of the shell hinge with a sharp knife. Cut away the beards. Cover the mussels with water, add the cornmeal, and let the mixture sit at least 30 minutes. The cornmeal is supposedly washed through the shellfish to carry out sand and grit.
2. Rinse the mussels thoroughly under running water.
3. Combine the wine, garlic, parsley, and bay leaf in a non-aluminum saucepan, cover, and bring to a boil. Add the mussels, cover, and boil until shells open, about 5 minutes.
4. Lift cooked mussels with a slotted spoon to a bowl. Chill the mussels. Discard the bay leaf from the broth.
5. Line a strainer with a double thickness of cheesecloth or a heavy paper towel wrung out in water. Pour mussel cooking broth through strainer. Let liquid rest 5 minutes, then pour through again, discarding the sediment that sinks to the bottom of the pan. Set aside while preparing sauce.

To Prepare the Sauce

1. Put the whole egg, yolk, lemon juice, and salt in a food processor and blend 20 seconds.
2. Dribble in the oil in a very fine, steady stream, almost drop by drop, while machine runs.
3. Meanwhile, heat strained mussel broth in a 1-quart nonalumimun saucepan. When boiling, dribble into the egg-oil mixture while machine runs.
4. Pour sauce into the now-empty saucepan and whisk until thickened over low heat, about 1 minute.
5. Remove from heat and stir in mustard, capers, cayenne, and parsley. Taste and adjust seasoning, add more lemon juice if sauce is too bland. You will have about ¾ cup of sauce.

To Serve

1. Remove one half of mussel shell, discard. Free mussel from the

other half, but leave in the shell, and arrange on a platter in a spoke fashion. Place a dab of sauce on each and garnish with a tiny sprig of parsley if desired.

VARIATION: Mussels may be served warm or cold, removed from the shell and tossed with the *remoulade* sauce, then mounded on a lettuce cup. Garnish with lemon slices dipped in parsley.

Yield: 20 mussels   Fat in each: 4g
Calories in each: 25   Carbohydrates in each: 1g
Protein in each: 2g   Sodium in each: 40mg

Curried Clam Fingers

❖

This curried clam appetizer is a moist, spicy mouthful that can be offered wrapped in lettuce leaves or more simply, mounded on baking shells. If you don't have a Chinese steamer, you may fashion one by positioning a cake rack on 4 ramekins set in a deep electric skillet. These finger rolls may be done through Step 6 up to 4 hours ahead.

6 ounces mushrooms, chopped
1 1/2 teaspoons curry powder
8 ounces canned clams, minced (about 1 1/2 cups)
2 small ribs celery, minced
1 tablespoon minced fresh parsley
3 tablespoons grated Parmesan or Romano cheese
a few drops hot pepper sauce
4–6 drops lemon juice
1 large head iceberg lettuce, outer leaves not
removed
chutney (optional)

1. Spray an 8-inch skillet with cooking spray and "saute" the mushrooms until limp.
2. Sprinkle curry powder over mushrooms, cook over medium heat another 30 seconds.
3. Remove from heat, combine mushrooms with clams, celery, parsley, grated cheese, pepper sauce, and lemon juice. Set aside.
4. Bring 1 quart of water to a boil.
5. Core the lettuce. Remove the outer leaves without tearing. Cut away and discard the white "spine" at the base of the lettuce leaf. Cut the leaves in half lengthwise if they are very large. Dip 16–18 leaves, one at a time, into the hot water (it doesn't have to remain boiling). Immerse 2 seconds or just until wilted. Drain on a towel.
6. Place a tablespoon and a half of the clam filling on the base of each leaf. Roll tightly, tucking in the sides as you go. Place the rolls, seam side down, on a bamboo steamer. Rolls may be refrigerated at this point.
7. Put approximately 1½ cups water in a wok. Bring to a boil. Place Chinese bamboo steamer over boiling water, and steam lettuce fingers about 4 minutes. Serve with chutney as a dipping sauce if desired.

Yield: 16-18

Calories in each: 32

Protein in each: 4g

Fat in each: 1g

Carbohydrates in each: 2g

Sodium in each: 20mg

Sole and Crab Peppers

❖

These morsels may be made ahead and reheated, but for best flavor make them through Step 5, cooking just before serving. This recipe makes use of the seafood flakes (usually 35 percent crab-65 percent whitefish) now widely available. Or use 5 ounces uncooked shrimp or the real McCoy, of course. The sauce may be made ahead and reheated or omitted altogether if black bean or oyster sauce is unavailable.

4 ounces sole or other whitefish fillets
1 scallion, minced
4 water chestnuts, fresh or canned, chopped
a pinch cayenne pepper
1/2 teaspoon red wine vinegar or rice wine vinegar
1 egg white
1 teaspoon cornstarch
5 ounces crabmeat or seafood flakes
2 medium red or green peppers
1 teaspoon oil
1/2 cup chicken broth

The Sauce

1 tablespoon cornstarch
1/2 cup chicken broth
1 tablespoon black bean or oyster sauce (available at
*   Oriental or specialty food shops)*
1 teaspoon sesame oil

1. Put the fish in a food processor or through a meat grinder and process to a paste. Scrape into a bowl.
2. Add the scallion, water chestnuts, cayenne, vinegar, egg white, and cornstarch. Mix well.

3. Dice the crabmeat. Stir into the fish mixture.
4. Wash the peppers, cut in half, discard seeds, and cut each half in four pieces. (Don't wash the inside of the pepper or the filling won't adhere.)
5. Pack a heaping teaspoon of filling on each pepper.
6. Film a 12-inch skillet with the oil. Place filled peppers in skillet, pepper side down. Saute at high heat until peppers are just browned, add chicken broth, cover, and steam 3–4 minutes. Serve hot with black bean sauce dabbed on top or as a dip.

To Make the Sauce

1. Dissolve the cornstarch in the broth. Add black bean sauce and sesame oil. Stir over medium heat until thickened. Sauce may be reheated.

Yield: 15-16
Calories without sauce: 26
Protein without sauce: 3g

Fat without sauce: 1g
Carbohydrates without sauce: 2g
Sodium without sauce: 30mg

❖ **THINKING THIN TIP** ❖

Take a cooking course if you're not yet comfortable in the kitchen. Even if a reduced-calorie cooking course isn't offered in your area, learning your way around a kitchen will help you prepare fine reduced-calorie meals.

Seviche

❖

Seviche is the Latin American cousin of Japan's sashimi. Unlike sashimi, which is strictly raw, seviche is prepared by marinating the fish several hours in lemon juice. This firms the flesh, turning it opaque; in essence, cooking it. Like sashimi, the freshness of the fish is imperative. However, once it's marinated, seviche will keep for 2–3 days. Seviche makes a nice luncheon dish or first course as well as an appetizer. To give it a bit more body, do as a Peruvian friend of mine does; add a boiled, cubed sweet potato.

> 1 1/2 pounds scallops or delicate white-fleshed fish, such as sole, cut into bite-size pieces
> 1 cup lemon juice
> 1 tablespoon finely chopped Bermuda or Spanish onion
> 1/4 green pepper, finely chopped
> 1/2 red pepper, finely chopped
> 1/2 blanched, skinned, and seeded tomato, cubed
> 1/3 cup lime juice (about 2 limes)
> 2 tablespoons orange juice, freshly squeezed preferred
> 3 tablespoons lemon juice
> freshly ground pepper to taste
> minced fresh parsley
> lettuce

1. Marinate the seafood in the lemon juice in a nonmetallic container overnight.
2. Drain seafood, discarding marinade. Rinse with water.
3. Combine the onion, green pepper, red pepper, tomato, citrus juices, and fish. If desired, add the remaining halves of tomato and green pepper, also chopped. Season with pepper to taste. Garnish with a bit of parsley.

4. To serve, line individual plates or a platter with lettuce, mound mixture on top.

Yield: 10 appetizer servings
Calories: 94
Protein: 16g

Fat: 1g
Carbohydrates: 5g
Sodium: 190mg

Yield: 6 first course servings
Calories: 157
Protein: 27g

Fat: 2g
Carbohydrates: 8g
Sodium: 310mg

Shrimp-Stuffed Mushrooms

❖

Stuffed mushroom caps are far from innovative, but their versatility and easy preparation make them enduringly popular. For variety, try filling the blanched caps with the red or yellow pepper puree (pages 72 or 261), or a *duxelle* (page 52) or chèvre mixed with a bit of milk. These may be made and assembled through Step 5, heating at the last moment.

> 7–8 ounces mushrooms, chosen for broad caps
> juice of ½ lemon or 2 tablespoons lemon juice
> 1 tablespoon butter
> 1 small rib celery, minced
> 2 ounces salad shrimp, chopped
> additional few drops lemon juice
> a few sprigs fresh thyme or ¼ teaspoon dried thyme
> ⅛ teaspoon salt
> freshly ground pepper to taste
> 2 tablespoons dried bread crumbs

1. Wipe the mushrooms with a paper towel to remove dirt. Remove and mince the stems.

2. Bring a 2-quart saucepan half full of water with the lemon juice to a boil. Immerse cleaned mushroom caps and boil 2 minutes or just until softened. Drain on a towel, rounded-side up.

3. Meanwhile, melt the butter in an 8-inch skillet over medium heat. When foamy, add the minced mushroom stems and celery and cook, covered, 2–3 minutes, stirring often.

4. Add the shrimp, lemon juice, thyme, salt, pepper, and bread crumbs. Turn heat to high, cook 30 seconds more, uncovered.

5. Remove shrimp mixture from heat. Place a heaping teaspoon on each mushroom cap. Place stuffed mushrooms on a baking sheet.

6. Broil until bubbly, 6–8 minutes.

Yield: 12 to 14 caps
Calories in each: 22
Protein in each: 2g

Fat in each: 1g
Carbohydrates in each: 1g
Sodium in each: 30mg

❖ **OIL-DRIED BASIL** ❖

It's no wonder certain varieties of basil are used to manufacture perfume, for culinary basil has a sweet aroma matched by no other herb. Yet when dried, that special fragrance and flavor are greatly diminished. Before cold weather turns your verdant green basil crop into a blackened skeleton of its former self, try this simple curing technique. While nothing matches the fragrance of fresh, I think this comes close to its flavor.

Rinse and spin dry the basil leaves. Dishwasher sterilize a crock, such as that stone-ground mustard comes in. Lay basil leaves about 2 deep in the crock. Sprinkle lightly with salt, drizzle with oil, and repeat. Push the leaves down with a spoon handle, and continue to salt and oil the layers. Cover tightly and refrigerate. To use, pat or rinse the leaves free of oil and salt, mince and enjoy. The oil-cured leaves will keep under refrigeration until next year's new, bright growth is ready. Note: Remove leaves with very clean utensils only.

Fresh Mozzarella
and Tomato Pizza

❖

This quick recipe makes a nice lunch as well as a cocktail snack. It's a little messy to eat, so make this a casual offering. Assemble no more than an hour before serving or the tortilla will get soggy. Fresh mozzarella, the kind sold in brine and available at some specialty food stores, makes a delicious change from the supermarket variety.

> 1 flour tortilla (sold refrigerated in the supermarket dairy section)
> 1 large, fully ripe tomato, thinly sliced, slices cut in half
> 1 ½ slices (3 ounces) mozzarella cheese, cut into strips
> 4 or 5 fresh basil leaves, snipped, or ½ teaspoon dried basil
> 1 teaspoon extra-virgin olive oil
> ⅛ teaspoon salt and freshly ground pepper to taste

1. Preheat oven to 475 degrees. Place the tortilla on a baking sheet. Arrange the tomato slices, overlapping them spoke fashion, on the tortilla.
2. Cover the tomato with the cheese strips.
3. Sprinkle basil over cheese, dribble on oil, then season with salt and pepper.
4. Bake in a 475-degree oven about 6 minutes until cheese is melted. Then broil until lightly browned, about 3 minutes more. Cool slightly before cutting into quarters with a pizza cutter.

Yield: 4 servings   Fat: 5g
Calories: 95   Carbohydrates: 7g
Protein: 6g   Sodium: 170mg

Chapter 4

THE SOUP BOWL

The Soup Bowl

❖

Of soup and love, the first is best.
—Spanish Proverb

Soup—what diversity in a single bowl! From the elegance of a sparkly clear consomme to an unpretentious potato soup, from a trendy blueberry bisque to a plain old clam chowder, soups come in a fashion for every taste and occasion. Whether you're looking for a meal in a bowl or just a tasty starter, even a dessert, soup fills the bill.

Many cooks today are rediscovering the natural goodness of homemade soups. Perhaps the food processor is partly responsible for the newfound popularity, maybe it's because most soups freeze so well—a boon for today's busy cook. Maybe it's just the down-home appeal of a good bowl of soup. Regardless, soups are a natural in *Gourmet Light* cooking, for a deliciously satisfying first course can be enjoyed for less than 100 calories, or a nutritionally balanced meal consumed for under 300 calories. Naturally, you won't find heavy cream soups here, but you will find their updated, lightened versions and more. Some of the soups are skinny by nature such as Gazpacho and Two Mushroom Consomme; others have been run through the calorie reducer such as the Spinach and Oyster Bisque. Some are a snap to fix, others require a lengthier kitchen commitment.

Bouillabaisse of Scallops

❖

This soup perfumes the air. Serve it with the Fire and Ice Salad, page 102, for a fine, light cold-weather meal, or serve it chilled in summer.

2 leeks, white part only, thinly sliced
1 medium onion, thinly sliced
4–5 tablespoons chicken broth or bottled clam juice
4 large tomatoes or 2 cups canned tomatoes
2 cloves garlic, minced
4 cups fish stock or 3½ 8-ounce bottles clam juice
    mixed with 3 ounces vermouth and 1 ounce
    water
2 tablespoons orange zest
2–3 tablespoons orange juice, freshly squeezed
    preferred
6–7 fresh basil leaves, snipped, or 1 teaspoon dried
    basil
a pinch of saffron
1 bay leaf
¼ teaspoon thyme
½ teaspoon fennel seeds
1 pound scallops or white fish fillets, cut into chunks
2 tablespoons minced fresh parsley
a bowl of freshly grated Parmesan

1. "Saute" the leeks and onion in a 10-inch skillet with the broth. Cover the pan while cooking, adding more liquid if necessary.
2. To peel and seed the tomatoes, bring a 2½-quart saucepan ¾ full of water to a boil. Core the tomatoes, and cut a cross in each one's bottom. Immerse the tomatoes in boiling water for 15 seconds or until the skins loosen. Drain, cool under running water, and peel off the skins. Cut the tomatoes in quarters and squeeze over a

strainer to remove seeds. Press the seeds with the back of a wooden spoon to extract the juice. Reserve the juice.

3. When the leeks and onion are limp, add the garlic, tomatoes, reserved juice, stock, orange zest, orange juice, basil, and saffron. Tie the bay leaf, thyme, and fennel in a cheesecloth bag (a bouquet garni) and add to the skillet. Simmer, covered, for 30–40 minutes.

4. Add the scallops, raise heat to medium, and cook covered, until they are opaque, about 4–5 minutes.

5. Remove the bouquet garni, stir in the parsley, and taste for seasoning. Ladle the finished soup into warmed bowls and pass grated Parmesan cheese at the table.

Yield: 3-4 servings
Calories per serving: 235
Protein per serving: 31g

Fat per serving: 3g
Carbohydrates per serving: 20g
Sodium per serving: 360mg

Broccoli-Cheddar Soup

This hearty soup would make a Grilled Pork and Veal Croquette, page 142, a good companion. Double the recipe and freeze half for an easy meal at a later date. Serve the soup hot or just slightly chilled.

> 1 bunch broccoli
> 1/2 cup chicken broth
> 1/2 cup milk
> 1 tablespoon cornstarch dissolved in 2 tablespoons
>   chicken broth
> 1 tablespoon butter

¾ cup (2 oz.) grated cheddar cheese, lightly packed
1 tablespoon sherry
½ teaspoon salt
freshly ground pepper to taste
freshly grated nutmeg to taste
a few shakes paprika
additional chicken broth, optional

1. Separate the broccoli into flowerets and stalks. Peel the stalks with a knife or vegetable peeler. Dice the stalks, chop the flowerets. Bring a 2½-quart saucepan ¾ full of water to a boil, immerse broccoli, and boil, uncovered, until tender but crisp, about 8 minutes. Drain and set aside.
2. Meanwhile, heat the broth with the milk until bubbles appear at the edge of the pan.
3. Remove the pan from the heat and whisk in the dissolved cornstarch. Return to low heat and cook, whisking, about 1 minute.
4. Whisk in the butter, cheese, sherry, salt, pepper, nutmeg, and paprika.
5. Cook over low heat until well blended, about 2 minutes.
6. Combine broccoli with cheese mixture in a food processor or in batches in a blender. Taste for seasoning; overseason if serving chilled. Thin with additional chicken broth if soup is too thick.

Yield: 4-5 cups
Calories per cup: 160
Protein per cup: 11g

Fat per cup: 8g
Carbohydrates per cup: 15g
Sodium per cup: 540mg

❖ BOUQUET GARNI ❖

To make a bouquet garni, cut a piece of cheesecloth about 6 inches by 4 inches. Place the herbs called for, generally thyme, garlic (no need to peel), fresh parsley stems, and peppercorns (crushed, please) in the center. Roll the cloth in jellyroll fashion, then bring the ends together and knot. The flavors suffuse the soup, stew, or broth, but the herbs can be easily removed before serving.

Cauliflower "Cream" with Yellow Pepper Swirl

❖

"Cauliflower is nothing but a cabbage with a college education."
—Mark Twain

In a class ahead of its cousin the cabbage or not, cauliflower is a calorie counter's dream, supplying only 28 calories a cup and a good supply of vitamin C. Here, it's pureed in a soup to be served hot or cold and garnished with a swirl of Yellow Pepper and Basil Puree, an economical way to serve the delicious but rather dear yellow peppers now coming to market. The puree also makes a delightful dip for vegetables at cocktail time. You may substitute red peppers for the yellow.

3 small leeks, white part only
1 tablespoon olive oil, extra-virgin recommended
3 cups blanched cauliflower (about 1/2 head)
2 cups milk
1 small potato, peeled and diced
3/4 teaspoon salt
freshly ground pepper to taste
freshly grated nutmeg

For the Garnish

2 yellow peppers
1 cup loosely packed snipped fresh basil leaves or 2
      tablespoons dried basil
4 tablespoons Parmesan or Romano cheese, grated
1 tablespoon olive oil

To Prepare the Soup

1. Slice the leeks and rinse thoroughly. Place the leeks in a 1-quart

saucepan with the oil and enough water to half cover. Cover the pan, turn heat to high. When a boil is reached, reduce the heat so the liquid simmers. Uncover after 10 minutes and continue to cook until the leeks are soft, about 5 minutes more. Drain and reserve liquid.

2. Meanwhile, core the cauliflower and blanch the head in boiling water for about 5 minutes. Drain and chop it. Combine the cauliflower with the milk, potato, salt, pepper, and leeks in a 2-quart saucepan.

3. Cover the pan, bring to a boil, and reduce heat to a simmer. Simmer for 20 minutes.

4. Puree the mixture in a food processor or in batches in a blender. Thin if desired with the reserved liquid from Step 1, or milk. Add nutmeg and taste for seasoning adjustment. Overseason if serving the soup cold. Serve with a tablespoon of the yellow pepper puree swirled in.

To Prepare the Yellow Pepper Puree

1. Cut the peppers in half, flatten them with the heel of your hand, and place peppers on a baking sheet, skin side up, under a hot broiler. Broil until the peppers are completely blackened and charred, which can take as long as 10 minutes. Remove peppers to a plastic or paper bag and chill until cool enough to handle.

2. Peel the loosened skin from the peppers and discard. Chop the peppers and puree them in a food processor, blender, or food mill. See the illustrations on page 260.

3. Add the basil, cheese, and olive oil to the peppers. The puree will be thick and chunky. It will keep up to one week chilled, or it may be frozen.

Yield of soup: 4 cups	Fat per cup: 4g
Calories per cup: 137	Carbohydrates per cup: 19g
Protein per cup: 9g	Sodium per cup: 480mg
Yield of garnish: 1 cup	Fat per tablespoon: 1g
Calories per tablespoon: 18	Carbohydrates per tablespoon: 1g
Protein per tablespoon: 1g	Sodium per tablespoon: 11mg

Chilled Tomato Soup
with Tarragon Ice

❖

This is one of my favorite summertime soups because of its delightful combination of flavors and colors. There's no need to buy perfect tomatoes for this recipe, the "seconds" or bruised tomatoes offered at many farm stands are ideal. The soup freezes well, too, making it possible to enjoy the flavor of summer in the dead of February. The tarragon ice is fashioned after a basil sorbet served at the famed Four Seasons Restaurant in New York City, which like many other restaurants today offers a health-conscious menu.

For the Soup

3 pounds ripe tomatoes, cored
8–10 fresh basil leaves, snipped, or 1 teaspoon
    dried basil
2 medium onions, sliced
2 cloves garlic, minced
1–2 teaspoons sugar
1 tablespoon fresh tarragon, snipped, or 1 teaspoon
    dried tarragon
3/4 teaspoon salt
freshly ground pepper to taste
1/2–3/4 cup chicken broth, if needed

For the Tarragon Ice

1 small, ripe avocado
juice of 1/2 a lemon
2 tablespoons finely minced fresh tarragon leaves or
    1 tablespoon dried tarragon leaves
1 cup water

2 tablespoons sugar
pinch of salt

To Prepare the Soup

1. Quarter the tomatoes. Put them in a large saucepan with the basil, onions, garlic, sugar, tarragon, salt, and pepper. Turn heat to medium high, cover, and simmer until tomatoes are completely soft and pulpy, about 20 minutes. Stir occasionally.
2. Uncover the pan, lower the heat to medium-low, and cook about 30 minutes or until reduced by ⅓.
3. In batches, process soup in a food processor, blender, or food mill. Strain if desired to remove the seeds and skins. Chill and serve the soup garnished with a dollop of tarragon ice. Thin with chicken broth if needed.

To Prepare the Tarragon Ice

1. Peel and pit the avocado. Puree it in a food processor or blender with the lemon juice.
2. In a saucepan, simmer the tarragon leaves in the water for 20 minutes. Remove from the heat, add sugar and salt, and stir until dissolved.
3. Add tarragon water to the avocado in a food processor. Blend.
4. Place in an ice cream freezer and follow manufacturer's instructions to freeze. Soften before serving. It's best used within 24 hours.

Yield of soup: 4 cups
Calories per cup: 95
Protein per cup: 4g

Fat per cup: 1g
Carbohydrates per cup: 20g
Sodium per cup: 410mg

Yield of ice: ¾ cup
Calories per tablespoon: 20
Protein per tablespoon: 0

Fat per tablespoon: 1g
Carbohydrates per tablespoon: 3g
Sodium per tablespoon: 9mg

Chinese Egg Drop Soup

❖

A filling, very good lunch. Even if you haven't shopped for a week, you're likely to have the ingredients.

1 ½ cups chicken broth
1 egg
1 tablespoon soy sauce, or less, to taste
1 tablespoon minced chives

1. Bring the broth to a boil in a small saucepan.
2. In a bowl, beat the egg and soy sauce with a fork. Stir into the boiling broth, creating a small whirlpool. Continue stirring until the egg cooks, about 45 seconds.
3. Garnish the soup with chives and serve. Slices of bean curd, peas, and cooked chicken may be added for variety.

Note: Sodium-reduced soy sauce is available in many markets for those wishing to restrict the amount of sodium.

Yield: 1 good serving
Calories: 125
Protein: 9g

Fat: 6g
Carbohydrates: 8g
Sodium: 640mg

❖ **THINKING THIN TIP** ❖

If making a chicken stock you'll use immediately, skin the chicken before making the stock. It will save time when you degrease the pan. To slip skin from the wings and backs, put them in a roasting pan, cover with aluminum foil, and bake 15 minutes in a 500-degree oven.

"Cream" of Lettuce Soup

❖

This cream soup owes its richness more to the vegetable itself than cream, making it as healthful as it is calorie conservative. Make it in quantity when garden lettuce is in season and freeze for a taste of summer in the chill of winter. This soup is good hot or cold and may be made as much as 24 hours in advance.

> 1 head lettuce, preferably romaine (about ³⁄4 pound)
> 2½ quarts water
> 1 can (13³⁄4 ounces) chicken broth
> ³⁄4 cup fresh or frozen peas
> 2 scallions, roughly chopped
> 1 tablespoon minced fresh parsley
> ½ teaspoon salt
> freshly ground pepper to taste
> ½ cup milk
> 4 tablespoons crème blanc, page 37 (optional)

1. Wash and core the lettuce, and tear the leaves in half. Bring the water to a boil. Add the lettuce leaves and boil, uncovered, for 3–4 minutes or until wilted and somewhat softened.
2. Drain the lettuce and place it in a food processor or blender in small batches, with the broth, peas, scallions, parsley, salt, and pepper. Process the mixture and leave it slightly coarse.
3. Pour the mixture into a saucepan, add milk, and simmer 15–20 minutes.
4. Before serving add a dollop of crème blanc to each serving.

Note: Overseason if serving the soup cold.

Yield: 4 cups
Calories per cup: 73
Protein per cup: 6g

Fat per cup: 1g
Carbohydrates per cup: 12g
Sodium per cup: 380mg

"Cream" of Mushroom Soup

◆

Use this recipe as an example of how to rewrite old favorites in the *Gourmet Light* way. To update, add a half ounce of sherry-soaked cepes or chanterelles at Step 8.

> 1 quart chicken broth plus an additional ½ cup
> 1 small onion, minced
> 1 tablespoon butter
> 3 tablespoons flour, instant blending recommended
> 12 ounces mushrooms, wiped clean
> juice of half a lemon or 1 tablespoon lemon juice
> 2 egg yolks
> ½ cup milk
> 1 tablespoon sherry
> ¼ teaspoon salt
> freshly ground pepper to taste
> freshly ground nutmeg

1. Bring ¼ cup broth to a boil in a 10-inch skillet. "Saute" the onion at high heat until it becomes limp and transparent.
2. Meanwhile, bring 1 cup of broth to a boil in a 2½-quart saucepan.
3. When the onion is limp and the broth almost evaporated, reduce the heat to medium. Add the butter. When it's melted and foamy, stir in the flour. Stir with a wooden spoon for 1 minute over low heat.
4. Remove the skillet from the heat. Whisk in the hot broth. Whisk in an additional cup of cold broth. Transfer the ingredients to the now-empty saucepan. Add the remaining 2 cups broth.
5. Remove stems from the mushrooms. Mince the stems and slice caps. Add the stems to broth-onion mixture. Simmer, covered, for 20 minutes.

6. Place the caps in now-empty skillet, add lemon juice, and remaining ¼ cup broth, and "saute" at high heat until mushrooms are soft and liquid is evaporated. Set aside.
7. Strain the stems and onions from the broth-onion mixture. Press the vegetables with the back of a wooden spoon to extract their juices.
8. Beat the egg yolks with milk in a small bowl. Drizzle ½ cup strained hot soup base into yolks while beating with a fork. Slowly pour yolks into remaining soup base, and whisk over low heat until thickened, about 4 minutes.
9. Add mushroom caps to the soup. Add the sherry, season with salt, pepper, and nutmeg.

Note: Do not boil soup once the egg yolks have been added.

Yield: Approximately 4 cups
Calories per cup: 150
Protein per cup: 7g

Fat per cup: 6g
Carbohydrates per cup: 17g
Sodium per cup: 190mg

❖ **NUTMEG** ❖

Recipes in this book frequently specify using freshly grated nutmeg, for it is considerably more flavorful than the ground variety. Whole nutmegs—the pit of a West Indian peachlike fruit—are available at some supermarkets and specialty food shops. Mace, a similar but stronger taste than nutmeg, is the outside sheathing that covers the nutmeg. It is sold already ground. Nutmeg grinders, (similar to small pepper mills) are available as are small, inexpensive graters that often have a hinged top to store the nutmeg.

Gazpacho

❖

This zesty bowl of garden goodies, which is really improved the second day, is naturally low in calories. A friend gave me this version of the Spanish classic. Here it is with a bit less oil. For a special treat, serve with the tarragon ice on page 74.

> 1 ¾ pounds ripe tomatoes
> 1 medium onion, chopped
> 1 cucumber, peeled, seeded, and chopped
> 1 green pepper, seeded and chopped
> 1 red pepper, seeded and chopped (optional)
> 1 clove garlic, minced
> 24 ounces tomato juice
> 1 tablespoon extra-virgin olive oil
> 4 tablespoons red wine vinegar
> 1 teaspoon salt
> a few drops hot pepper sauce
> 2 tablespoons chopped chives (from scallion tops)
> oven-dried croutons, optional

1. Core the tomatoes and cut a cross in each one's bottom. Immerse tomatoes in boiling water for 15 seconds. Cool them under running water and strip the skins. Quarter the tomatoes. Squeeze the tomatoes in a strainer supported over a bowl to remove the seeds. Press the seeds with the back of a spoon to extract the juice. Discard the seeds.
2. In a food processor or blender, combine half of the seeded tomatoes, all the juice from the same, the onion, half of the cucumber, green pepper, red pepper, all the garlic, and half the tomato juice. Process until somewhat smooth.
3. Stir in the remaining tomato juice, oil, vinegar, salt, pepper sauce, the remaining tomato, cucumber, peppers, and all the chives.

Chill at least 2 hours; also chill the soup bowls. Serve with oven-dried croutons if desired.

Oven-Dried Croutons

1. Dice 4 slices of bread. Place on a cookie sheet in a 325-degree oven for 15 minutes, and stir the cubes occasionally. To brown slightly, spray a frying pan with cooking spray and "saute" oven-dried cubes over medium heat until lightly browned.

Yield: 6 cups
Calories per cup: 90
Protein per cup: 3g

Fat per cup: 3g
Carbohydrates per cup: 15g
Sodium per cup: 610mg

Potato and Sorrel Soup

This soup is very good served cold with a simple chicken salad for a tempting hot-weather meal. If sorrel is unavailable, substitute fresh spinach seasoned with a few drops of lemon juice.

> 2 *large or 4 small leeks*
> 4 *cups chicken broth*
> 3 *potatoes, about 1 pound (Idaho or all-purpose white), peeled*
> 1/2 *teaspoon salt*
> *freshly ground pepper to taste*
> *freshly grated nutmeg*
> 4 *or 5 leaves sorrel, or spinach seasoned with lemon juice*

1. Discard the green ends from the leeks. Slice the white part and rinse it thoroughly.
2. Place the sliced leeks in a 2½-quart saucepan with enough chicken broth to half cover, cover the pan, and boil gently for 8 minutes or until leeks are softened.
3. Dice the potatoes. Add them to the leeks with the remaining chicken broth, salt, and pepper. Simmer, covered, for 30–35 minutes.
4. Rub potato-leek mixture through a sieve into a bowl or puree in a food processor or blender. Scoop what won't go through the sieve into the soup.
5. Season with nutmeg. Stack sorrel or spinach leaves, roll tightly in jellyroll fashion, and slice thinly crosswise (known as *chiffonade*). (See drawing on page 201.) Add the leaves to the hot soup until wilted. If serving the soup cold, allow at least 4 hours chilling time and overseason slightly as chilling weakens the flavors.

Yield: 5 cups
Calories per cup: 75
Protein per cup: 3g

Fat per cup: trace
Carbohydrates per cup: 16g
Sodium per cup: 230mg

Curried Zucchini Soup

Omit the curry if it's a spice you'd rather live without. This recipe makes good use of baseball bat–size zucchini, but remove the seeds first. Because the soup freezes well, you might like to double the recipe.

2 large onions, diced
1 quart plus 6 tablespoons chicken broth

1 clove garlic, minced
3–4 pounds zucchini, diced
1 cup cooked rice
1 tablespoon curry powder
8–10 fresh basil leaves, snipped, or 1 teaspoon
    dried basil
5–6 fresh sage leaves, snipped, or ½ teaspoon dried
    sage
1 teaspoon fresh thyme leaves or ½ teaspoon dried
    thyme
1 teaspoon salt (less if using canned broth)
freshly ground pepper to taste
½ cup grated cheddar cheese
1 cup milk

1. "Saute" the onions in a 10-inch skillet in the 6 tablespoons of chicken broth until they're limp. Add the garlic and cook 1 minute more.
2. In a 4-quart or larger saucepan, combine the onions, garlic, zucchini, remaining broth, rice, spices, and herbs. Cover and simmer at least 1 hour or as long as two.
3. Puree the zucchini-onion mixture in a food processor or food mill in batches. Strain the soup if desired.
4. Stir in the grated cheese and milk. Heat to blend.

Yield: Approximately 6 cups   Fat per cup: 3g
Calories per cup: 155   Carbohydrates per cup: 24g
Protein per cup: 9g   Sodium per cup: 580mg

Gingered Carrot Soup

❖

The ginger root in this refreshing chilled summer soup lends peppery zip. Make this a day or two before serving if desired.

4 large carrots, scrubbed and grated
1 medium onion, diced
3 cups chicken broth
½ teaspoon salt
lots of freshly ground pepper to taste
1½ teaspoon sugar if using carrots sold in cello bags,
    less for those with greens attached
a 1-inch x ½-inch piece of fresh ginger root, peeled
    and minced
1 slice white bread, stale or lightly toasted
freshly ground nutmeg
6 tablespoons crème blanc, page 37
a bit more grated ginger root

1. In a 2½-quart saucepan, combine the carrots, onion, broth, salt, pepper, sugar, and ginger root. Cover, turn the heat to high, and reduce it to medium once it begins to boil. Uncover, simmer 40 minutes or until about ¾ to 1 cup liquid remains.
2. Puree the soup in a food processor or in a blender in batches. Crumble bread in your hand, add it to the soup, and process until smooth.
3. Add nutmeg, taste for additional salt, sugar, or pepper. Overseason if serving chilled. Top each serving with a dollop of crème blanc mixed with a little more ginger root.

Yield: 4 cups
Calories per cup: 80
Protein per cup: 4g

Fat per cup: trace
Carbohydrates per cup: 16g
Sodium per cup: 380mg

Spinach and Oyster Bisque

Traditionally, a bisque is a puree of shellfish finished with cream. Today, bisque has come to mean almost anything the recipe writer wants it to be, as long as it's a creamy puree of something. Here's a *Gourmet Light* bisque that's based on shellfish, cheats on cream, and is enhanced with spinach, making it an emerald-hued soup rich in vitamin A and potassium.

> 6 ounces shucked oysters, liquor reserved
> 3 tablespoons cornstarch
> 1½ cups milk
> 1 10-ounce package fresh spinach, stems removed
> ½ teaspoon salt
> a few drops pepper sauce
> freshly grated nutmeg

1. Mix the reserved oyster liquor with the cornstarch to dissolve.
2. Chop the oysters in a food processor or meat grinder.
3. Simmer the ground oysters in milk for 8 minutes, stirring often.
4. Meanwhile, wash the spinach. Place it in a 2½-quart saucepan with the water that clings to the leaves. Cover, turn heat to high, and cook until just wilted, about 45 seconds. Drain, and chop finely, or place it in a food processor to puree.
5. Add the spinach to the oyster-milk base. Stir dissolved cornstarch into the oyster-spinach base. Cook the mixture over low heat, stirring until thickened, about 4 minutes. If a smoother texture is desired, puree it in a food processor.
6. Season the bisque with salt, pepper sauce, and nutmeg. Serve with unsalted crackers.

Yield: 4 cups
Calories per cup: 110
Protein per cup: 10g

Fat per cup: 1g
Carbohydrates per cup: 15g
Sodium per cup: 420mg

Two Mushroom Consomme

❖

If consomme brings to mind images of Victorian ladies presiding over sherry parties, this version holds a surprise for you. It is updated with cepes, which are dried mushrooms imported from France. Their earthy scent perfumes this light soup. Although this is easily made with store-bought consomme, you might enjoy the satisfaction and rich flavor of making your own.

> 5 cups degreased homemade beef stock or 3 cans
>   (10½ ounces) beef consomme
> 2 egg whites and the eggshells
> 8 ounces mushrooms, wiped clean with a cloth
> 3 tablespoons beef broth
> 2 tablespoons lemon juice
> ½ ounce cepes (available at specialty food stores),
>   soaked in sherry or water to cover
> ⅓ cup Madeira or sherry
> 2 tablespoons finely minced chives

To Clarify Homemade Stock

1. Beat 1 cup cold stock with the egg whites and eggshells (yes, shells!) in a large bowl. Meanwhile, bring remaining stock to a boil.
2. Gradually pour the hot stock into the egg whites, beating all the while. Pour the whites and stock back into the saucepan and set over moderate heat. As the stock regains a simmer, stir with a spoon. As soon as the simmer is regained, stop stirring.
3. Turn the heat to low. Move the pan very gently partially off the heat, the liquid must not bubble or move too much. Let it rest for 15–20 minutes.
4. Line a colander with a double layer of cheesecloth that has been wrung out in water. Gently ladle stock-egg mixture through the

cheesecloth. Discard the shells and whites. The resulting soup should be crystal clear.

For Canned Consomme or to Finish Soup

1. Slice the mushrooms. "Saute" them in a little broth and lemon juice in an 8-inch skillet.
2. Drain the cepes, mince them, and discard the wine or strain it through a double-thick, wrung-out piece of cheesecloth before adding it to soup. Add cepes to mushrooms and heat through.
3. Combine clarified stock (or canned consomme diluted according to directions) with the mushrooms, Madeira, and chives. Serve hot in small cups.

Yield: 6 servings
Calories per serving: 45
Protein per serving: 2g

Fat per serving: trace
Carbohydrates per serving: 9g
Sodium per serving: 20mg

❖   **THINKING THIN TIP**   ❖

There are times when it might be better to eat a little of something fattening than a lot of something skinny.

Chapter 5

SALADS AND THEIR DRESSINGS

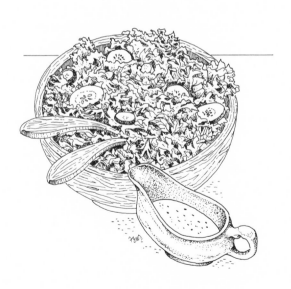

Salads

❖

Salads have risen to new heights, both in popularity and design in recent years. Where once a few leaves of iceberg, chopped cucumber, and minced onion would suffice as a side dish, one now finds a range of rare goodies artfully presented as main-course meals. Radicchio, lamb's lettuce, and baked chèvre cheese are but a few of the new salad items popular today. To support the demand, fancy greengrocers are popping up like mushrooms from coast to coast, offering an enormous selection of fresh produce from near and—thanks to modern transportation—far.

This chapter focuses on salads as a side course. The majority of the main-dish salads are found in the chapter of the predominant ingredient. For example a Sole, Scallop, and Pea Pod Salad is found in the seafood chapter, and a Sesame Chicken Salad is found in the poultry chapter.

The Greens

❖

A simple tossed salad is so much more interesting with two or three greens. Why limit yourself to one when there's such a big garden of salad things to choose from, everything from arugula to watercress. While iceberg is probably the most popular salad green, it is also probably one of the dullest. It has its place, keeping the bread from getting soggy in a tuna salad sandwich, but it is far outclassed by other, less well known varieties. Three other types of lettuces to consider are:

Cos or romaine—large, almost rectangular leaves, dark green at the tip, paler green at the base. This is the lettuce of choice for Caesar salad, it is also excellent torn into small pieces for a tossed green salad.

Butterhead—The lettuces of this group offer soft, velvety leaves that unfortunately bruise and rust quickly. This perishable type includes Boston, a medium-size, light green head, and Bibb, a smaller, more compact head. Limestone lettuce is another Butterhead variety. For longer storage life, rinse, dry, and chill these lettuces as soon after purchase as possible. These soft-leafed lettuces are excellent for simple salads composed of mixed greens, or even alone, tossed with a vinaigrette and possibly a scattering of freshly made croutons.

Leaf lettuces—The lettuces in this group grow as clumps of leaves rather than as heads. It is quite a hardy lot, ranging from red leaf (mostly green turning to red at the tip) to salad bowl, a tangle of curly, narrow leaves. Leaf lettuces are best in combination with other greens.

Less well known, but fun to experiment with, are beet, dandelion, and mustard greens; even nasturtium leaves lend a salad distinction. And there's watercress with its peppery crunch, chicory, endive, and . . . of course spinach. Radicchio, a red "green," and lamb's lettuce are specialty items you'll find on trendy restaurant menus or in chic produce markets. With such a wealth of greens, most of which are available year round, it seems sad to reach for the old standby every time.

Select greens with an eye for color and texture. An excellent combination is a salad of Bibb, red leaf, and watercress, the softness of the Bibb offset by the crunch of the watercress, and the red leaf adding vibrant color.

While my personal bias leans toward a salad of mixed greens graced only by a sprinkling of freshly made croutons or a bit of grated cheese, many enjoy other additions. Any vegetable in its prime that can be eaten raw is a candidate. Again, keep color, texture, and flavor in harmony.

There is no written rule that demands a tomato in every salad. When they are out of season, which sadly is most of the year, get color from other sources. Roasted, julienned red peppers (see page 260) are delicious, a bit of grated red cabbage or carrot will do the trick, as will a few leaves of red leaf lettuce. Put nothing in the salad that is tasteless, such as a winter tomato. For a change of pace, "saute" mushroom slices before adding them. I find the flavor enhanced when they're cooked.

Purchase greens that look perky, without yellow or rust spots, and if possible with most of the outer leaves intact, because these contain more nutrients than the delicate centers. Generally, the greener the leaf, the greater the source of vitamins A, C, and E as well as iron and calcium. A quarter of an average-size head contains a meager 15 calories.

Salad greens retain their nutrients best when held at near-freezing temperatures in high humidity. Head lettuce will keep in the vegetable crisper of the refrigerator for 3–4 days; some varieties will last even longer. Leaf lettuces are more perishable and keep best if rinsed, spun dry, and stored in a loose plastic bag with a few paper towels on every other layer to absorb moisture, a leading cause of rust and bad spots. Lacking a lettuce spinner, wash the lettuce, shake off excess moisture, lay leaves in a single layer on an old thick bath towel, roll loosely, and refrigerate. The lettuce will keep this way about 24 hours. Washing, drying, and chilling any lettuce about 4–5 hours before serving will make for a beautifully crisp salad. For those special occasions, don't forget to chill the plates too.

Don't store lettuce near apples, melons, or avocados because the ethylene gas these fruits give off acts as a ripening agent, maturing the lettuce before its time and turning it brown.

The Salad Syndrome or The Invisible Calorie

❖

It's become common knowledge that the culprit is the butter not the potato, but the fats in salads remain invisible to many—that is, until they show up on the waistline. "All I ever have for lunch is a salad, and I still gain weight!" is a common lament. The demon is the salad dressing. Most dressings are very high in fat, contributing 150 to 200 calories in just 2 tablespoons to an otherwise skinny bowl of greens. *Gourmet Light* dressings are based mostly on stocks or consomme, and contribute far fewer calories than commercial preparations. The recipes that follow are dressings for mixed-green salads, beyond that are recipes for specialty salads.

Vinaigrettes

Vinaigrette, a classic combination of oil and vinegar with or without additional seasonings, is the true French dressing. Following are several variations on the simple vinaigrette theme, all prepared the *Gourmet Light* way. (For more on skinny dressings, see the Primer, page 6.) First, these tips:

1. If you don't make your own naturally thick chicken or beef stock, use commercially prepared consomme or canned chicken broth. The former, because of its added gelatin, will give the best results.
2. When using homemade stock, double the amount called for in the recipe and boil it until reduced by half. This double-strength stock will give your dressings body. Don't reduce commercial broths though, for they will be too salty.
3. If you do not use canned consomme, you will need to add salt to taste.
4. If possible prepare the dressing at least 2 hours before serving, to let the flavors marry.
5. A dressing made with homemade stock or store-bought consomme will jell in the refrigerator. Remove it an hour before serving or heat briefly to liquefy.

Other Dressings

Vinaigrettes do not all salads make, of course; occasionally, we yearn for something cool and creamy. Either of the *Gourmet-Light* mayonnaises (page 26 and 27) take kindly to herb, cheese, or mustard additions. In the event that time is tight, a half-and-half mixture of plain yogurt and store-bought mayonnaise will save you 340 calories over straight mayonnaise. To use a homemade mayonnaise as a salad dressing, simply add flavorings and thin it with a bit of chicken broth. Roquefort Skinny Dip and the Sauce Verte, both in the appetizer chapter, are also excellent for salad dressings—again, thinned with a bit of broth.

Herbed French Vinaigrette

❖

A true French dressing is not the mayonnaise/ketchup variety commonly called "French," but an emulsion of oil and vinegar. Here is a skinny version.

> 5 tablespoons double strength homemade beef or
>   chicken stock or canned consomme
> 2 tablespoons red wine vinegar
> 1 teaspoon sugar
> ½ teaspoon Dijon-style mustard
> 1 tablespoon extra-virgin olive oil
> 1 clove garlic, minced
> 2 teaspoons chives, minced
> 1 teaspoon paprika

1. Combine all the ingredients in a jar, shake well, check for seasoning, and refrigerate.

Yield: ⅔ cup
Calories per tablespoon: 16
Protein per tablespoon: trace

Fat per tablespoon: 1g
Carbohydrates per tablespoon: 1g
Sodium per tablespoon: 4mg

❖   **THINKING THIN TIP**   ❖

Because *Gourmet Light* cooking uses so little oil, buy the best. Extra-virgin olive oil is the first pressing of the olives and the most flavorful. Virgin quality is the next, and so on until the final pressings, which rely on hot water poured over the pits to coax the final droplets of oil.

Lemon Vinaigrette

❖

Easy on your time and waistline.

> 5 tablespoons double-strength homemade beef or
>   chicken stock or canned consomme
> 1 tablespoon extra-virgin olive oil
> 1 tablespoon lemon juice
> 1 tablespoon red wine vinegar
> 1 teaspoon sugar
> freshly ground pepper to taste
> 1 teaspoon minced fresh parsley (optional)

1. Combine all the ingredients in a jar, shake well, check for seasoning, and refrigerate.

Yield: ½ cup
Calories per tablespoon: 20
Protein per tablespoon: trace

Fat per tablespoon: 2g
Carbohydrates per tablespoon: 1g
Sodium per tablespoon: 2mg

❖   **VINEGARS**   ❖

Once used as a medicine or as a drink when heavily diluted with water and often used as a preservative with salt, vinegars are the slightly aging darling of the growing gourmet food industry. Where most kitchen cabinets once stored pretty much your basic cider variety, many shelves are now crowded with enough labels and flavors to rival a modest wine cellar. Indeed, some vinegars carry a higher price tag than jug wines! Some vinegars, such as balsamic, are even aged like spirits in oak barrels. The added cost is offset by the wonderful flavor they impart.

Balsamic-Walnut Oil Vinaigrette

❖

Balsamic vinegar, a malt vinegar aged in wooden casks, and walnut oil have become buzz words in culinary circles. Both are available at specialty food stores. Here they are combined to create a delicious dressing for mixed greens.

double-strength homemade beef or chicken stock or
canned consomme
walnut oil (refrigerate after opening)
balsamic vinegar
1 tablespoon water
1/2 teaspoon prepared mustard
1/2 teaspoon sugar
freshly ground pepper to taste

1. In a 1-cup glass measure, pour in the consomme until the liquid reaches the 1/4-cup mark. Add walnut oil until the liquid measures 1/3 cup. Add the balsamic vinegar until the liquid measures 1/2 cup. Add water, mustard, sugar, and pepper. Shake well, check for seasoning, and refrigerate.

Yield: 1/2 cup
Calories per tablespoon: 18
Protein per tablespoon: trace

Fat per tablespoon: 2g
Carbohydrates per tablespoon: 1g
Sodium per tablespoon: 3mg

Caesar Salad Dressing

❖

Make this salad with romaine lettuce, freshly grated Parmesan or Romano cheese, and if you like, a handful of freshly made croutons. Arrange the lettuce leaves in spoke fashion around the plate, sprinkle cheese and croutons on top, and drizzle with the following dressing. To eat, pick up the leaves in your fingers, using them as scoops to hold the croutons and cheese. Delicious!

> 2 cups water
> 1 egg
> 5 tablespoons double-strength homemade beef or
>   chicken stock or canned consomme
> juice of ½ lemon
> 1 tablespoon extra-virgin olive oil
> 6 or 7 drops Worcestershire sauce
> a few drops hot pepper sauce to taste
> 1 clove garlic, minced
> freshly ground black pepper to taste
> 2 tablespoons freshly grated Parmesan cheese

1. The egg will need to be coddled. Bring 2 cups water to a boil. Add the egg, cover, and boil for 1 minute. Drain and cool under running water.
2. Crack the coddled egg open into a jar. Combine all the remaining ingredients, except the cheese. Sprinkle cheese over the salad greens, then drizzle with dressing.

Note: For instructions on making croutons see page 81.

Yield: ⅔ cup
Calories per tablespoon: 30
Protein per tablespoon: 2g

Fat per tablespoon: 2g
Carbohydrates per tablespoon: 1g
Sodium per tablespoon: 17mg

Sesame Seed Dressing

❖

This dressing is the perfect partner for a spinach salad with shredded hard-cooked egg and sliced "sauteed" mushrooms.

2 tablespoons sesame seeds
4 tablespoons double-strength homemade beef or
*   chicken stock or canned consomme*
2 teaspoons sesame oil, available at specialty food
*   shops*
2 tablespoons lemon juice
1 teaspoon sugar
freshly ground pepper to taste

1. Spray a baking sheet with cooking spray. Sprinkle sesame seeds over sheet. Turn oven to 350 degrees, put baking sheet in oven, and remove 10 minutes later.
2. Combine sesame seeds in a jar with all the other ingredients. Shake well, check for seasoning, and refrigerate.

Yield: ½ cup
Calories per tablespoon: 26
Protein per tablespoon: trace

Fat per tablespoon: 2g
Carbohydrates per tablespoon: 1g
Sodium per tablespoon: 1mg

Fresh Herb Vinaigrette

❖

This is the dressing of choice for herb gardeners looking for ways to preserve summer's fragrant gifts, for it freezes nicely. Delicious on vine-ripened tomatoes (which have twice the vitamin C of hothouse winter tomatoes) or cold fish salads tossed with leftover corn cut from the cob.

> 1 cup loosely packed fresh basil leaves
> 1/2 cup loosely packed fresh tarragon leaves
> 2 tablespoons homemade chicken or beef stock or canned consomme
> 1 tablespoon raspberry or red wine vinegar
> 1 tablespoon safflower oil
> 1 scant teaspoon sugar
> freshly ground pepper to taste

1. Put the herbs in a bowl or measuring cup and snip repeatedly with scissors until they're reduced to about half the original volume.
2. Combine the herbs in a food processor or blender with the remaining ingredients. Blend until herbs are mostly minced and sauce is a lovely pale green. Check for seasoning. May be frozen.

Yield: ¾ cup
Calories per tablespoon: 14
Protein per tablespoon: trace

Fat per tablespoon: 1g
Carbohydrates per tablespoon: 1g
Sodium per tablespoon: 2mg

Japanese Dressing
for Snow Peas

❖

Yet another alternative to a mayonnaise dressing is tofu, a soybean product. The following recipe is excellent tossed with blanched snow peas or broccoli.

4 *ounces tofu*
5 *tablespoons double-strength homemade chicken*
   stock or canned consomme
1 *tablespoon sesame oil*
1 *tablespoon walnut oil*
2 *tablespoons rice wine vinegar, available at Oriental*
   or specialty food stores
1 *teaspoon soy sauce*
1 *quarter-size piece of fresh ginger, peeled and*
   minced

1. Combine all the ingredients in a food processor or blender and blend. Chill.

Yield: 1 cup
Calories per tablespoon: 21
Protein per tablespoon: trace

Fat per tablespoon: 2g
Carbohydrates per tablespoon: trace
Sodium per tablespoon: 12mg

Beyond Simple Tossed . . .

❖

No matter how innovative and imaginative your mix of greens, there are times when you yearn for something different. Perhaps a Fire and Ice Salad or the pleasant bite of Counter Slaw, or maybe the cool creaminess of a Dilled Zucchini and Carrot Salad. Whatever your pleasure, scan these offerings for that which tempts you. These are side dishes, lunches, or light dinners; heavier offerings are found in the seafood and poultry chapters.

Fire and Ice Salad

❖

This salad gets its name from the flame of the brandy and the chill of the greens. Often when a recipe indicates flaming it is purely for effect; here, igniting the liquor renders it mellow. A wonderful salad for chilly nights.

The Salad

1 pound fresh spinach, stems and backbones
    removed
1 hard-cooked egg
4 or 5 black olives, pitted and chopped
4 ounces mushrooms, cleaned and sliced

The Dressing

2 strips bacon
1/2 can canned consomme or double-strength
    homemade chicken or beef stock

3 tablespoons malt or balsamic vinegar
1 tablespoon lemon juice
2 teaspoons sugar
½ to 1 teaspoon Worcestershire sauce
1 teaspoon oil
2 tablespoons brandy or bourbon

To Prepare the Salad

1. Wash and spin dry the spinach. Tear it into bite-size pieces in a large bowl.
2. Sieve the hard-cooked egg over the greens. Add the olives and mushrooms (cooked or uncooked as you like). Set aside while preparing the dressing.

To Prepare the Dressing

1. Fry the bacon strips in a small skillet. When crisp, remove and drain on paper towels. Reserve 2 tablespoons fat and discard the rest.
2. In the now-empty skillet, combine the consomme, vinegar, lemon juice, sugar, Worcestershire sauce, oil, and reserved 2 tablespoons fat. Bring to a boil.
3. Meanwhile, heat the liquor in a small pot with a long handle and a spout. When bubbles appear at the edge of the pot ignite the liquor by tipping it into the flame of a gas stove, or light it with a match. Pour the liquor into the hot dressing.
4. When the flames die out, boil just 20 seconds longer. Remove from the heat and toss with the chilled greens.

Yield: 4 servings
Calories per serving: 163
Protein per serving: 7g

Fat per serving: 11g
Carbohydrates per serving: 9g
Sodium per serving: 308mg

Dilled Zucchini
and Carrot Salad

❖

This salad may be made early in the day and placed on lettuce at serving time. Plump out the offering with cooked salad shrimp and a bit of minced green pepper if you like.

> ½ cup Reduced-Calorie Mayonnaise, page 26
> 2 tablespoons freshly minced dill or 1 tablespoon
>   dried dill weed
> 1 tablespoon plain yogurt
> 1 · medium zucchini
> 3 carrots, scrubbed
> 1 teaspoon salt
> freshly ground pepper to taste
> lettuce to line individual bowls or serving plate

1. Combine the mayonnaise, dill, and yogurt in a bowl. Stir to combine.
2. Grate the zucchini and carrots by hand or with the julienning disk of a food processor. Place them in a bowl.
3. Season the vegetables with salt and pepper. Stir to combine. Add the dilled mayonnaise, and mix. Chill until serving time.

Yield: 4 servings
Calories per serving: 170
Protein per serving: 4g

Fat per serving: 14g
Carbohydrates per serving: 8g
Sodium per serving: 623mg

Wilted Cucumber Salad

❖

If soft-leafed lettuce dressed with vinaigrette is the national salad of France, a wilted cucumber salad is the fingerprint of Germany. Here's a reduced-calorie version that's as good the second day as the first.

1 *cucumber*
2 *teaspoons salt*
2 *tablespoons canned consomme*
1 *tablespoon red wine vinegar*
1 *teaspoon honey or sugar*
1 *teaspoon oil*
freshly ground pepper to taste

1. Peel the cucumber and seed by slicing it in half the long way and removing the seed core with a teaspoon. Slice the cucumber very thinly by hand or in a food processor, and place it in a sieve or colander. Sprinkle salt over it and let it drain 20–30 minutes over a bowl or in sink. This removes excess water from the vegetable.
2. Rinse the cucumber repeatedly. Taste it to be sure the salt is removed. Press cucumber to help remove water. Drain it on an absorbent towel.
3. In a small saucepan, combine the consomme, vinegar, honey, and oil. Reduce the liquid over high heat until 2 tablespoons are left. Pour it over the drained cucumber, season with pepper, and chill until serving time.

Yield: 2 servings
Calories per serving: 58
Protein per serving: 1g

Fat per serving: 2g
Carbohydrates per serving: 9g
Sodium per serving: 12mg

Counter Slaw

❖

Cynthia Young, a fine Nantucket cook, gave me this recipe some years ago when we honeymooned at her Polpis guest house. It's quick, easy, and delicious, just the thing to take on a picnic to Great Point—or your favorite summer afternoon getaway spot. Coleslaw prepared with mayonnaise-type dressings contains as many as 225 calories in a ³/₄-cup serving; this counter slaw lets you save room for dessert. Add grated carrots, raisins, or a bit of onion for variety.

1   small green pepper, grated
6   cups loosely packed, shredded cabbage (about ¹/₂ small head)
¹/₃ cup chicken broth
2   tablespoons light oil, such as safflower
2   tablespoons sugar
2   tablespoons red wine vinegar
1   teaspoon caraway seeds
¹/₂ teaspoon salt
    freshly ground pepper to taste

1. In a medium-size bowl, combine the green pepper with the cabbage.
2. In a 1-quart nonaluminum saucepan, combine the broth, oil, sugar, vinegar, and caraway seeds. Cook over high heat until the sugar is dissolved, about 1 minute.
3. Toss hot dressing with the vegetables. Season to taste with salt and pepper. Cover the slaw with plastic wrap and leave it at room temperature for 4 hours. Chill until serving time.

Yield: 6 servings
Calories per serving: 73
Protein per serving: trace

Fat per serving: 5g
Carbohydrates per serving: 7g
Sodium per serving: 186mg

Pear and Gouda Salad
with Pine Nuts

❖

A halved pear broiled until a cloak of Gouda cheese bubbles and browns, resting on a lightly dressed bed of curly salad bowl lettuce, makes a dish of pasta tossed with Basil-Walnut Sauce (page 32) a wonderful dinner partner. You can have it on the table in less time than it will take to drive to McDonald's.

> 1 pear, any variety, slightly underripe is fine, peeled
>   if desired
> 2 tablespoons (1 ounce) Gouda cheese, grated
> 2 tablespoons pine nuts
> 1/4 head salad bowl or other leaf lettuce
> 4 tablespoons Herbed French Vinaigrette, page (95)

1. Preheat the broiler. Cut the pear in half the long way, and remove its core and woody fiber leading to the stem. Sprinkle it with lemon juice if holding more than 20 minutes before broiling. Slice a sliver from the curved side of the pear so it will sit evenly. Place on a baking sheet.
2. Divide the grated cheese over the pear halves. Broil about 8 minutes, or until the pear is softened and cheese is bubbly and browned.
3. Meanwhile, toast the pine nuts by putting them in an 8-inch skillet over high heat. Shake the pan constantly for about 1 minute until nuts turn golden brown. Remove from skillet.
4. Wash, rinse, and dry the lettuce. Divide on two plates. Center each broiled pear half on lettuce. Drizzle 2 tablespoons dressing on each salad, and sprinkle pine nuts over.

Yield: 2 servings
Calories per serving: 183
Protein per serving: 5g

Fat per serving: 11g
Carbohydrates per serving: 16g
Sodium per serving: 126mg

Bibb, Tuna, and Green Bean Salad

❖

One of my favorite lunchtime or light dinner salads.

½ pound green beans
1 small head Bibb lettuce
2 slices thin-sliced bread
1 teaspoon butter
1 6½-ounce can water-packed tuna, drained
4 tablespoons Balsamic-Walnut Oil Vinaigrette (page 97) or other reduced-calorie vinaigrette dressing

1. Prepare the beans for cooking by aligning several at a time and cutting off their tips. Turn the beans around, align again, and slice ends again. Continue until all are ''tipped and tailed.''
2. Bring a 2½-quart saucepan ¾ full of water to a boil. Add the beans and boil 4 minutes or until softened but still crisp. Drain and cool under running water. Pat dry.
3. Core and wash the lettuce. Spin dry the leaves or dry them on an absorbent towel. Chill until serving time.
4. With one slice bread atop the other, dice it into tiny cubes. Spray a baking sheet with cooking spray. Place the bread on the baking sheet and bake in a 325-degree oven for about 10 minutes.
5. Melt the butter in an 8-inch skillet. Saute bread cubes over medium heat until toasty. Remove from heat.
6. Remove chilled, washed lettuce from the refrigerator. Tear it into bite-size pieces and arrange it on individual plates or in a bowl. Arrange the beans, flake the tuna over, and sprinkle the salad with croutons. Dribble on the dressing.

Yield: 2 servings
Calories per serving: 250
Protein per serving: 29g

Fat per serving: 8g
Carbohydrates per serving: 16g
Sodium per serving: 115mg

Apple-Artichoke Salad
with Hollandaise

❖

The ingredients are reminiscent of a Waldorf salad, but the light Hollandaise adds a different dimension. You may expand the salad to a main-dish meal by grilling and dicing a swordfish steak, toss it with the celery and so on, and serve at room temperature or only slightly chilled. Make this salad early in the day so flavors may meld before serving time.

> 4 artichokes
> 2 tablespoons lemon juice
> 1/4 cup flour
> 1 quart water, plus a little more
> 2 celery ribs, diced
> 1 apple, Red Delicious recommended, diced
> 1 ounce walnuts, roughly chopped
> 1/2 cup Hollandaise, page 21, or mayonnaise, page 26
> 1/4 teaspoon salt
> freshly ground pepper to taste

1. With a stainless-steel knife, cut off the stem and upper third of each artichoke. Using scissors, remove the sharp tips of the leaves. Cut around the artichoke with a sharp knife as if paring an apple, removing the tough outer leaves. When you get to the soft inner core, slice it off. Be sure all dark green skin is removed from the bottom of the artichoke. Drop each artichoke bottom into water with the lemon juice added.
2. Make a paste of about 1/4 cup flour with enough water to moisten. Bring a quart of water to a boil, stir in the flour paste, and bring to a boil in a nonaluminum saucepan. Add the artichokes and simmer for 10 minutes or until easily pierced with a fork. Remove the

artichokes from the cooking liquid with a slotted spoon and drain until cool.

3. With a grapefruit spoon, remove each artichoke's fuzzy center and discard. Set artichokes aside while preparing remaining salad.
4. In a bowl, toss together the celery, apple, walnuts, and Hollandaise (which may be cold). Season with salt and pepper. Add swordfish here if desired.
5. Line individual plates with a lettuce leaf. Place an artichoke bottom on lettuce. Fill to overflowing with celery-walnut mixture.

Yield: 4 servings
Calories per serving: 180
Protein per serving: 6g

Fat per serving: 8g
Carbohydrates per serving: 21g
Sodium per serving: 178mg

Confetti Rice Salad

Carbohydrates, the bugaboo of the diet world for years, are no longer a dirty word. The calorie conscious, particularly those who exercise regularly, need complex carbohydrates for energy; otherwise, the body will break down proteins for fuel, proteins better used to build and maintain tissues. Sadly, most carbohydrates taste better when lathered with fats: the butter on the bread, the sour cream on the potato, the dressing on the salad. Here's a cool salad, great for picnicking because it's ultimately portable, which makes the most of the carbohydrates and the least of the fat. A few smoked shrimp would make a wonderful addition.

2 medium tomatoes
2 medium green peppers
1 medium red pepper
3 cups cooked rice

2 tablespoons minced fresh parsley
10 fresh basil leaves, snipped, or 1 teaspoon dried
basil
½ teaspoon salt
freshly ground pepper to taste
3 tablespoons oil, safflower or corn oil recommended
1 tablespoon plus 2 teaspoons rice wine vinegar,
available at specialty food stores or Oriental
markets

1. Dice the tomatoes. Seed and dice the peppers.
2. Place the vegetables in a bowl with the rice, parsley, basil, salt, and pepper. Sprinkle all with oil and vinegar.
3. Spray a 1-quart mold or 6 1-cup ramekins with cooking spray. Fill each ramekin ¾ full with rice mixture, press salad down with a glass or any utensil slightly smaller than the diameter of the ramekin. Cover with plastic wrap and chill at least 3 hours. (Note: For a decorative design, fashion a "flower" from a thin carrot slice and a "stem" from a parsley stem on the bottom of each ramekin.)
4. To unmold, run a flexible-bladed metal spatula between the salad and the mold. Invert a plate on mold, flip over, and lift mold off.

Yield: 6 servings
Calories per serving: 187
Protein per serving: 3g

Fat per serving: 7g
Carbohydrates per serving: 28g
Sodium per serving: 183mg

Pasta Salad
with Basil-Walnut Sauce

❖

I could eat this salad, which is best at room temperature, nearly every day and not tire of it. The sauce is reminiscent of pesto, but it's much lighter. Delicious with garden-ripe tomatoes and a simple tossed salad, or flesh the meal out with a Chicken Breast Paillard.

> 12 ounces egg noodles, fresh if possible
> ¾ cup Basil-Walnut Sauce, page 32
> ¼ teaspoon salt
> freshly ground pepper to taste
> freshly grated Parmesan cheese

1. Cook the noodles according to package directions. Drain.
2. Toss noodles with the Basil-Walnut Sauce, salt, and pepper. Serve at room temperature or warm. Top with Parmesan cheese.

Yield: 4 servings
Calories per serving: 436
Protein per serving: 14g

Fat per serving: 13g
Carbohydrates per serving: 67g
Sodium per serving: 168mg

❖ **THINKING THIN TIP** ❖

Carbohydrates, which used to be taboo for any weight-loss program, are now recognized as a necessary and vital part of any diet plan. To avoid them is to court fatigue, irritability, and failure for any prolonged weight reduction.

Pea Pod and
Water Chestnut Salad with
Sherry Ginger Dressing

❖

Make the dressing, blanch the pea pods, and grate the water chestnuts early in the day, then assemble this salad at the last minute.

> *½ pound pea pods, strings removed*
> *5 tablespoons double-strength homemade beef or chicken stock or canned consomme*
> *1 tablespoon vegetable oil*
> *2 tablespoons sherry wine vinegar, available at specialty food shops*
> *1 tablespoon soy sauce*
> *1 teaspoon sesame oil, available at Oriental or specialty food shops*
> *1 teaspoon peeled and minced fresh ginger*
> *1 scant teaspoon sugar*
> *4–6 radicchio lettuce leaves or soft-leafed lettuce such as Bibb*
> *2 fresh mandarin oranges, peeled and sectioned, or 1 7-ounce can mandarin oranges packed in light syrup, drained*
> *8 or 9 fresh water chestnuts, peeled and blanched, or 4 ounces canned chestnuts*

1. Bring a 2½-quart saucepan ¾ full of water to a boil. Immerse pea pods, remove from heat, and let peas sit 4 minutes. Drain and rinse the peas under cold running water until they're no longer warm. Drain peas on absorbent towels.

2. Combine the consomme, oil, vinegar, soy sauce, sesame oil, ginger, and sugar in a jar. Shake well to combine.
3. In a small bowl, combine half the dressing with the cooked pea pods. Let the mixture rest at least 15 minutes or up to several hours at room temperature or in the refrigerator.
4. Arrange the lettuce on individual plates or a serving platter. Arrange the pea pods and orange sections alternately in a circle on the lettuce.
5. Grate the water chestnuts in a Mouli grater or food processor. Arrange in the center of the pea pods and oranges. Dribble the salad with the remaining dressing.

Yield: 4 servings
Calories per serving: 130
Protein per serving: 4g

Fat per serving: 5g
Carbohydrates per serving: 19g
Sodium per serving: 142mg

Chapter 6
MEATS

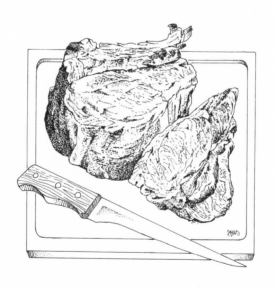

Meats

❖

America produces more meat than any other country, and we eat almost all of it. Beef is still the national favorite; it's estimated every man, woman, and child will consume 120 pounds in a single year. While there are those who will view this as eating our way to the grave, others will claim it as evidence Americans are among the best-fed people in the world. Is eating meat a dietary liability or insurance of good nutrition? And what is its place in a reduced-calorie format?

Those on the pro side of the meat question will have us know that, ounce for ounce, meat is nutrient dense. Quite simply, it supplies outstanding nutritive value. It is an excellent source of high-quality protein and essential minerals such as iron, phosphorus, and copper while contributing vitamins, too. Those on the con side point to meats, particularly red meats, as major contributors of saturated fats, which have been linked to high cholesterol levels and heart disease. And because most meat is high in fat, as a rule it is a caloric pill of no little consequence.

Does that imply one should eschew meat for tofu? Give up taste for health? After all, *Gourmet Light* professes to be a "waist not—want not" style of eating, and for many, eating red meats is one of the pleasures of the table. Others enjoy a juicy pork chop or succulent veal cutlet, and with 4 billion pounds of hamburger consumed in 1982, it's not only children who hanker for America's signature food. Whether you're interested in reducing your intake of saturated fats, calories, or both, limiting—not eliminating—the amount of fatty meats in your diet may be the answer. Selection is also key.

Disavowing Spartanism, which meat to choose when the carnivorous hunger strikes? Must one feel guilty savoring a fork-tender rib eye? No, moderation is the simple answer. And if meat is an important part of your diet, perhaps a look at sample calorie counts of each type will help when selecting a type of meat.

Veal, of course, is the leanest of the meats, because the 3-month or younger calf has developed little fat. A 4-ounce portion is roughly 176 calories. Lamb, marketed at about 6 months, has a hefty fat cover, but that can be removed before cooking. A 4-ounce serving contains about 298 calories; less when all the fat is removed. Pork weighs in at about 340 calories for a 4-ounce serving, although that is based on data from the early 1960s, and a leaner animal is now being bred. And finally, all America's favorite, beef ranges from 342 calories in a moderately fatty 4-ounce portion to a surprisingly low 163 calories in lean flank steak.

In moderation, any of these meats are perfectly permissible for the calorie conscious. But while 4 ounces of beef—about 340 calories—is within most people's limits, 6–7 ounces may not be. And you may be eating more than you think. Take careful note of package weights before cooking and determine just how much a 3½- or 4-ounce serving truly is. Or perhaps get in the habit of weighing portions for a while to train the eye to recognize how much (or little) the recommended portion size amounts to. "But it's good for me!" comes the lament. "What's wrong with a little extra meat?" For children, who need protein to grow, nothing; for the adult it may mean added pounds.

Just how much protein do we really need? And will it really make us strong? Here's a look at some protein myths and realities.

The Protein Pedestal

❖

Of the three food classifications of protein, carbohydrates, and fats, protein has long been ballyhooed to all too often mythical proportions.

MYTH 1: To be healthy we need to eat lots of protein.

Nutritionists recommend that protein constitute the smallest percentage of the daily diet. It's been estimated that most Americans eat 2 to 3 times the amount of protein they need. And more is not necessarily better. Excess protein is burned for calories, stored as fat, or simply excreted.

The recommended daily allowance of protein is 42 grams for a 120-pound person and up to 73 grams for a 200-pound person. If in a typical day you eat something like this—a glass of 2 percent low-fat milk (4 grams protein), a ham sandwich on white bread (14 grams), and a 4½-ounce hamburger (30 grams)—you've received 48 grams of protein, to say nothing of protein also eaten in the course of the day in other forms, from vegetables to the flour in desserts.

MYTH 2: Protein isn't fattening.

In truth, protein supplies the same amount of calories per gram (4) as carbohydrates. And excess protein turns to the same kind of body fat as excess carbohydrates or fats.

MYTH 3: Protein increases athletic performance.

There are no magic potions for increasing athletic prowess. Protein alone will make no one a better athlete, or even increase one's stamina. The proverbial balanced diet (with protein on the low end) will allow us to perform at our individual best. Foods don't make for athletic performance, skill and training do. But without proper nutrition we can't live up to our potential. Good nutrition is but one rung on the ladder.

For all these reasons—from a high concentration of saturated fats to bulging calorie counts—this chapter is necessarily lean. Those wishing to curb calories will do well to incorporate a larger percentage of fish and poultry in their diet. But when meat and only meat will do, by all means enjoy. Veal, selected cuts of beef and lamb, and even a lean pork tenderloin or cutlet are within the bounds of the calorie-conscious diner. Unfortunately, the leanest meats are often the toughest, and the tastiest cuts are the fattest. But even lean meats can be coaxed into tenderness if the cook understands a bit about the science of tender meat. The following factors apply mostly to beef. Tenderness for veal, pork, and lamb are discussed in the recipes for those meats.

The Science of Tender Meat

❖

The tenderness of meat is the cumulative effect of these factors:

1. *Connective tissue*

There are two kinds of connective tissue in the muscles: collagen, which melts into gelatin quickly in the presence of heat, and elastin, which stubbornly refuses to melt unless subjected to long, slow cooking and even then may remain unchanged. If there is a great deal of either collagen or elastin in the meat, it is likely to be tough. Connective tissue is not to be confused with the streamlets of fat that run through the muscles; this marbling is an indication of tender meat.

2. *Where the cut is from*

As a general rule, the less exercised a muscle is the more tender it will be. Choosing any cut that lies on either side of the backbone (the loin) will be the most tender, and, of course, the most fatty.

3. *Aging*

When beef is aged, enzymes in the meat naturally soften the connective tissue creating literally fork-tender meats. Aged meats are more costly because of the refrigeration and warehouse space involved. Home aging of meats is possible for good cuts of meat that are at least 4 pounds in weight, when they're covered with a protective flap of fat.

4. *Grade of the cut*

Meat is graded by government inspectors prior to sale. The carcass is inspected for conformation, quality, and finish—gibberish to you and me but the meat of the matter for the inspector before it is labeled prime, choice, or good. There are actually 5 lesser grades but not for retail sale. While prime meat is regarded as the best, the quality of choice meats is also excellent and because of reduced marbling, may be slightly less fatty.

A naturally tender steak, then, has a lot of marbling, has little connective tissue, was cut from the loin, and was hopefully aged at least a week or more. It can be either of prime or choice quality. Meat that is not naturally tender can be made so by attention to the cooking technique used.

Moist vs. Dry Heat Cooking

Virtually all the recipes you've ever read for meat fall under one of but two categories, moist or dry heat cooking. Moist heat (stewing, braising, etc.) breaks down the collagen if the meat is allowed to cook at low temperatures for a long time. Naturally, a piece of meat may not be cooked rare if it is a tough cut, it will need to cook beyond the 120 internal degrees of pink meat. Not even meat tenderizers can transform a tough cut into fork-tender steak.

It is my experience that meat tenderizers promise more than they can deliver, much as a sparkling wine is not, after all, a fine champagne. Tenderizers for the most part are made from papain, an enzyme found in papayas. This enzyme, which incidentally is injected into humans to dissolve calcium deposits on the spine, does soften tissue. However, it has some drawbacks. It is only effective on the meat's surface, unless the meat is punctured, making little escape tunnels for the juices. Further, the tenderizing activity is slow unless the meat is quite warm—reaching its peak at 176 degrees—so it may actually do nothing at all on refrigerator cold meat.

Marinating meat is another popular method for tenderizing tough cuts. Its effectiveness remains a moot point. While some cooks claim soaking meat in an acid (wine or vinegar) solution with oils and seasonings will tenderize it, there are scientific studies that both contradict and confirm the practice. It is an indisputable fact that marinating meats in an acid will result in some loss of minerals.

It seems wise then to choose the cooking method that best complements the meat. Dry heat cooking (sauteing, grilling, broiling, and roasting) is suitable for cuts that are naturally tender. These meats may be cooked rare. You can broil, pan-fry, or grill tender meat (not at too high a heat, which can destroy some of the protein) for a quick, delicious, and somewhat fattening meal. For beef lovers who wish to curb both calories and cholesterol, a bit of finagling is called for, because the cut of choice for them is a leaner, thus a tougher cut. Top round, eye of the round, flank steak, and lean sirloin steaks are lower in fat. Of the tender cuts, filet mignon (tenderloin) is the better choice.

For those who relish a moist, juicy, rare beefsteak, the Roasted Tenderloin of Beef may be the answer. For others, there are Beef Paupiettes with Sausage and Zucchini, Braised Beef with Pineapple and Papaya, and more. This section is thin, however, because of the generally high calorie count of most meats.

Beef

Despite a slightly tarnished reputation because of a bit of bad press, I'll bet the hamburger is still one of America's favorite foods. From Monday's meat loaf to Saturday's prime rib, beef has been the backbone of the American diet. But unless you've been orbiting in space for the last decade or so you also know that it is high in saturated fat, which has been fingered as a contributor to heart disease, and it is high in calories. Nutritionists have warned against indulging in too much fatty meat, which has sent the American Beef Council scrambling to remind the public that beef . . . indeed, is good food. With 3 1/2 ounces of beef round supplying more than 1/2 the daily requirement of protein, more than 1/4 the phosphorus, 1/6 the iron, and 1/4 of the niacin for a 120-pound woman for only 261 calories, one wonders, what's the fuss? The *rest* of the story, of course, is the high concentration of saturated fats, which, if you're prone to high cholesterol levels, are health threatening. But one needn't give up fatty meats altogether. With proper cooking techniques and wise selection, moderate amounts of beef can be enjoyed.

From a caloric and a quality viewpoint, there is beef and there is beef. Unfortunately, the tastiest beef is the most fattening, the leaner the beef, the tougher and the more tasteless. Following the guidelines given above about tender meat, select and cook lean meats so as to maximize their tenderness and flavor.

Braised Beef
with Pineapple and Papaya
❖

Call it boeuf en daube, boeuf à la mode, estouffade de boeuf, braised beef, or pot roast, the technique is all the same. A tough and often fatty cut of meat is browned, liquid and vegetables are added for flavoring, and the whole is simmered until tender. It's the sort of robust meal that justifies the existence of cold weather. But because it is often made with relatively fatty cuts that drip their fat into the sauce rather than into a broiler pan to be discarded, it should not be a common meal for the calorie concerned. This *Gourmet Light* version, made with a leaner cut than the more traditional chuck, uses the natural tenderizing effects of two tropical fruits, pineapple and papaya. Both contain papain, a common ingredient in commercial meat tenderizers. Long ago, natives of tropical islands found that meat was more tender if wrapped in papaya leaves and slow roasted. Papaya leaves might be hard to come by, but most markets carry the fruit. And if need be, canned pineapple, rather than fresh, may be used. Both not only add flavor but serve as a natural tenderizer, helping to dissolve the connective tissues in the meat as it cooks. Start this recipe about 3 1/2 hours before dinner, or make it in advance and reheat.

4 pounds top or bottom round beef roast
2 medium onions, chopped
1 clove garlic, mashed
2 cups beef broth
½-liter bottle dry red wine such as a Burgundy
2 cups fresh or canned pineapple, chunked
1 green pepper, seeded and chopped
1 bay leaf
a few sprigs fresh thyme or ½ teaspoon dried thyme
½ teaspoon salt
freshly ground pepper to taste
4 large carrots, cut into bite-size pieces
8 small or 4 large potatoes, peeled and halved or
    quartered
1 papaya, peeled, seeded, and sliced
2 tablespoons cornstarch

1. Spray a Dutch oven or other deep-sided heavy-bottomed skillet with cooking spray. Brown the meat at high heat on all sides and remove to a plate.
2. "Saute" the onions and garlic over medium heat in the Dutch oven in ¼ cup beef broth, covering the pot until the vegetables are soft and transparent.
3. Add the beef, wine, and remaining beef broth.
4. Add the pineapple, green pepper, herbs, salt, and pepper. Cover the pot, leaving a sliver exposed so there will be some evaporation, and simmer for 2 hours and 35 minutes. Add the carrots, potatoes, and papaya and cook until tender, about 25 minutes more. Remove the meat from the pot. Moisten the cornstarch with a few tablespoons of cooking liquid, stir it into the remaining cooking liquid over medium heat, and stir until thickened.
5. To serve: Cut meat into serving-size chunks, serve with the vegetables and sauce.

Yield: 8 generous servings
Calories per serving: 460
Protein per serving: 48g

Fat per serving: 14g
Carbohydrates per serving: 34g
Sodium per serving: 366mg

Flank Steak
in Gingered Beer Sauce

❖

Flank steak, a strip of muscle that lies on either side of the loin, is the leanest of all beef cuts, with about 163 calories in a 4-ounce serving. Because the muscle fibers are coarse and there is little fat, it is most often cooked with moist heat, though occasionally it is broiled or grilled as a steak. With its long, thin configuration, which is ideal for stuffing, flank steak makes an attractive presentation. Here it is rolled around a fruit stuffing and slow cooked in a fragrant sauce of gingered beer. The meat may be readied for cooking early in the day.

The Stuffing

5   dried apricots
2   tablespoons rum or hot water
1   small onion, minced
2   tablespoons beef broth
3   small apples, peeled, cored, and chopped
2   teaspoons minced ginger root
1/4   teaspoon salt
freshly ground pepper to taste
dash ground cinnamon

The Meat

1 3/4   pounds flank steak
Dijon-style mustard
1   onion, chopped
2   celery ribs, chopped
1   carrot, chopped

½ teaspoon salt
freshly ground pepper to taste
a 12-ounce bottle dark beer
1½ cups beef broth
3 tablespoons tomato paste
3 or 4 allspice berries or ¼ teaspoon ground allspice
1 bay leaf
1 tablespoon fresh thyme leaves or ½ teaspoon
    dried thyme
2 unpeeled garlic cloves, halved
1 cinnamon stick
a quarter-size piece of fresh ginger root, peeled

To Prepare the Stuffing

1. Plump the apricots in the rum or hot water for at least 30 minutes or as long as 12 hours.
2. "Saute" the onion in the broth in a 10-inch skillet over medium heat until limp and the broth is evaporated.
3. Drain the apricot liquid into the onion skillet. Chop and add the apricots. Add the apples and ginger. Season with salt, pepper, and cinnamon. Cover and cook over medium-low heat for 4 minutes or until the fruits are soft. Remove from the heat and cool while preparing the pot vegetables and meat.

To Prepare the Meat

1. Place the meat between two sheets of wax paper and pound it with a cleaver until somewhat thinner and enlarged. Dip a pastry brush into a pot of mustard and brush it over the inside of meat. Set aside.
2. Spoon the stuffing (from Step 3) onto the meat, completely covering the surface; reserve any extra. Starting at the small end, roll the meat up in jellyroll fashion. Tie tightly with butcher's twine.

Gather what stuffing falls out and reserve with other stuffing.

3. Spray the skillet used for stuffing (no need to wash) with cooking spray. Add the onion, celery, and carrot, cover, and cook at high heat until the vegetables are lightly browned. Scrape them into a 5-quart Dutch oven or electric Crockpot.

4. Pat the meat dry. Spray the skillet with cooking spray. Sear the meat over high or medium-high heat, turning frequently. If the meat seems to be sticking, dribble in a bit of vegetable oil. When browned, remove to the Dutch oven. Season with salt and pepper.

5. Deglaze the skillet with ¼ of the beer, stirring with a wooden spoon over medium heat. Pour the deglazing juices, remaining beer, and broth onto the meat. Stir in the tomato paste. Add any extra stuffing.

6. Preheat oven to 350 degrees. Cut a piece of cheesecloth to make a bouquet garni of the allspice, bay leaf, thyme, and garlic. Enclose the herbs and knot the cheesecloth. Add to the Dutch oven.

7. Add the cinnamon and ginger to the pot. Cover and bake at 350 degrees for ½ hour. Reduce the heat to 300 degrees and cook an additional 2 hours. Flip the meat 2 or 3 times, spooning hot juices over. To cook in an electric Crockpot, simmer for 2½ hours. Don't let liquid boil. Check for evaporation, adding more broth if necessary.

To Serve

1. Remove the meat from the pot. Cut and discard strings. Let the meat rest, covered with a towel, while preparing the sauce.

2. Remove the bouquet garni, cinnamon, and ginger from the pot. Pour the sauce through a coarse strainer (or put through a food processor and then strain), pushing the vegetables with the back of a wooden spoon. Discard the pulp in the strainer, taste the sauce, and adjust seasoning. If it's too thin, boil until somewhat reduced. If there's not enough sauce, add broth or red wine, heat, and stir until it reaches the desired thickness.

3. Slice the meat in ½-inch slices, arrange in a circle on platter. Pour the sauce over and around the meat. Garnish the center of the platter with lightly buttered peas or glazed carrots or turnips.

Yield: 6 servings
Calories per serving: 267
Protein per serving: 30g

Fat per serving: 8g
Carbohydrates per serving: 19g
Sodium per serving: 375mg

❖ **GINGER** ❖

Ginger root is the up-and-coming spice of the 80's. It is being used in sauces, blanched and julienned like orange rinds as a garnish for poultry dishes, and used in everything from salad dressings to ice creams. Oriental cooking has long known the wonders of this root of an orchidlike plant. Of course, in powdered form ginger has been used in baked goods literally for centuries. Our grandmothers used it in pickles and chutneys, and it is a component of curry powder. To use fresh ginger root, peel the outer skin and small knobs with a knife, exposing the pale yellow woody flesh. Cut off as much as you need and mince it finely. The remaining ginger root may be stored at room temperature in an airtight container (how long will depend on the age of the root when you buy it) or immersed in oil or sherry and kept refrigerated for up to 6 months. The ginger-spiked oil or sherry is delicious anywhere ginger is welcome: eggs, fish, poultry, carrots, squash, sweet potatoes, or your favorite way.

Beef Paupiettes with Sausage and Zucchini

❖

Make the stuffing for these rolls a day in advance if you like, and assemble about an hour or so before cooking. The ground veal helps to reduce the caloric tally of the rolls while the sausage lends it zip.

> 1 pound thinly sliced beef; use bottom or top round
>   or use minute or thin-sliced sandwich steaks
> prepared horseradish
> 2 small zucchini
> 2 teaspoons salt
> 4 ounces ground veal
> 4 ounces bulk-type sausage
> 1/2 teaspoon fresh thyme leaves or 1/4 teaspoon dried
>   thyme
> 2 tablespoons grated mozzarella cheese
> Béarnaise Sauce (page 24) or Wine Sauce (page 34)

To Prepare the Beef

1. If using bottom or top round steak, partially freeze the meat, then slice it as thinly as possible. Place the meat between pieces of wax paper and pound it with a cleaver until thin.
2. Dip a pastry brush into the horseradish jar and spread it thinly on the meat. Set aside while preparing the stuffing.

To Prepare the Stuffing

1. Grate the zucchini into a sieve held over a bowl. Sprinkle with salt and let rest for 20 minutes. The salt removes excess moisture.
2. Remove the sausage casing. Crumble the veal and sausage into an 8-inch skillet, cook gently, stirring from time to time, over me-

dium heat until the sausage and veal are cooked through, about 7 minutes.

3. While the sausage cooks, rinse the zucchini thoroughly, then squeeze it hard to remove excess moisture. Taste to be sure salt is completely removed.

4. Add zucchini, thyme, and mozzarella to the sausage-veal mixture the last minute of cooking. Stir to combine. Remove from heat.

To Assemble the Rolls

1. Divide the sausage-zucchini mixture over the meat, don't overfill. Loosely roll up the beef, enclosing the stuffing. Tie with butcher's twine as you would a package, or secure the flaps with toothpicks (this does make cooking more difficult).

2. Spray a large skillet with cooking spray, place over high heat, and "saute" the rolls, reducing heat to medium once they've browned. Cover the pan and shake it occasionally to cook the meat evenly. The paupiettes will cook in about 12 minutes. Remove paupiettes from the pan. Snip and discard strings. Serve the rolls with Béarnaise Sauce, or Wine Sauce. They may also be grilled or broiled.

Yield: 6 servings
Calories per serving: 280
Protein per serving: 23g

Fat per serving: 20g
Carbohydrates per serving: 2g
Sodium per serving: 236 mg

Roasted Tenderloin
of Beef

❖

I've always felt that a tenderloin epitomized the best of beef. Fewer cuts are more tender, easier to carve, or serve. But tenderloin can lack flavor, for as meats go, it is fairly lean, particularly if well trimmed before cooking. Hence the tradition of wrapping a tenderloin steak in a slice of bacon before grilling, or serving the meat with a rich sauce such as Béarnaise.

To accentuate the tenderness, our *Gourmet Light* version calls for home aging (a process you may omit). For the ultimate in juicy perfection the meat is then slow roasted in a salt crust, which, rather amazingly, doesn't penetrate the roast. This makes an excellent party meal served with Reduced-Calorie Béarnaise Sauce, which holds better than the traditional sauce, for everything may be done ahead. For an even more festive treatment, butterfly the meat and stuff it, after aging, with langoustine (available frozen), crab, or lobster. Retie the roast and proceed as directed.

Tenderloins freeze well so take advantage of an occasional sale. A typical tenderloin weighs 5½ pounds to about 8 pounds, before trimming. Allow about three-quarters of a pound per person of un-trimmed weight for the generous servings you plan for when entertaining. A 7-pound tenderloin will weigh about 5 pounds after trimming, theoretically feeding 10 people with a generous half pound. However, I've never found this to be true. In my experience a 7-pound tenderloin (before trimming) will feed 6–8 with seconds for some. Ask the butcher to trim and tie the roast, reserving the fat if you wish to age it at home.

Prime meat has already enjoyed a lengthy aging, but choice meat often has not. For truly fork-tender meat, follow this procedure 3 days before your dinner party.

Remove the store wrappings from the meat weighing at least 4 pounds, trim any fat that remains. Place the meat on a cake rack over a baking sheet. Lay the reserved fat on the meat, covering it as much as possible. Crease a piece of aluminum foil large enough to cover the meat down the center. Position the tent of foil over the meat loosely, do not wrap tightly. Air must circulate. Refrigerate for 3 days, turning the meat and repositioning the fat once a day. During this time, the enzymes that are naturally present in the meat break down the fibers of the muscles, causing them to relax. In the process, the meat softens. You'll notice that any surface not covered by fat will darken and harden. To prepare the meat for cooking, untie the butcher's twine. Carefully pare away all the hardened flesh. Retie the roast, it is now ready for roasting.

> a whole tenderloin, about 7 pounds before trimming,
>   tied and trimmed
> 1   clove garlic, mashed or pressed
> 10 cups kosher salt
> 2½ cups water
> Béarnaise Sauce (page 24)

1. Preheat oven to 400 degrees. Pat the meat dry with paper towels. Rub the garlic over the meat.
2. In a large bowl, moisten the salt with the water bit by bit, stirring to form a paste. Because kosher salt has no additives to keep it free flowing, it is very susceptible to moisture and may or may not need the entire amount of water specified here. Add only as much (or more) as needed to form a thick paste.
3. Put half the salt paste in a roasting pan just large enough to hold the meat. Put the meat on top, add remaining salt paste, and pack tightly around the roast with your hands.
4. Place on the lowest shelf in a 400-degree oven and roast for 1 hour or until an instant-reading meat thermometer registers 120 degrees for rare or 135 degrees for medium rare. Begin temperature testing after 40 minutes to be on the safe side. The temperature of the meat at the time of roasting, the shape of the meat, and the density of the salt paste can all affect the actual roasting time; what worked last time may not work next time.

5. Remove the pan from the oven when the meat is the desired temperature. Let the meat sit for 10 minutes, and remove salt crust. Slice the meat before serving it, because the outside will be gray rather than brown since it was not seared. Serve with Béarnaise Sauce.

Yield: 8 servings
Calories per serving: 425
Protein per serving: 73g

Fat per serving: 14g
Carbohydrates per serving: trace
Sodium per serving: cannot be calculated

Beef Stroganoff

❖

Here's an exercise in transforming a classic recipe into one for the *Gourmet Light* files. The meat is browned in cooking spray rather than fat and the sour cream is replaced by crème blanc. There's another change. Because I enjoy meat rare, I've chosen to pan-fry a solid piece of beef, rather than cook bite-size pieces, which inevitably become overdone. The meat is then given the briefest of simmers in the sauce. The sauce may be made ahead and reheated just before serving time.

> 2 medium green peppers, seeded and thinly sliced
> 4 tablespoons beef broth
> 2 tablespoons tomato paste
> 1 tablespoon plus 1 teaspoon Worcestershire sauce
> 2 teaspoons prepared mustard
> 1 teaspoon prepared horseradish
> 1/2 teaspoon salt
> 1 cup crème blanc, made without milk, page 37
> 6 ounces mushrooms, sliced

1 1/4 pounds sirloin strip steak
1/2 cup dry red wine
1 clove garlic, minced

1. "Saute" the peppers in the broth in an 8-inch skillet over medium heat until just softened. Scrape them into a bowl when done.
2. While the peppers cook, stir the tomato paste, Worcestershire, mustard, horseradish, and salt into the crème blanc. Set aside.
3. Spray now-empty skillet (no need to wash) with cooking spray. Add the sliced mushrooms, cook over high heat, reducing to low, until mushrooms are lightly browned. Add to peppers in the bowl, cover, and keep warm in a 150-degree oven.
4. Pat beef dry. Spray pan again and heat it on high heat. When it is very hot, add meat. Sear at high heat 1 minute, reduce heat to medium, cook 2 minutes more. Turn meat over, cook another 2 to 3 minutes or until it has reached the desired degree of doneness.
5. Remove meat from pan and keep warm. Add wine and garlic to the pan. Cook on high heat until wine is reduced by half to about 1/4 cup. Remove from heat, add mushrooms and peppers, stir, and cool about 2 minutes. If the wine is too hot the crème blanc will curdle.
6. Add the flavored crème blanc, stirring. Add meat, simmer at very low heat just 4 to 5 minutes. The crème blanc must not boil. Serve on a heated platter on a mound of egg noodles if desired.

Yield: 4 servings
Calories per serving: 510
Protein per serving: 29g

Fat per serving: 38g
Carbohydrates per serving: 12g
Sodium per serving: 467mg

Veal Roast with Sun-Dried Tomatoes Roasted in Salt

❖

Lean meats such as veal are often dry meats, so it behooves the cook to look for ways to enhance the natural moisture of such foods. Cooking in salt seals in the juices while amazingly not contributing to the sodium content of the food. In fact, I find I often have to salt the roast at the table. Uncharacteristically, oil has been used in the stuffing. The meat is so lean as to benefit by this touch of fat, but it may be omitted if you prefer to cook the onions in broth.

> 1 ounce (about 5) sun-dried tomatoes, salt-cured not
> oil-cured type if possible, available at specialty
> food stores
> boiling water
> 1 small onion, chopped
> 1 clove garlic, minced
> 1 tablespoon extra-virgin olive oil
> 4 ounces mushrooms, sliced
> 1/4 cup cooked rice (substitute dried bread crumbs if
> you have no cooked rice)
> 1 teaspoon fresh tarragon leaves or 1/2 teaspoon
> dried tarragon
> 6–8 fresh basil leaves or 1 teaspoon dried basil
> 1 teaspoon raspberry or other fruit-flavored vinegar
> 2 slices bacon, fried, drained, and crumbled
> 1/4 cup minced fresh parsley
> freshly ground pepper to taste
> a veal shoulder roast, boned, about 2 pounds
> 5 cups kosher salt
> 3/4 to 1 cup water

1. Cover the tomatoes with the boiling water. Steep for 15 minutes. Drain and cut the tomatoes into thin strips.
2. Cook the onion and garlic in olive oil in a Teflon-coated pan over medium-low heat, covered, until softened.
3. Remove the onion and garlic to a small bowl. Do not wipe the pan. Add the mushrooms, cover and cook over high heat, lowering heat if needed. Remove the cover and stir mushrooms from time to time. Uncover the mushrooms when browned, add tomatoes, stir and cook 30 seconds. Scrape into the bowl with the onion and garlic.
4. Stir the rice, tarragon, basil, vinegar, bacon, parsley, and pepper into the bowl. Set one-half cup of stuffing aside for final step.
5. Preheat oven to 450 degrees. Open the meat if it has been tied. Some veal roasts that come in netting are actually two pieces of meat. Simply spread the stuffing over one layer, top with the second layer, and tie with butcher's twine for a roast. If needed, cut a cavity into the roast for the stuffing. Wipe the meat dry.
6. Place the salt in a bowl. Add only as much water as you need, bit by bit, to make a paste.
7. Place ⅓ of the salt paste in a 9-inch by 5-inch by 3-inch loaf pan. Place the dried roast on top. Cover with the remaining salt paste, packing it down with your hand. Be sure meat is completely encased by salt paste. Place the pan in the bottom third of the 450-degree oven. Reduce heat to 350 degrees after 30 minutes and cook an additional 45 minutes or until an internal meat thermometer registers 165 degrees. Let meat rest for 5 minutes. Crack the salt crust open and discard. Lift the meat to an ovenproof platter. Pat the remaining stuffing (from Step 4) over the roast and broil 5 minutes or until lightly browned on top. Remove strings and slice thinly.

Yield: 6 servings
Calories per serving: 380
Protein per serving: 32g

Fat per serving: 24g
Carbohydrates per serving: 8g
Sodium per serving: 597mg

Veal Chops
with Red Pepper Butter

❖

Really watching calories for a few days? How about a veal chop for lunch? Too much, too fattening? Would you believe these succulent chops slathered with red pepper butter actually have fewer calories than a tuna on white bread? More costly perhaps, but would you rather pay with your pocketbook or your waistline? Besides the calorie count, an added payoff is the feeling of satisfaction after such a pampered lunch that will last till dinnertime. Because the red pepper butter keeps in the freezer indefinitely, make it in quantity—even frozen, it is sliceable. It flames a simple green vegetable, chicken, or fish fillet with flavor and color.

For the Red Pepper Butter

5 *medium red peppers*
4 *tablespoons minced fresh parsley*
1 *clove garlic, minced*
½ *teaspoon salt*
freshly ground pepper to taste
1 *teaspoon fresh lemon juice*
2 *tablespoons butter*

For the Meat

4 *loin or shoulder (sometimes called arm) veal chops*
¼ *teaspoon salt*
freshly ground pepper to taste

To Prepare the Red Pepper Butter

1. Halve the peppers, discard the seeds, and flatten the peppers with your hand. Place on a baking sheet and broil until blackened and charred, about 8 minutes. Turn the sheet around once or twice to

ensure even cooking. *See the illustration on page 260.*

2. Scrape the peppers into a plastic or paper bag, roll it closed, and chill until cool enough to handle, about 10 minutes. (The freezer makes quick work if you're in a hurry.)

3. Peel and discard the skins and chop the flesh roughly.

4. Puree the roasted peppers in a food processor with the remaining ingredients, adding the butter after the other ingredients have been pureed. Lacking a food processor, puree the peppers in a blender or food mill, add the remaining ingredients, and puree again.

5. Scoop the pepper butter onto a double thickness of wax paper. Form it into a log shape, roll and twist ends to compact. Wrap in aluminum foil. Chill. The butter may be used as is or frozen and sliced as needed. You will only need about ½ the red pepper butter for the chops.

To Prepare the Chops

1. Preheat oven to 400 degrees. Sear the chops in a Teflon-coated skillet over high heat, a little less than a minute on each side. Season with salt and pepper.

2. Tear off 4 pieces of parchment paper (17 inches by 15 inches). The paper may be used as is, with the chops wrapped as you would a sandwich. Or for a more decorative presentation, stack the four sheets and fold in half the long way. Trim the corners so you're left with four heart shapes. Place a chop on a half of each heart. Place a tablespoon of red pepper butter on each. Fold top of heart over. Starting at the rounded top, fold and pleat the paper, making a tight seal. Tuck the pointed end under the packet. Place each packet on a baking sheet. Place in the lower third of the preheated 400-degree oven for 15 minutes or until the paper puffs. Remove the baking sheet from the oven, and let each diner open the paper at the table and enjoy the heady aroma.

Yield: 4 servings
Calories per serving: 160
Protein per serving: 25g

Fat per serving: 6g
Carbohydrates per serving: 1g
Sodium per serving: 100mg

Paupiettes of Veal
with Apple-Cabbage Stuffing

❖

A paupiette is the French term for a thin piece of meat that is pounded, stuffed, rolled, and then tied. Because of their resemblance to stuffed quail they are often called "birds." Paupiettes do require a bit of advance work: The meat needs pounding, the stuffing needs doing, and the whole needs tying. However, this is about 40 minutes work that may be done early in the day or even days before, then the paupiettes frozen for a delicious weekday meal prepared at the weekend's more leisurely pace. The cabbage and apple stuffing is also delicious served as a side dish with pork or chicken dishes.

For the Stuffing

1   *small onion, chopped*
1   *small clove garlic, minced*
6   *tablespoons beef or chicken broth*
2   *medium apples, peeled, cored, and chopped*
1   *cup shredded red cabbage*
1/2   *teaspoon salt*
freshly ground pepper to taste
4   *ounces ground veal*

For the Meat

8   *veal scallops (about 1 1/4 pounds)*
lemon juice
1/4   *teaspoon salt*
freshly ground pepper to taste
5   *tablespoons dry sherry*
5   *tablespoons chicken or beef broth or veal stock*
1   *tablespoon butter, at room temperature*
1   *tablespoon minced fresh parsley*

To Prepare the Stuffing

1. "Saute" the onion and garlic in 4 tablespoons of the broth over medium-high heat until they're limp and the broth is evaporated.
2. Add the apples, cabbage, and the remaining 2 tablespoons broth. Season with salt and pepper, cover, and cook over high heat 1 minute. Reduce heat to medium low, and continue to cook, covered, 10 minutes more.
3. Uncover, add the veal, and stir over high heat until the meat loses its pinkness, about 3 to 4 minutes, or until moisture evaporates. Remove from heat.

To Prepare the Meat

1. Pound the veal scallops between sheets of wax paper until very thin. Sprinkle with lemon juice, salt, and pepper.
2. Place 2 tablespoons stuffing in the middle of the veal slice, enclose like an envelope. (Reserve remaining stuffing.) Tie the bundle with butcher's twine as if tying a package. Repeat with remaining veal. Bundles may now be refrigerated up to 8 hours before cooking or frozen until ready to cook.

To Cook the Paupiettes

1. Spray a 10-inch or 12-inch skillet with cooking spray. Saute the bundles, turning frequently. When browned, add the sherry and stock (veal stock would be lovely!), half cover, and cook for 6 minutes. Remove the paupiettes to a serving platter with a slotted spoon, raise heat to high, and boil until juices are reduced to 1/3 cup. While the sauce is reducing, cut and discard the strings from meat.
2. Swirl the butter into the sauce over medium-low heat, and pour over the meat. Reheat the remaining apple-cabbage mixture and serve on the side. Sprinkle parsley over the veal. Serve 2 per person.

Yield: 4 servings
Calories per serving: 170
Protein per serving: 18g

Fat per serving: 7g
Carbohydrates per serving: 9g
Sodium per serving: 115mg

Veal Scallops with Prosciutto and Mozzarella

❖

When a normally skinny veal scallop is dipped in egg, bread crumbs, and flour and bathed in fat, its calorie index jumps about 150 points higher. Here is an attempt to capture the flavor of breaded, sauteed veal without the excess calories.

2 pounds veal scallops, pounded thin
lemon juice
1/2 teaspoon salt
freshly ground pepper to taste
8 paper-thin slices prosciutto
4 ounces part-skim mozzarella cheese, grated or torn
1 egg white
1 tablespoon milk
1/2 cup plus 2 tablespoons dried bread crumbs
1 tablespoon vegetable oil
1 tablespoon butter
1/4 cup beef or chicken broth
2 tablespoons Madeira or dry sherry
8 very thin lemon slices

1. Sprinkle the meat with lemon juice and season lightly with salt and pepper. Lay a piece of prosciutto on each veal scallop and divide the cheese over. Roll the scallop like a jellyroll.
2. Beat together the egg white and milk. Pour into a saucer.
3. Spread the bread crumbs on a sheet of wax paper. Roll the veal first in the milk, then in the bread crumbs. Chill for 20 minutes if possible to set the crumbs.
4. Heat the oil and butter in a 10-inch or 12-inch skillet until bubbly. Add the veal scallops, saute over medium-high heat a few at a time so they don't touch, until nicely browned, about 3–4 min-

utes. Return all meat to the skillet, turn heat to medium low, cover, and cook the rolls another 5–7 minutes, turning often. You may need to add a bit of oil or cooking spray. Remove the veal to a heated serving platter.

5. Add the broth to the skillet, boil until it's reduced to 2 table-spoons, add Madeira, and reduce the liquid to a syrupy glaze. Pour it over the veal and garnish with lemon slices.

Yield: 8 servings
Calories per serving: 275
Protein per serving: 30g

Fat per serving: 14g
Carbohydrates per serving: 3g
Sodium per serving: 333mg

Pork Cutlet
in Cider Cream Sauce

Here's a quick and delicious meal for midweek dining when time is of the essence. Pork cutlets are lean, boneless cuts taken from the loin, they cook with little waste. After an initial searing, the pork must be slowly cooked to avoid toughening.

> 2 teaspoons butter
> 1 teaspoon vegetable oil
> 1 to 1 1/4 pounds boneless pork cutlets
> 3/4 cup cider (hard or nonalcoholic sparkling cider recommended)
> 4 small apples, peeled, cored, and thinly sliced
> 1/4 teaspoon salt
> freshly ground pepper to taste
> 2 teaspoons (or to taste) stone-ground mustard (the kind made with horseradish is excellent)
> 1/2 cup crème blanc (page 37), made without milk

1. In a 10-inch Teflon-coated skillet, melt the butter and oil until foamy over high heat. Alternately, spray any 10-inch heavy-bottomed skillet with cooking spray, then add the butter and oil. Pat the cutlets dry. Sear the cutlets for about 1 minute on each side or until well browned.
2. Reduce the heat, add the cider and apples, season with salt and pepper, and half cover the pan. Stirring the apples occasionally, simmer for 8 minutes, or until the pork is cooked through and the apples are tender but not mushy.
3. Remove the cutlets from the pan to a serving plate, cover with a towel to keep them warm. Boil pan juices, if necessary, to reduce to ¼ cup. Cool about 1 minute, cider that's too hot will curdle the crème blanc.
4. Stir the mustard into the crème blanc. Whisk this mixture into the cider. Pour the sauce and apples over the pork cutlets.

Yield: 4 servings
Calories per serving: 472
Protein per serving: 22g

Fat per serving: 32g
Carbohydrates per serving: 24g
Sodium per serving: 513mg

Pork and Veal Croquettes with Lemon Caper Sauce

❖

Traditionally, a croquette is ground meat, poultry, or what have you bound by a white sauce and deep-fat-fried—two no-no's in *Gourmet Light* cooking. Here we temper the high-calorie ground pork with lean veal and zucchini, add cooked rice, and lightly bread the croquettes by dipping them in milk and egg white rather than the traditional whole egg. The croquettes may then be sauteed in a Teflon-coated pan, or baked. The sauce may be made ahead and gently reheated at serving time.

For the Croquettes

8 ounces ground veal
6 ounces ground pork
1 small zucchini, grated
1 onion, chopped
5–6 fresh sage leaves, snipped, or ½ teaspoon dried
    sage
1 cup cooked rice
2 teaspoons capers (optional)
½ teaspoon salt
freshly ground pepper to taste
1 egg white
2 tablespoons milk
¼ cup dried bread crumbs

For the Sauce

2 tablespoons lemon juice (about ½ a fresh lemon)
¾ cup chicken broth
1 teaspoon cornstarch
2 tablespoons milk
1 teaspoon capers
2 tablespoons chicken broth
1 tablespoon butter, at room temperature

To Prepare the Croquettes

1. Combine first 9 ingredients in a bowl; mix well.
2. Beat together the egg white and milk and pour them into a saucer.
3. Spread the bread crumbs on a piece of wax paper.
4. With your hands form the meat mixture (Step 1) into "logs," each about 2 inches wide by 4 inches long.
5. Roll the meat mixture in the egg and milk, then in the bread crumbs. If sauteing the croquettes, chill for 20 minutes if time allows to set the crumbs. Spray a 10-inch nonstick skillet with cooking spray. When the pan is hot, add the croquettes, and saute, covered, over medium-high heat. Turn the croquettes of-

ten, until they are cooked through, about 10-12 minutes.
6. If you have decided to bake the croquettes, bake them in a preheated 400-degree oven. Turn them after 15 minutes in the oven to brown them evenly; they will cook in 25 to 30 minutes.

To Prepare the Sauce

1. Reduce the lemon juice to a glaze in a heavy-bottomed 1-quart saucepan over high heat.
2. Add the broth and bring to a boil.
3. Dissolve the cornstarch in the milk. Remove the boiling broth from heat and whisk in the dissolved cornstarch. Return the pan to medium-high heat and bring back to a slow boil, whisking all the while.
4. Whisk in the capers, additional broth (more or less to desired consistency), and butter. Sauce may be reheated.

Yield: 9 croquettes
Calories in each: 116
Protein in each: 12g

Fat in each: 4g
Carbohydrates in each: 8g
Sodium in each: 251mg

Yield of Sauce: ¾ cup
Calories per tablespoon: 13
Protein per serving: trace

Fat per tablespoon: 1g
Carbohydrates per tablespoon: 1g
Sodium per tablespoon: 3mg

❖ UNOPENED FLOWER BUDS ❖

Two spices in your kitchen are actually unopened flower buds: cloves, from a kind of evergreen tree, and capers, from a Mediterranean shrub. Capers are priced by their size, the smaller the more costly. They are most frequently preserved in vinegar, occasionally in salt. Used in salads, sauces, and as a garnish for egg dishes they lend a distinction totally their own. They will keep in the refrigerator for up to one year. Cloves are dried flower buds; they come powdered or whole. Add a few to a bouquet garni destined for a tomato dish for a pleasant, peppery sweet taste.

Roasted Pork Tenderloin with Curried Fall Fruit Compote

❖

Pork has always been considered a fatty meat, but with better breeding today's animal is less fatty than in previous years. The tenderloin, a long thin strip of meat taken from the unexercised backbone area, is among the leanest of the cuts. Pork tenderloins range from 2 inches to 3 inches thick tapering down to a mere flap of meat. If you're only able to buy the thinner tenderloin, purchase two and tie them together with one thin tail abutting the thick body of the other. This way you'll have a "log" of meat of uniform thickness. This recipe may be prepared early in the day and roasted just before serving. Serve it with the Curried Fall Fruit Compote for a delicious dinner worthy of a festive occasion.

> *Dijon-style mustard*
> *1 3/4 pounds pork tenderloin*
> *1/2 teaspoon salt*
> *1 clove garlic, minced*
> *1/4 cup unseasoned dried bread crumbs*
> *freshly ground pepper to taste*
> *4 to 5 fresh sage leaves, snipped, or 3/4 teaspoon*
> *dried sage*

1. Preheat oven to 450 degrees. Brush the mustard over the meat with a pastry brush. Sprinkle half the salt over the meat.
2. Spray an 8-inch skillet with cooking spray, add the garlic, and cook over medium heat about 30 seconds. Add the bread crumbs and sage. Cook, stirring until the crumbs begin to brown. Season with remaining salt and pepper.
3. Put half the crumbs in a roasting dish just large enough to hold the meat. Put the roast on top, pat remaining crumbs around and on top of roast.

4. Place roast in the bottom third of the preheated 450-degree oven for 10 minutes. Then reduce heat to 325 degrees and roast for an additional 50 minutes. Check meat's internal temperature after it has roasted 45 minutes. It is done when internal temperature registers 160 to 165 degrees. Let the tenderloin rest 5-10 minutes before slicing. Serve with Curried Fall Fruit Compote.

Curried Fall Fruit Compote

½ small onion, chopped
4 tablespoons beef or chicken broth
1 teaspoon curry powder
½ teaspoon ground cumin
1 pear, peeled, cored, and chopped
1 Granny Smith apple, peeled, cored, and chopped
1 Red Delicious apple, peeled, cored, and chopped
2 dried apricots, soaked 20 minutes in 2 tablespoons
 apricot or other fruit-flavored brandy
4 tablespoons golden raisins

1. "Saute" the onion in 2 tablespoons of the broth until limp. Sprinkle on the curry powder and cumin. Cook over medium-high heat, stirring, about 15 seconds.
2. Add the remaining ingredients, including the brandy, cover, and cook over low heat 20 minutes or until flavors are blended. Serve with pork dishes. Leftovers are easily reheated in a bit of broth or cider.

Yield of meat with compote:
 4 servings
Calories per serving: 275
Protein per serving: 32g

Fat per serving: 15g
Carbohydrates per serving: 2g
Sodium per serving: 360mg

Yield of Compote: 4 servings
Calories per serving: 120
Protein per serving: 1g

Fat per serving: trace
Carbohydrates per serving: 29g
Sodium per serving: 7mg

Mock Tenderloin

❖

This is one of my favorite ways to enjoy lamb, pink and succulent with a texture and taste much like that of a fine beef tenderloin. A lamb leg is completely stripped of fat, the muscles separated, marinated, cut into noisettes, and then grilled. Serve this with the Mustard Hollandaise (page 174). Alternately, the muscles may be left whole and roasted in a 450-degree oven for 15 minutes for rare meat.

> ½ leg of lamb, the shank half (about 3½ pounds total)
> 4 tablespoons red wine vinegar
> 4 tablespoons red wine
> 2 tablespoons vegetable oil
> 2 tablespoons minced fresh parsley
> 1 clove garlic, minced
> a few drops hot pepper sauce
> Dijon-style mustard
> ⅛ teaspoon salt
> freshly ground pepper to taste
> Mustard Hollandaise

1. Have the lamb boned or do it yourself. Lay the meat flat on the counter top with what was the skin side facing up. Trim and discard all the fat and gristle from the meat.
2. Cut off and freeze for another use the thin flap of meat that you'll find on one side. Pull the meat with your hands; you'll notice natural "breaks" in the muscles. Separate the muscles by pulling the white veil of connective tissues. You'll need a knife in only a few places. You'll have three separate muscles. Fold the thin ends of each muscle toward the middle and tuck underneath. Cut each muscle into rounds (noisettes), about 1½-inches thick. Each noisette will be about 3 inches across and look like a slice of beef

tenderloin. Reserve and freeze any untidy chunks of meat with the flap and use for a curry or kebabs.

3. Combine the vinegar, wine, oil, parsley, garlic, and hot pepper sauce in a jar and shake to combine. Put the meat and marinade in a leak-proof plastic bag and refrigerate, turning occasionally, for about 12 hours.

4. Pat the meat dry, brush with the mustard, season with salt and pepper, and grill until done to your liking. Or "saute" in a non-stick skillet, or broil. Serve with Mustard Hollandaise.

Note: If you sear the meat on both sides, then remove it from the fire and let it rest 20 minutes before finishing the cooking, the noisettes will be even juicier.

Yield: 4 servings
Calories per serving: 325
Protein per serving: 41g

Fat per serving: 17g
Carbohydrates per serving: 2g
Sodium per serving: 170mg

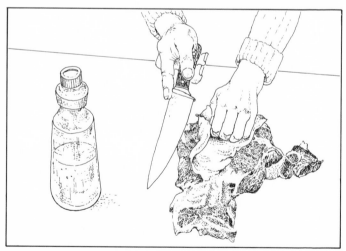

HOW TO CUT LAMB NOISETTES

   1. Lay the boned lamb on the counter. Trim and discard the fat and gristle from the meat.

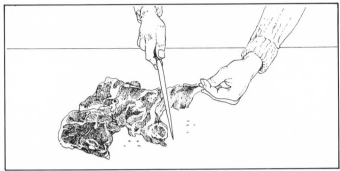

2. Turn the lamb over so what was the fat side is now facing down. Remove the thin triangular flap of meat. It may be saved for another use.

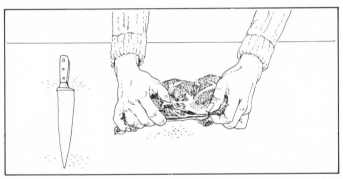

3. The meat will pull apart into three segments that are held together by a white, gossamer tissue and some gristle. Use your fingers and a small knife to separate the meat into three muscles.

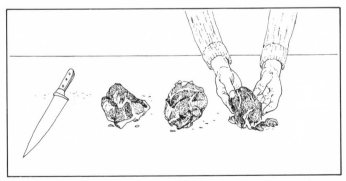

4. Fold the thin ends of each muscle toward the middle and tuck underneath.

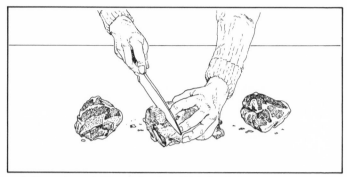

5. Slice each muscle into noisettes about 1½-inches thick.

6. The finished noisettes will be about 3 inches across and look like a slice of beef tenderloin.

Chapter 7

POULTRY
AND
GAME

Chicken

❖

Back when Grandma simmered a pot of baked beans on the wood stove all day long and whipped up a mess of biscuits, mile high and puffy as you please, chicken was Sunday fare, a to-do worthy of company. Today, thanks to scientific advancements in the breeding and feeding of the barnyard birds, chicken has become a standard rather than a luxury. Because the birds now come to market in a matter of weeks, rather than months, the reduced production costs translate into reduced consumer prices, making chicken not only one of our more economical but also nutritionally bountiful buys, as well. Just 4 ounces of white meat, without skin, supplies about half an adult's protein needs for less than 150 calories. But half a cup of skinned, boned chicken is hardly something to feast on, and certainly no culinary inspiration. This chapter offers more tempting treatments for chicken as well as some for turkey, duck, and quail.

Chicken, like meat, must be inspected for wholesomeness, but there's no law stating it must be graded—a letter classification (A or B) based on the bird's physical appearance. Chickens wearing a Grade A shield do so because the processor has paid USDA inspectors to grade the product, a cost that the producer, and ultimately the consumer, must pay for. And it's not likely you'll spot a Grade B shield boldly displayed on a chicken breast—who wants the world to know your product is second best? This is not to say that nongraded birds are necessarily of poor quality, only that they've not been graded. You can be assured they'll be less expensive, and in some cases, just as good.

Here are some tips when purchasing chicken:

1. The bird should be fresh, not previously frozen.

Each time a chicken is thawed it loses some of its juices. If you suspect your market is selling previously frozen birds, or ones that have unintentionally frozen when shipped on ice, snap a leg bone after roasting. It will appear reddish-black if the bird was once frozen.

2. Match the cooking technique to the bird's size.

Roasters, over 3 pounds—roast or fricassee
Fryer, 2–3 pounds—saute, roast, or fricassee
Broiler, 1 ½ to 2 ½ pounds—grill or roast

Chickens range from broiler/fryers (smallest) to roasters (largest), which is not to say a fryer couldn't be broiled or a broiler roasted. However, the long, slow cooking such as that required for a Coq au Vin might render a small bird mushy and grilling a cut-up roaster might take far too long, burning the skin before it was ever done at the bone. Adapt the recipe to the bird, remembering (logically) that large birds do best with long, slow cooking, while small birds are better suited to shorter cooking methods. Old, tough birds—fowl—need long, slow cooking in a liquid to make them tender.

3. Look for a plump bird, with a good covering of fat.

The plumper the bird, the more tender the meat. While buying only Grade A chickens pretty much ensures the best, buying plump ungraded chickens will get you to the same place for a few pennies less per pound.

4. Skin color is not an indication of flavor.

Some chicken producers routinely monitor the birds' skin pigment by taking blood samples from a few chickens. Those to be marketed in the Northeast, where yellow-skinned chickens are preferred, may have their feed bolstered by marigold petals, a completely natural substance that yellows the skin color but does not affect the flavor.

The very methods responsible for the relative inexpensiveness of chicken are held responsible by some cooks for production of a bland, flavorless bird. Free-range chickens, available at some specialty markets, are brought up "the old-fashioned way," pecking away in the barnyard. These same cooks feel the increased exercise and natural feed supplements make for a better-flavored bird. If you can find a supplier of free-range chickens, you can test the theory yourself . . . but because the old-fashioned method is more dear, be prepared to pay more.

Like fish, chicken is very perishable. It is best to freeze it if not using it within 24 hours of purchase. If you choose to rinse the chicken before cooking and it is to be browned, pat it thoroughly dry or it will more likely stew than saute.

A frozen chicken, or any other poultry, is best thawed under refrigeration, well wrapped, to inhibit water loss. This can take anywhere from 1–3 days, depending on the size of the bird.

Boning Chicken Breasts

❖

Chicken breasts are a favorite in *Gourmet Light* cooking for they make a tidy serving and neatly solve the "just one more bite" temptation. A typical chicken breast weighs 3 ounces, supplies a mere 125 calories (150 with the skin) and supplies 20 grams of protein—about half the daily requirement for most women. It's wonderfully versatile, nutrient dense, skinny, and economical, too—don't be caught without a supply in the freezer.

Although chicken breasts are readily available boned and skinned, you may wish to do the work yourself. Not only is it more economical but the bones are almost indispensable for enriching store-bought chicken broth or making your own. As you bone the breasts, toss the bones into a plastic bag in the freezer. You may add to and use from your stash as needed.

You may use any sharp knife for boning chicken breasts, you don't need a special boning knife. Place the breast on the work surface, skin side up. If whole, flatten with the heel of your hand and split by cutting through or just to one side of the breastbone. With the breastbone to the right and the rib cage section to the left, slice against the breastbone and scrape down the bones, pulling back the meat with your fingers. Always angle the knife toward the bones. Don't worry about making gorgeous, clean cuts. The meat is very gelatinous and will "glue" together as it cooks, and the bit of meat left on the bones will only serve to enrich your stock. When the meat is scraped free of the bones, cut loose at the shoulder end. This is called a supreme. Turn the supreme so the skin side is down. Notice the small strip of meat, called the filet mignon, with the white tendon running its length. By the way, if the filet became detached in cutting, don't despair, just stick it back on! Grasp the end of the tendon in your finger tips and pull it free by scraping the meat away with the tip of a small, sharp knife. Although this is a pesky task and may be omitted, the tendon, if left, tends to pull the breast out of shape as it doesn't shrink with the cooking meat. The breasts may now be skinned or not as you please. To skin, simply lift the skin in your finger tips, cutting loose where needed. With your finger tips check to be sure the supreme is free of any remaining cartilage. Trim away yellow fat. Freeze the breasts or use within 24 hours.

❖ BUTTER AND OIL ❖

Frequently in this book you'll notice small amounts of both butter and oil are called for in the sauteing of foods. Using both combines the benefits of each—the flavor of butter (which burns at a low temperature) with the higher smoking point of oil, allowing for rapid browning with good butter flavor.

Chicken Paillards

❖

A paillard is the culinary term for a piece of beef, chicken, or veal that is cooked without fat. Although this can be accomplished in a good heavy nonstick skillet, it is best suited for grills, either the indoor models with their wonderfully effective fans or a more typical outdoor version. What follows are basic instructions for preparing chicken paillards and some suggestions for varying the routine. You'll soon devise some wonderful alternatives that reflect your own tastes for this simplest and skinniest of meals. Technically, a chicken paillard is the breast boned and skinned. Should you choose to leave the skin on, add 60 calories a serving.

For the Paillards
4 boneless chicken breasts
juice of half a lemon
⅛ teaspoon salt
freshly ground pepper to taste

1. Skin the chicken breasts or not as you desire. Place the chicken between sheets of wax paper and pound to an even thickness, not to make thin.
2. Heat a grill or skillet with grill ridges. Place the chicken perpendicular to the grill rungs. After the chicken has seared, turn ¼ turn (90 degrees) to make customary grill marks. Season with a few drops lemon juice. Turn over after 3 minutes. Repeat above procedure to make grilling pattern. Season with salt, pepper, and lemon juice, continue to cook until chicken is firm when poked with your finger in several places, about 6–7 minutes. Because the grill's heat and the thickness of chicken will vary, watch it closely. Chicken may be cooked in anywhere from 4–8 minutes.

Yield: 4 servings
Calories per serving: 115
Protein per serving: 23g

Fat per serving: 1g
Carbohydrates per serving: trace
Sodium per serving: 130mg

Mustard Paillards

Dip a pastry brush in stone-ground mustard and lavish over uncooked chicken. Spread on additional mustard if desired during cooking. This is also delicious with some of the sweet mustards on the market, such as Russian or champagne mustard. (The nutritional content is not available.)

Basil-Walnut Paillards

When fresh basil is in season, make several batches of the wonderfully delicious Basil-Walnut Sauce on page 32. It is an all-purpose flavor booster with a tiny caloric price tag. Brush 2 tablespoons on each chicken paillard before and as it cooks and serve with sauteed cherry tomatoes.

Yield: 4 servings
Calories per serving: 175
Protein per serving: 25g

Fat per serving: 7g
Carbohydrates per serving: 2g
Sodium per serving: 150mg

Red Pepper Butter Paillards

When red peppers are plentiful in early spring and fall, make the Red Pepper Butter on page 136 in quantity and freeze it. Sliced right from the freezer it cloaks a simple chicken paillard with a scarlet robe at once subtle yet piquant. Add a slice after the chicken has cooked on one side, and another when the chicken is done, just before serving, covering briefly while still on the grill to melt the butter.

Yield: 4 servings
Calories per serving: 155
Protein per serving: 24g

Fat per serving: 4g
Carbohydrates per serving: 5g
Sodium per serving: 30mg

Sesame Chicken Salad

❖

This chicken salad is Chinese in spirit with its soy marinade, Japanese in soul with its yolk-enhanced grilling technique, and very much "today" with its lightness, attention to color, and emphasis on vegetables. It is served warm, not chilled.

> 6 *tablespoons soy sauce*
> 2 *tablespoons rice wine vinegar, available at Oriental or specialty food shops*
> 1 *scallion, minced*
> *a quarter-size piece of fresh ginger root, peeled and diced*
> 1 *teaspoon sesame oil, available at Oriental or specialty food shops*
> 4 *boneless, skinless chicken breasts*
> 1 *egg yolk*
> 3 *tablespoons chicken broth*
> 1 *scant teaspoon sugar*
> 1 *carrot, cut into narrow strips about 3 inches long*
> 1 *small zucchini, cut like the carrot*
> 1 *small summer squash, cut like the carrot*
> *red leaf lettuce*
> 2 *tablespoons sesame seeds, toasted*

1. Combine the soy sauce, vinegar, scallion, ginger, and sesame oil in a bowl. Pour the mixture into a leakproof plastic bag or shallow baking dish, add the chicken, and marinate overnight or at least 4 hours in the refrigerator.
2. Drain the chicken, reserving marinade. Mix 4 tablespoons marinade with the egg yolk, set aside.
3. Mix the remaining soy marinade with the chicken broth and sugar. Set aside.

4. Bring a 2½-quart saucepan three quarters full of water to a boil. Add the carrots, 30 seconds later add the zucchini, and 30 seconds later add the squash. Time 1 minute more, drain and cool under running water. Toss the vegetables with half the soy-broth-sugar mixture from Step 3. Set aside while preparing chicken.
5. Grill chicken 3 minutes on each side, basting frequently with the yolk-enriched marinade. When the chicken is cooked (firm when poked with a finger), remove and slice in thin strips on the diagonal.
6. Line a serving platter with the lettuce. Drizzle with the remaining dressing from Step 3. Place dressing-tossed vegetables on lettuce and chicken strips arranged in a V-shaped column down the center. Sprinkle with toasted sesame seeds.

Note: To toast sesame seeds, place them in a skillet over high heat until they pop, shaking constantly. Sodium-reduced soy sauce is available in many markets for those wishing to restrict the amount of sodium.

Yield: 4 servings
Calories per serving: 195
Protein per serving: 26g

Fat per serving: 6g
Carbohydrates per serving: 9g
Sodium per serving: 900mg

❖ **THINKING THIN TIP** ❖

Portion control is vital to weight control. Invest in a small food scale and use it until you can pretty well judge what a 4-ounce portion looks like.

Breast of Chicken Salad

❖

Minimum cooking with minimum effort, but the dish is pretty, appealing, and no insult to your new bathing suit. It is served warm. Or, if you wish, serve it chilled by preparing the chicken and the sauce a few hours ahead, refrigerating them, and assembling the dish just before serving.

4 chicken breasts (no need to skin or bone)
2 scallions
a 3-inch chunk of ginger root, peeled and sliced
1 cup chicken broth
4 egg yolks
½ teaspoon salt
1 tablespoon lemon juice
1 teaspoon prepared Dijon-style mustard
freshly ground pepper to taste
½ teaspoon sugar
¾ cup safflower or other vegetable oil
¼ cup reduced cooking juices from chicken
1 head soft-leafed lettuce such as red leaf or Bibb
small bunch red or green seedless grapes
½ a ripe cantaloupe

To Prepare the Chicken

1. Place the chicken breasts, skin side down, in a skillet just large enough to hold them.
2. In a food processor, combine the scallions, ginger, and broth. Pour the mixture over the chicken and add just enough cold water to cover. Cover the pan and turn heat to high. When a boil is reached, immediately reduce to a simmer for 15 minutes.
3. Remove the chicken from pan, cool under running water. Turn the heat to high under cooking liquid and boil until reduced to

about 1/4 cup. Strain if there are large pieces of scallion or ginger visible.
4. Discard the chicken skin, lift the meat from bones in one piece, and set chicken aside while preparing the sauce.

To Prepare the Sauce

1. Combine the egg yolks and salt in a food processor or blender. Process for 1 minute.
2. Add the lemon juice, mustard, pepper, and sugar. Process 30 seconds more.
3. A few drops at a time, dribble in the oil. After 1/4 cup has been incorporated, the oil may be added in a thin stream instead of drops.
4. Dribble in the hot reduced chicken-cooking juices from Step 3. The sauce will thicken on standing.
5. Place a bed of lettuce on each plate. Cut the chicken on the diagonal in thin strips. Arrange the strips in spoke fashion on the lettuce. Place a small cluster of grapes in the center, and two half-moons of cantaloupe at either side. Drizzle the sauce over chicken and pass the remaining sauce at the table.

Yield: 4 servings
Calories per serving: 460
Protein per serving: 27g

Fat per serving: 32g
Carbohydrates per serving: 17g
Sodium per serving: 280mg

Chicken Saute with Cepes

❖

This recipe is ideal for today's overscheduled cook who's bored with routine meals. In just 15 minutes you can turn out a moist chicken breast with a sauce perked by raspberry vinegar and cepes. Serve it with Pea and Leek Puree (page 253) and a simple rice studded with a handful of golden raisins.

> 3/4 cup chicken broth
> 1 ounce dried cepes (or porcini), available at
>   specialty food shops
> 1/2 teaspoon kosher salt
> 4 boneless chicken breasts, with skin
> 3 tablespoons raspberry or red wine vinegar
> 1 clove garlic, minced
> 12 mushrooms, sliced
> 1 tablespoon plus 1 teaspoon butter
> 1 tablespoon minced fresh parsley (optional)

1. Bring the broth to a boil. Break the cepes up in your fingers, add them to the hot broth, cover, and steep 20 minutes. Set aside.
2. Sprinkle a 10-inch nonstick skillet with the salt. Place on high heat. When hot, add the chicken, skin side down. Cover and saute 3 minutes, reducing heat if needed to avoid burning. Turn the chicken, cover, and continue to saute 3 minutes more, again reducing heat if needed. When chicken is firm to the touch, place it on a serving platter in a 150-degree oven while completing the sauce.
3. Remove the skillet from heat. Deglaze it with vinegar. Return the skillet to heat when sizzling stops, boil until the vinegar is reduced to a film on the bottom of skillet.
4. Wet a coffee filter (or a piece of cheesecloth or heavy paper towel), and suspend it in a wide-mouthed jar or measuring cup.

Pour the mushroom-broth liquid through, removing cepes with a slotted spoon.

5. Pour the strained mushroom liquid into the vinegar skillet. Add garlic, mushrooms, and cepes. Boil until the liquid is reduced to about ⅓ cup.
6. Reduce heat to medium-low. Whisk in the butter, pour sauce over chicken, and sprinkle with parsley if desired.

Yield: 4 servings
Calories per serving: 250
Protein per serving: 24g

Fat per serving: 14g
Carbohydrates per serving: 9g
Sodium per serving: 340mg

Chicken Fricassee with Leeks and Carrots

This economical meal makes the most of some rather simple ingredients. Boned chicken thighs (you may use the whole leg for larger servings) are wrapped around a filling of leeks and carrots, then browned, braised, and served up in a rich sauce that promises everything but high calories. True to its word, this dish pleases children and parents alike. The chicken thighs may be made ahead and kept chilled for up to 6 hours before cooking. You also may freeze them. This dish is also good reheated.

8 or 9 chicken thighs (about 2½ pounds)
¼ teaspoon salt
freshly ground pepper to taste
1 cup chicken broth
1 cup dry red wine

1 sprig fresh tarragon or 1 teaspoon dried tarragon
1 bay leaf
1 clove garlic, speared on a toothpick
a few grindings fresh pepper
4 leeks, white part only
2 carrots, scrubbed and julienned
3 tablespoons chicken broth
1 teaspoon butter
1 teaspoon vegetable oil
1 teaspoon cornstarch
1 tablespoon chicken broth or wine
8 to 10 washed and dried fresh spinach leaves, stems
and spines removed

1. Bone the chicken thighs by slicing through the meat on the inner thigh to the bone and scraping the flesh free working from the top of the thigh down to the leg joint. When one end of the bone is free from flesh, pull bone away, and cut remaining knuckle free. Be careful not to cut through to the skin. Be sure all cartilage is removed. Reserve bones.
2. Place chicken between sheets of wax paper, flesh side up, and flatten it slightly with a cleaver or heavy flat-bottomed skillet. Season chicken with salt and pepper. Set aside.
3. Spray a 12-inch nonstick skillet with cooking spray. Add the bones, cover, and brown for 5 minutes over high heat. When browned, add broth, wine, tarragon, bay leaf, garlic, and pepper. Cover, and simmer while continuing with recipe.
4. Slice the white part of the leek on the diagonal and rinse thoroughly.
5. "Saute" the leeks and carrots in the 3 tablespoons broth over medium-high heat in a 10-inch skillet, covered, until leeks are soft, about 5 minutes, or until all the liquid is evaporated. Remove from the heat and cool slightly.
6. Place about 2 tablespoons of leeks and carrots on center of each chicken thigh, on the flesh side. Roll loosely and secure with butcher's twine as you would tie a package. Reserve any remain-

ing vegetables for the next step.

7. To brown the chicken, spray a 10-inch or 12-inch nonstick skillet with cooking spray. Heat the butter and oil in the skillet until bubbly. Brown the chicken pieces, a few at a time, so they don't touch. Remove them to the simmering broth-wine when browned. Add any remaining carrots and leeks, cover, and simmer over medium heat for about 35 minutes.

8. Remove the chicken to a heated platter. Snip and discard strings. Dissolve the cornstarch in the remaining broth. Remove and discard the bones, bay leaf, and garlic from cooking broth. Whisk in the dissolved cornstarch and stir until thickened over medium heat.

9. Make a stack of the spinach leaves. Roll them tightly. Slice them crosswise into thin strips (known as chiffonade). (See page 201.) Add the spinach to the sauce over high heat. Stir for 30 seconds or just until wilted. Pour the sauce around chicken.

Yield: 4 servings
Calories per serving: 330
Protein per serving: 38g

Fat per serving: 14g
Carbohydrates per serving: 11g
Sodium per serving: 280mg

Parchment Chicken
with Tomato Vinaigrette

❖

Oven poaching a chicken breast in oodles of sweet butter is neat, simple, and fattening. Neat and simple is nice, but fattening is as welcome as the taxman. Here the French technique of oven poaching is adapted, omitting the butter and encasing the poultry in parchment paper, which seals in the natural juices of the bird and anything else you might add, such as the tangy Tomato Vinaigrette used here. Or the chicken may be oven poached in its packet and lathered with a sauce after the fact. This Tomato Vinaigrette is one with panache. The feather in its cap is a dash of vinegar—just the right touch for a moist and juicy chicken breast. Because the sauce is actually better the second day, make some ahead; it will keep under refrigeration for about a week. The Hollandaise, the Béarnaise, the Basil-Walnut Sauce, all in Chapter 2, or the Lemon Caper Sauce (page 142) also would be appropriate.

For the Chicken

1 boneless, skinless chicken breast
⅛ teaspoon salt
freshly ground pepper to taste
2 tablespoons Tomato Vinaigrette, recipe follows
2 or 3 mushrooms, sliced
parchment paper, available in specialty food shops

To Prepare the Chicken

1. Preheat oven to 425 degrees. Trim the breast of fat and gristle. Place on a square of parchment paper (see page 209 for instructions on wrapping food in parchment paper hearts if preferred). Sprinkle the chicken with salt and pepper, spoon on the Tomato Vinaigrette, and place mushrooms on top. Fold the paper around the chicken as you would for a sandwich. Place on a baking sheet in the preheated 425-degree oven. Cook for 12–15 minutes.
2. To serve, open and discard the paper and spoon juices over chicken.

Tomato Vinaigrette

A wonderfully versatile sauce, Tomato Vinaigrette may be a thick but thinning hot or cold soup, tossed with marinated chilled zucchini as a salad, and used as a braising sauce for veal chops or grilled chicken. It is best, though, made with tomatoes plump with the sun, rather than those ripened by ethylene gas.

1½ pounds tomatoes (2–3 large), quartered
1 tomato, blanched, peeled, seeded, and chopped
2 teaspoons olive oil
1 tablespoon raspberry or red wine vinegar
4–6 fresh or oil-cured basil leaves or 1 teaspoon
    dried basil
1 tablespoon minced fresh parsley
1 teaspoon sugar
½ teaspoon salt
3–4 drops hot pepper sauce

1. Quarter the tomatoes, place in a heavy-bottomed saucepan, cover, and bring to a boil over medium heat. Simmer, uncovered, 45–50 minutes or until somewhat reduced.
2. Puree the tomatoes in a food processor, blender, or food mill. Strain the tomatoes into a bowl to remove the seeds and skin.
3. Add the remaining tomato to the bowl along with the oil, vinegar, basil, parsley, sugar, salt, and pepper sauce. Stir to combine.

Yield of Chicken: 1 serving
Calories per serving: 140
Protein per serving: 25g

Fat per serving: 2g
Carbohydrates per serving: 5g
Sodium per serving: 280mg

Yield of Vinaigrette: 1¾ cups
Calories per tablespoon: 10
Protein per tablespoon: trace

Fat per tablespoon: trace
Carbohydrates per tablespoon: 2g
Sodium per tablespoon: 40mg

Simply Roasted Chicken

❖

Among my favorites is this recipe for roasted chicken with its simple sauce. It may be a bit more elaborate than the standard with the prebrowning of the bird and vegetables, but I think you'll find the added goodness worth the effort. A degreaser, a measuring cup with the spout coming off the bottom, is a useful gadget for defatting the pan juices. It is available at most cooking supply stores. Grapeseed oil, available at specialty food shops, is recommended because it smokes at a much higher temperature than other oils. The calorie count will be less than what is listed below if you are careful to drain away all fat.

a 3-pound chicken
½ teaspoon salt
freshly ground pepper to taste
1 tablespoon oil (grapeseed recommended), or other
    vegetable oil
1 carrot, diced
2 small onions, diced
a sprig fresh tarragon or 1 teaspoon dried tarragon
¾ cup chicken broth
¼ cup dry sherry or red or white wine
1 tablespoon butter, at room temperature

1. Dry the chicken, salt and pepper the cavity. Truss the chicken if desired, as illustrated.
2. Heat the oil in a Dutch oven. Brown the chicken on all sides, moderating the heat, because too high a temperature will cause the skin to tear. Turn the chicken with wooden spoons to avoid tearing skin.
3. Remove the browned chicken from the Dutch oven. Brown the carrot and onions in the same fat. Remove the vegetables and pat them free of fat with paper towels.

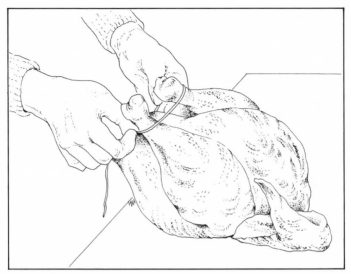

HOW TO TRUSS A CHICKEN

1. Fold a three- or four-foot length of butcher's twine in half, then lay the mid-section over the knee joints of the whole chicken.

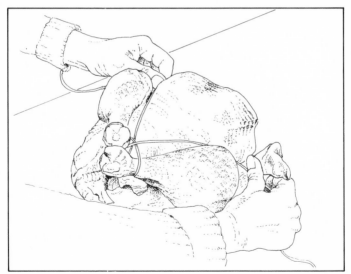

2. "Lasso" the leg ends by pulling the twine up, then lay the twine in the hollow between the leg and the breast.

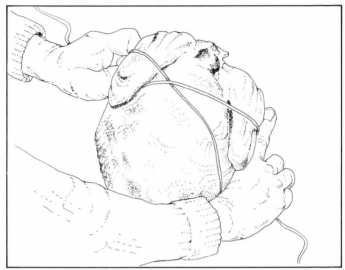

3. Flip the chicken over and cross the twine. Pull the wings snug to the body by laying the twine over them.

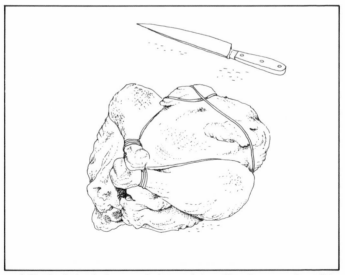

4. Flip the chicken back over so the breast side is up. Knot the twine and cut off the excess.

4. Preheat oven to 350 degrees.
5. Strew the vegetables over the bottom of a baking dish. You may use the same Dutch oven, wiped free of fat. Add the tarragon and broth. Place a rack on top of the vegetables and place the chicken, back side up, on the rack. Place the chicken in the preheated 350-degree oven.
6. Baste the chicken about every half hour. Turn it over so the breast side is up after 30 minutes. The 3-pound chicken will be done in 70-80 minutes (a 4-pound chicken in 75-90 minutes). It is done when the juices run clear. To test, hold the chicken vertically by upending it on a spoon held in the cavity. The first drops will be bloody, but if done the final drops will be clear. Alternately, you may prick the thigh to see if the juices run clear. Keep chicken warm, covered on a platter, while making the sauce.
7. Strain the cooking juices into a degreaser or glass measuring cup, pressing the vegetables with the back of a wooden spoon to extract the juices. Let the juices rest for 1 minute, allowing the fat to rise to the top. If using a degreaser, pour the juices into a 1-quart saucepan, or extract the fat-free juice from the bottom of the measuring cup with a bulb baster. Add the sherry and boil until reduced to ⅔ cup. Remove from heat. Whisk in butter, pour some of the sauce over the carved chicken, and pass the remainder at the table.

Yield: 4 servings
Calories per serving: 513
Protein per serving: 54g

Fat per serving: 27g
Carbohydrates per serving: 12g
Sodium per serving: 360mg

Stir-Fried Chicken
and Vegetables

❖

The signature of the world's oldest cuisine, the stir-fry, may be tailored to fit the modern principles of good nutrition perfectly. This recipe is rich in carbohydrates, while frugal with both proteins and fats. Just 10–12 ounces of meat or poultry with the bountiful use of vegetables and rice easily feeds 4. Stir-frys are also quick to cook once the chopping and slicing are accomplished, a task that can often be done as much as 5 hours in advance. This stir-fry is made spicy with hot red pepper and chili paste—both may be omitted if a milder dish is preferred. All this dish needs is a side of rice or Chinese noodles to complete the meal. The Oriental ingredients are available at specialty or Chinese food shops.

> 2 tablespoons soy sauce (light soy recommended)
> 1 tablespoon rice wine or semisweet sherry
> 1 tablespoon rice wine vinegar (white wine vinegar
>   may be substituted)
> 1 teaspoon sesame oil
> 2 tablespoons chicken broth
> 2 teaspoons sugar
> 1 clove garlic, minced
> 1 stalk green onion, minced
> a 1-inch piece of ginger root, peeled and minced
> ¾ pound skinless, boneless breast of chicken
> 1 tablespoon vegetable or peanut oil
> ½ red bell pepper, sliced
> ½ green bell pepper, sliced
> 8 ounces fresh mushrooms, sliced
> 1 cup Chinese cabbage, sliced
> 1 carrot, blanched 5 minutes and julienned

4 ounces snow peas, strings removed
1/2–1 teaspoon minced hot chili pepper (optional)
1/2–1 teaspoon chili paste with garlic (optional)
2 teaspoons cornstarch
1/3 cup chicken broth

1. Combine the soy sauce, wine, vinegar, sesame oil, broth, sugar, garlic, onion, and ginger in a measuring cup. Mix well. Pour it into a plastic bag.
2. Cut the chicken into thin strips, marinate in the above soy mixture for 2 hours in the refrigerator or 20 minutes at room temperature.
3. Heat the oil in a wok or heavy 10-inch skillet until very hot. Lift the chicken from the soy marinade a few pieces at a time (reserving the marinade for Step 7), stir-fry in hot oil until flesh firms and becomes opaque, about 4 minutes.
4. Remove the chicken with a slotted spoon or chopsticks and drain on paper towels. Continue stir-frying until all the chicken is cooked.
5. Add the peppers and mushrooms to wok. Add a bit of chicken broth or oil if necessary. Stir-fry for 1 minute. Add the Chinese cabbage, stir-fry another minute. Add the carrots and snow peas, stir-fry about 1 minute more or until pea pods are done.
6. Stir in the chili pepper and paste if desired.
7. Moisten the cornstarch in the chicken broth, combine with the reserved marinade from Step 3. Add to the vegetables along with the cooked chicken. Stir until thickened over high heat. Serve with boiled rice or noodles.

Yield: 4 servings
Calories per serving: 205
Protein per serving: 24g

Fat per serving: 6g
Carbohydrates per serving: 14g
Sodium per serving: 360g

Poached Chicken Breast
with Mustard Hollandaise

❖

Reheating a traditional Hollandaise is a bit like space-walking: There's little room for error. You won't find yourself in orbit, though, with the *Gourmet Light* version; it may be made early in the day and reheated over low heat. Or you may choose to keep it warm in a bowl set atop an electric warming tray. Serve this Chicken Breast with Hollandaise with the Pea and Leek Puree (page 253) and some broccoli or a rice pilaf.

> 1 *recipe Hollandaise, page 21*
> 2 *tablespoons stone-ground mustard, or to taste*
> 1 *scallion or half a small onion, minced*
> 1 *sprig fresh tarragon or ½ teaspoon dried tarragon*
> 1 *cup water*
> 4 *chicken breasts, with skin and bones*
> *juice of half a lemon*
> *minced fresh parsley or watercress (optional)*

1. Make the *Gourmet Light* Hollandaise. Stir in the mustard and set aside.
2. In a food processor or blender combine the scallion, tarragon, and water. Blend.
3. Pour into a skillet just large enough to hold the chicken. Add chicken, skin side down. Add the lemon juice. Add water to cover. Bring to a boil, immediately reduce to a simmer. Cover and cook for 8–9 minutes or until the chicken flesh feels firm when poked with a finger.
4. Remove the chicken with a slotted spoon (cooking liquid may be reserved for making stock). Cool briefly under running water.
5. Discard the skin. Lift the chicken from bones in one piece, place

on warmed plates. Spoon Hollandaise over and garnish with the
parsley or watercress if desired.

Yield: 4 servings
Calories per serving: 255
Protein per serving: 28g

Fat per serving: 14g
Carbohydrates per serving: 4g
Sodium per serving: 170mg

Scotch Chicken

Chicken, cream, and mushrooms make for a tempting trilogy often
found in French cooking. What a pity the cream brings out the calorie-conscious cringes. Fortunately, there's crème blanc, the *Gourmet
Light* replacement for overfatted dairy products. The sauce base must
be cooled a full minute as directed to avoid a curdled mess. Vary this
simple supper with the addition of some dried mushrooms such as
cepes or chanterelles.

> 2 *boneless chicken breasts, skin on*
> 1/8 *teaspoon salt*
> *freshly ground pepper to taste*
> 2 *tablespoons Scotch*
> 1/2 *cup chicken broth*
> 4 *ounces mushrooms, sliced*
> 1 *tablespoon crème blanc, page 37*
> *a few gratings fresh nutmeg*

1. Place the chicken, skin side down, in a 10-inch nonstick skillet.
   Season chicken with salt and pepper. Sear it, covered, over high
   heat 3 minutes. Turn the chicken over, reduce heat to medium,
   cover, and continue cooking another 3–4 minutes.

2. Remove the chicken from skillet to plate. Off the heat, deglaze the skillet with the Scotch. When the liquor quiets down, return to high heat, stirring constantly with a wooden spoon to loosen the particles stuck to pan bottom. Reduce the liquid until it's just a film.
3. Add the broth and mushrooms to the skillet, cover, and boil, stirring occasionally until it's reduced to about 3 tablespoons liquid.
4. Remove the skillet from heat, stir, and cool about 1 minute. Stir in crème blanc, season with nutmeg, and pour it over the chicken.

Yield: 2 servings
Calories per serving: 220
Protein per serving: 25g

Fat per serving: 10g
Carbohydrates per serving: 10g
Sodium per serving: 230mg

Herbed Chicken Breasts

This recipe calls for stuffing the breast with an herbed rice mixture. Bag the proverbial two birds with one stone by doubling the stuffing portion and serving it as a side dish. All you need then to complete the meal is a salad or possibly some broccoli with Reduced-Calorie Hollandaise, which will also complement the chicken. Although this needs no sauce you might like to nap it with the Tomato Vinaigrette, page 165; the Lemon Caper Sauce, page 142, or the Reduced-Calorie Béarnaise, page 24.

> ½ small green pepper, diced
> ½ small onion, diced
> 4 tablespoons chicken broth
> ½ cup cooked white or brown rice

5–6 *mushrooms, sliced*
5 *leaves fresh or oil-cured basil, snipped, or 1 tea-*
spoon dried basil
½ *teaspoon salt*
freshly ground pepper to taste
4 *boneless chicken breasts with skin*

1. "Saute" the green pepper and onion in 3 tablespoons broth (re-serving 1 tablespoon for Step 3), covered, in an 8-inch skillet until limp.
2. Combine the pepper and onion with the rice.
3. "Saute" the mushrooms in the same skillet with the remaining tablespoon broth until limp. Add it to the rice-pepper mixture.
4. Stir basil, ¼ teaspoon salt, and pepper into the rice mixture.
5. Cut a pocket in the chicken breast by pressing down on the skin side with one hand while slicing parallel with the counter top almost, but not all the way, to the back of the breast. Open the breast (like a book) and stuff it with a tablespoon of the rice-pepper mixture. Lay the meat back over stuffing, it will "glue" together while cooking. Lift a chicken breast onto a baking dish, skin side up. Repeat with the remaining chicken breasts. Sprinkle with the remaining salt. Refrigerate, if desired, up to 6 hours, until ready to cook.
6. Roast the chicken breasts in a preheated 350-degree oven for 20 minutes. Broil about 5 minutes to brown skin.

Yield: 4 servings
Calories per serving: 215
Protein per serving: 22g

Fat per serving: 9g
Carbohydrates per serving: 9g
Sodium per serving: 430mg

Chicken Baked in a
Salt Crust

❖

Meats and poultry roasted in a crust of salt are amazingly succulent, flavorful, and juicy. The moistened salt forms a shell, locking in moisture that would otherwise evaporate. Happily, the salt doesn't penetrate the food either. For this family meal, a broiler is stuffed with rice seasoned with a garlic puree (made mild by a long simmer), trussed to keep the legs from breaking through the salt crust, then roasted. Carve the bird and serve on a platter with the natural juices retrieved from the carving board. The rice stuffing may be prepared a day ahead or early in the day, the chicken stuffed and packed in salt just before roasting. Although the bird does take 2 hours to cook, it is not lengthy to prepare for roasting and all you need to complete the meal is a green vegetable or salad.

> 1 2- or 3-pound broiler chicken
> 1 whole head garlic, cloves separated
> 2½ cups cooked rice
> 1 small tomato, diced
> 4–5 fresh or oil-cured basil leaves (see page 64) or
>   1 teaspoon dried basil
> ½ teaspoon salt
> freshly ground pepper to taste
> 10 cups kosher salt
> 1¾ cups water

1. Prepare the bird for roasting by cutting off the excess fat at the cavity opening. Cut off the wing tips at the joint, add them to your bone collection for making stock, or discard. Set aside the bird while preparing the stuffing.
2. Separate but don't peel the garlic cloves. Bring a 1-quart saucepan

¾ full of water to a boil. Boil the garlic cloves 1 minute, lift with a slotted spoon to a sieve, and cool under running water. Slip skins off. Return peeled cloves to boiling water and simmer 30 minutes. Drain, reserving 2–3 tablespoons cooking water. Puree the garlic in a food processor, adding reserved cooking water as needed, or force through a fine mesh sieve with a wooden spoon.

3. Combine the cooked rice, garlic puree, tomato, basil, salt, and pepper. Adjust seasoning if necessary.

4. Stuff the cavity of the chicken with the rice mixture, don't pack too tightly; any remaining rice may be heated in a small casserole the last 20 minutes of roasting. To truss the bird, which will keep the legs from breaking through the salt crust during baking, cut a piece of butcher's twine a yard long. Place the chicken so the cavity opening faces you. Fold the twine in half, drape midsection over drumsticks so the ends point to floor. Grasp twine 1 inch below the drumsticks on both the left and right sides, lift and twist twine so each drumstick is "lassoed" and the twine now points upward. Laying twine in the crease formed between the drumsticks and the breast, flip chicken so back is up and string is still held. Cross the twine in back, flip the chicken over again so breast side is up, and tie the string. (See illustration, page 169.) Or use any other trussing technique. Pack any stuffing that might have come loose back into cavity.

5. Preheat oven to 475 degrees.

6. Line a roasting pan big enough for the chicken with a sheet of aluminum foil which extends 10 inches over short sides.

7. Moisten the salt with some of the water, don't use all the water at once. Paste should be just wet enough to hold together when packed with your hands. Place about a third of the paste on the foil-lined roasting pan. Place the chicken on top. Pack the remaining salt all around the bird, covering any exposed spots. Pull the foil up snug to the bird, use to help pack down the salt. Place in the lower third of a preheated 475-degree oven for 2 hours.

8. To serve, peel back the foil. Break and discard the top salt crust. Lift the chicken from roasting pan by the trussing string to a cutting

board or plate, one that will trap the juices. Snip and discard string. Brush away any clinging salt. Pull and discard skin from bird. To carve, cut off legs first, cut in half at the joint. Cut off breast meat. Flip bird, remove skin, cut back in half. Scoop stuffing on to serving platter. Dribble juices from cutting board on to chicken.

Yield: 4 servings
Calories per serving: 275
Protein per serving: 28g

Fat per serving: 2g
Carbohydrates per serving: 33g
Sodium per serving: 820mg

Turkey Cutlet with Cranberried Apple Sauce

Turkey cutlets—thin slices from the breast—make a quick and satisfying meal not unlike veal. If cutlets aren't available in your market, they may be cut from a whole turkey breast and the remainder of the breast may be roasted or smoked (page 182). Purchase cranberries in the fall and freeze them whole in the plastic bag for up to a year, scooping out just what you need for this sauce, which may be made ahead and reheated.

> ½ cup chicken broth
> ½ cup uncooked cranberries
> 2 medium apples, McIntosh recommended, peeled, cored, and chopped
> ⅓ cup flour
> ½ teaspoon salt
> freshly ground pepper to taste

1 ¼ pounds turkey cutlets
1 teaspoon vegetable oil
1 teaspoon butter
4 tablespoons dry sherry
6 tablespoons chicken broth
½ cup of the cranberry-apple sauce
thin orange slices for garnish (optional)

1. In a 1-quart saucepan, combine the broth, cranberries, and apples. Bring to a boil, reduce heat, and simmer 10 minutes. Puree in a food processor, food mill, or blender. Set this cranberry-apple sauce aside.
2. Season the flour with the salt and pepper. Dredge the cutlets in the flour.
3. Spray a 12-inch nonstick skillet with cooking spray. Add the oil and butter, heat until foamy. Add the floured cutlets, sear over high heat 1 minute. Reduce heat, cook 1 minute more, turn and repeat the procedure. Meat is done when it feels firm to the touch. Remove to a heated platter while completing the sauce.
4. Deglaze the skillet with sherry, stirring over high heat with a wooden spoon to loosen the coagulated proteins. When reduced to a syrupy glaze, add the broth, reduce it until ¼ cup remains. Stir in ½ cup or to taste of the cranberry-apple sauce. Remaining cranberry-apple sauce may be kept in the refrigerator for a little more than a week. Serve the sauce over turkey cutlets. Garnish the platter with orange slices if desired.

Yield: 4 servings
Calories per serving: 310
Protein per serving: 36g

Fat per serving: 12g
Carbohydrates per serving: 14g
Sodium per serving: 360mg

Chinese Tea-Smoked Turkey

❖

Tea smoking is a lovely way to impart smoked flavor to fish or poultry without a major investment of time or expensive equipment. You need a wok or any pan with a tight cover such as an electric skillet, and Chinese black tea. While the instructions are written for a boned turkey, you may use a turkey breast or even a chicken. Start the recipe a day before serving, and if using a frozen turkey or breast, 2 days before. The smoked turkey may be served simply sliced warm or at room temperature or used in other recipes such as a turkey salad. It is wonderful sliced for the buffet table accompanied with small pumpkin biscuits and pots of herbed jellies.

> 1 *4-pound boned turkey or turkey breast*
> 1 *tablespoon whole black peppercorns*
> 3 *tablespoons kosher salt*
> 2 *tablespoons Chinese black tea or contents of 4*
>   *Chinese tea bags (available at specialty food*
>   *shops)*
> 2 *tablespoons uncooked rice*
> 2 *tablespoons brown sugar*

1. Thaw the turkey if frozen and wipe it dry.
2. Combine the peppercorns and salt in a small skillet and saute over medium-high heat until the mixture is fragrant, about 2–3 minutes. Let the mixture cool and rub it into the turkey breast. Wrap the turkey in aluminum foil and refrigerate overnight.
3. Rinse the turkey breast free of peppercorn-salt mixture. Steam the breast in a steamer over 3 inches of water for 40–50 minutes. Remove the breast from steamer, let it stand at room temperature (or refrigerate overnight) until cool (about 2 to 3 hours); pat thoroughly dry. This step is important for if the meat is not cool and continues to "sweat," the moisture will prevent it from browning in the smoking step.

4. Line a wok or other deep pot that has a tight-fitting lid with a double thickness of aluminum foil. Combine the tea, rice, and sugar. Spread them over the foil. Set a rack in the pot. Place the breast on rack, skin side up. Cover and place over medium heat until the tea leaves crackle or wisps of smoke escape. Smoke the turkey for 10 minutes. Remove the lid. If the meat is not browned, cover and smoke another 5 minutes. Turkey is ready to serve or use in any turkey recipe.

Yield: 12 servings
Calories per serving: 180
Protein per serving: 17g

Fat per serving: 12g
Carbohydrates per serving: 0
Sodium per serving: 30 + mg

❖ SMOKED FOODS ❖

Smoking foods, used as a preservation technique in a time without refrigeration, has enjoyed a revival of late. Many restaurants feature smoked foods or garnish dishes with smoked tidbits. Smoked turkey breasts, hams, fishes, and shellfish are available by mail from many a modern smokehouse. Those on sodium-restricted diets should know that most smoked foods are treated heavily with salt. Some companies will supply salt-free smoked foods.

Grilled Duck Zinfandel

❖

There are a few foods that by their very presence mark a meal an occasion. Duck is one, but it does have two drawbacks: It is bony and it is fatty. This recipe compensates for both. The breast meat and legs are detached from the bird and cooked separately so the former comes to the table pink and tender while the legs, which would be too chewy if rare, are roasted to a crispy succulence. The sauce is based on a stock made from the remaining duck carcass, enriched with Zinfandel wine and a hint of light cream. It may be made the day before the event or started early and completed hours before serving. Serve both the breast and leg if the rest of the menu is small, serve only the breast (1 duck serves 2) meat if the menu is large. The breast may be grilled or roasted, the legs are roasted only.

> 2 whole ducks
> ½ teaspoon salt
> freshly ground pepper to taste
> 2 carrots, scrubbed and diced
> 1 medium onion, diced
> 2 ribs celery, diced
> 1 cup Zinfandel or other red wine
> 2½ cups chicken broth or 1 ½ cans (13¾ ounces)
>   chicken broth
> 1 quart plus 1 cup cold water
> 1 tablespoon fresh thyme or 1 teaspoon dried thyme
> 1 clove garlic, split in half, no need to peel
> 6–8 parsley stems
> 1 cup additional Zinfandel wine
> 2 tablespoons light cream

8 hours or up to 24 hours before dinner

1. Remove any large flaps of fat from the duck. To bone the duck: Slice off the wings and set them aside. Pull the leg from the body, slice off at the ball joint, and set it aside. Repeat with the other leg. The legs may be frozen for another use if you don't wish to use them in this recipe. Cut along the top ridge of the breastbone, freeing the breast meat by scraping down the rib cage with a knife angled toward the bones. Cut around the wishbone. Repeat on the other side. Score the skin of breast and leg, cutting through the skin but not the meat. Lightly salt and pepper the pieces. Refrigerate until 1 hour before cooking time.

2. With a cleaver or other heavy knife, chop the remaining carcass into quarters and the wings in half. Place the duck bones and wings in a heavy-bottomed skillet with a cover. Brown the bones over high heat, covered, about 25 minutes. There should be enough fat on the wings to brown the bones, but if they are sticking add a small piece of discarded fat from Step 1. When browned, remove to a stockpot or large (at least 4-quart) saucepan.

3. Without cleaning the skillet, brown the carrots, onion, and celery. Again, add a bit of fat if needed. When browned, about 10–12 minutes, remove to the stockpot.

4. Deglaze the skillet with the wine, stirring with a wooden spoon to loosen coagulated proteins. When reduced by half, add the liquid to the stockpot.

5. Add the broth, water, thyme, garlic, and parsley to the stockpot.

6. Bring to a boil, scrape any scum that rises to the surface with a slotted spoon. Reduce the heat and simmer, covered, 1½ hours.

7. Strain (if a clearer sauce is desired strain through a moistened coffee filter or a piece of cheesecloth), discard bones and vegetables, and chill at least 4 hours so the fat will solidify for easy removal. (Recipe may be done 24 hours ahead to this point.)

8. As much as 8 hours before dinner but at least 1 hour before, remove the sauce base from the refrigerator and scrape off bits of floating, hardened fat. Return the sauce base to high heat and boil down to 2 cups, about 45 minutes.

9. Add remaining wine and boil down to ½ to ¾ cup, about 15–20 minutes. Be careful, the sauce evaporates very rapidly at the end and scorches easily if allowed to boil below ½ cup. Remove the sauce from heat and stir in the cream. Taste for seasoning. Sauce may be reheated, even boiled.

To Cook the Duck

1. Preheat the oven to 425 degrees or turn on the grill. If serving the legs, place them, skin side down, in a nonstick skillet over high heat. Sear until lightly browned, about 3–4 minutes on each side. Place in a roasting dish and roast 30 minutes. Cut in half at the joint to serve.
2. To grill the breasts, place them, skin side down, on the grill. When browned, flip them and brown the underside. Turn and finish cooking on the skin side. The meat is done when firm but still slightly soft. Times vary radically from grill to grill, an indoor grill may take as long as 10–14 minutes to cook the breast, while a hotter outdoor grill might take only 6–8 minutes. The meat continues to cook when removed from the grill, so undercook slightly.
3. To roast the breasts, place them skin side up, on the rack of a broiler pan. Roast 15 minutes in a 350-degree oven.

To Serve

1. The breasts may be skinned or not as you please. Slice the long way, with a knife slanted so the strips of meat are thin, ½ inch wide and the length of the breast. Film the entire plate bottom with warm Zinfandel sauce. Arrange the duck strips in a fan, with base at center of the plate. Place the leg pieces at base of the fan. Serve with wild rice. Pass extra sauce at table. The plate is pretty garnished with a bit of red—sauteed cherry tomatoes or strips of roasted red pepper tossed with pea pods.

Yield of duck breasts: 4 servings
Calories per serving: 385
Protein per serving: 25g

Fat per serving: 25g
Carbohydrates per serving: 14g
Sodium per serving: 590mg

Grilled Quail

❖

If quail are difficult to come by, try this recipe with game hens or squab. These would be delicious served on a bed of whole wheat pasta or Chinese noodles and a tossed salad.

> ⅔ cup chicken broth
> ½ cup red wine vinegar
> 2 tablespoons extra-virgin olive oil
> 1 tablespoon freshly snipped tarragon or 1 teaspoon
>   dried tarragon
> 1 clove garlic, split and minced
> freshly ground pepper to taste
> 4 quail
> ⅓ cup flour
> ½ teaspoon salt
> 1 egg yolk

1. In a glass or other nonaluminum bowl, combine the broth, vinegar, oil, tarragon, garlic, and pepper. Cut the birds in half the long way, flatten them with the heel of your hand. Marinate the birds in the herbed broth for 4–6 hours.
2. Remove the birds from the marinade. Pat dry on paper towels. Combine flour and salt in a bag. Add birds, shake.
3. Set the marinade in a 1-quart saucepan and boil over high heat until reduced to ⅔ cup. Beat the egg yolk in a cup. Dribble 2 tablespoons hot marinade into the yolk while stirring with a fork. Pour yolk-marinade mixture back into the remaining marinade, stirring vigorously with a fork, over medium heat until thickened.
4. Place the birds on a grill, brush frequently with yolk-thickened marinade. Turn often. They will cook in about 25 minutes.

Yield: 4 servings
Calories per serving: 365
Protein per serving: 27g

Fat per serving: 23g
Carbohydrates per serving: 9g
Sodium per serving: 340mg

Chapter 8

FISH AND
SHELLFISH

Fish and Shellfish

❖

"Food is meant to tempt as well as nourish and everything that lives in the sea is seductive." —Jean-Paul Aron

Fish is to the calorie-conscious gourmet what polish is to wood—a gleam on the palate. Few foods are as calorie economic or as nutritionally rich. Yet, fish varies in calorie count from variety to variety. So-called fat fish (tuna, salmon, trout, and pompano) with a higher percentage of natural oils, are higher in calories than lean fish (cod, flounder, and red snapper). But a fat fish may need less fats added to it during cooking to avoid drying out. All fish is high in protein and relatively low in fat. A 3½-ounce serving of flounder supplies 30 grams of protein (¾ the daily requirement for a 120-pound woman) and 8 grams of fat for a very reasonable 202 calories. A similar-size serving of beef rump supplies somewhat less protein (24 grams) and 3 times the amount of fat (27 grams) for 347 calories. All other things being equal, substituting fish for beef 2 nights a week for 12 weeks would save 3,500 calories—the energy that when unused our body transforms into a pound of fat.

Care must be taken in the purchase and storage of fish, perhaps more so than with any other food, or the delicate flavor suffers. Today, most of us purchase fish that is already dressed, eviscerated, and scaled, with the head, fins, and tail cut off. Unfortunately, this convenience erases some of the freshness indicators, making it impossible to know if the eyes were bright, clear, and bulging; if the scales were firmly affixed; and if the internal body walls were bright in color with no bones protruding. It really isn't practical to poke fillets, either, but if you were so minded you could judge the fish's freshness by its resiliency, for your fingerprint would not make a lasting impression on a truly fresh fillet. Given the lack of physical evidence, what is a buyer to do?

Your most important clue in shopping for fresh fish is the odor of the fish. A strong smell indicates age, which in turn means poor taste. Unfortunately, fish begins to deteriorate almost as soon as it leaves the water, unlike beef which actually improves with age. This deterioration may be slowed if the fish is kept at about 30 degrees, which does not freeze the flesh but seems to stabilize it. So look for fish sold on ice. There's no way of knowing, of course, if the fish was iced aboard ship or during any processing. But again, the odor of fish cannot be masked, so if the fish you're buying smells fishy, it's time to find a new supplier. Buying from a reputable store should erase fears of purchasing something second rate. A reputable store is one supplied daily, not twice a week—don't hesitate to ask when the product came in.

With the freshest possible fish at hand, the rest is up to the consumer. Just as at market, the fish should be put in a bowl of ice (protected in a plastic bag) in the refrigerator if held more than 4 hours before cooking. Very fresh fish, just 1 or 2 days out of the water, will keep this way with very little flavor loss for 3–4 days. Remember to replenish the ice and pour off the water.

Not all parts of the country can get fresh fish, some must use frozen. Properly prepared it can be quite good. Again, there should be no odor, the package should be intact, and the edges of the fish should not be freezer burned.

In most cases, fish cooks quickly. And if it's impeccably fresh, fish needs little adornment. It is one of the few foods that truly needs only "a little lemon juice" to be enjoyable. Following are recipes for more elaborate treatments, as well as instructions for your basic broiled fillet, because even the most ardent fish fan must yearn for something a little different now and again. I urge you to substitute your local varieties of fish in these recipes. Unlike beef or poultry, products which are largely uniform from Anaheim, California, to Bangor, Maine, fish types vary from coast to coast, and in between.

Shellfish, other than shrimp, may be even more regional than fish fillets. Bivalves, such as mussels and clams, should be alive when purchased and cooked. Frozen langoustine is a somewhat credible substitution for lobster. Having been spoiled by Nantucket's November scallops, I am admittedly biased, but many feed happily on the frozen Florida bay variety.

If you've never much cared for fish but are somewhat tempted by its high-nutrition/low-calorie ratio, I urge you to give it a try with the freshest catch money will buy. Good food with little fat, what better lure is there?

Coquilles St. Jacques

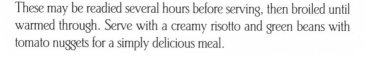

These may be readied several hours before serving, then broiled until warmed through. Serve with a creamy risotto and green beans with tomato nuggets for a simply delicious meal.

> 1 cup dry white wine or vermouth
> 1 tablespoon lemon juice
> 1 shallot, minced
> 1 small clove garlic, minced
> 1 teaspoon fresh tarragon leaves or ½ teaspoon
>   dried tarragon
> 1¼ pounds scallops
> 1 tablespoon sherry
> ½ cup crème blanc, page 37, made without milk
> a few gratings fresh nutmeg
> 1 teaspoon butter
> 2 tablespoons dried bread crumbs
> 2 teaspoons grated Parmesan cheese
> 1 tablespoon minced fresh parsley (optional)

1. Bring the wine, lemon juice, shallot, garlic, and tarragon to a boil in a 10-inch skillet. Reduce heat, simmer 2–3 minutes.
2. Add the scallops, cover, and simmer over low to medium heat until scallops turn an opaque milky white, about 4 minutes. Remove the scallops with a slotted spoon to ovenproof baking shells or a quiche dish.
3. Boil the wine sauce over high heat, uncovered, until reduced to ½ cup. Stir in sherry. Remove from heat, cool 1 minute, stir in crème blanc, and season with nutmeg. Pour the sauce over the scallops.
4. Melt the butter in skillet. Saute the bread crumbs until lightly toasted. Sprinkle over scallops along with grated cheese and broil until bubbly. Garnish with parsley.

Note: If the recipe has been made ahead and chilled, warm in a 350-degree oven for 10 minutes before broiling.

Yield: 4 servings
Calories per serving: 215
Protein per serving: 36g

Fat per serving: 4g
Carbohydrates per serving: 8g
Sodium per serving: 468mg

❖   **THINKING THIN TIP**   ❖

If you eat very quickly and in large bites, eat with chopsticks. It will slow you down at least until you become proficient with them.

Seafood Crepes
in Champagne Sauce

❖

The components of this dish, the crepes and fish, may be readied ahead of time, and the whole assembled as much as 2 hours before serving. Any longer though and the crepes will be sloshed with champagne, though one supposes there are worse fates. Serve with asparagus or some other aristocratic vegetable (artichoke? snow peas?). A starter of Cream of Lettuce or Gingered Carrot Soup would set the right tone.

For the Crepes

1 *egg, beaten*
½ *cup milk*
¼ *cup flour*
pinch salt
1 *tablespoon butter*

For the Seafood

1¼ *pounds assorted seafood, such as ½ pound*
      white fish fillets with ¾ pound shrimp, any
      combination you like, cut into bite-size pieces
1 *shallot, minced*
5 *ounces mushrooms, sliced*
1 *tablespoon lemon juice*
½ *teaspoon salt*
freshly ground pepper to taste
1 *cup champagne*

For the Sauce

1 *tablespoon butter, softened*
2 *tablespoons flour, instant blending recommended*

1 1/4 cups to 1 1/2 cups champagne cooking juices
      from fish
2 tablespoons light cream
1 tablespoon sherry
a few gratings fresh nutmeg
1 tablespoon minced fresh parsley

To Prepare the Crepes

1. Beat the egg and milk together, add the flour sifted with the salt, stir just to combine. Chill 2 hours.
2. Melt 1/2 teaspoon of the butter in a nonstick 8-inch skillet until foamy. Ladle just enough batter into the pan to film bottom. Pour the excess batter back into bowl after bottom sets. Cook crepe over medium-high heat until browned on one side. Flip, cook on underside just to firm, slide onto a plate and continue cooking, adding butter to skillet as necessary and placing a sheet of wax paper between the crepes as they are slid from the pan. Crepes are now ready for use or may be chilled up to 8 hours or frozen until needed. The recipe makes six 8-inch crepes.

To Prepare the Seafood
(May be done as much as 6 hours ahead)

1. Preheat oven to 350 degrees. In a nonaluminum baking dish just large enough to hold the fish, place the fish, shallots, and mushrooms. Season with lemon juice, salt, and pepper. Pour in the champagne. Cover with aluminum foil or a buttered piece of parchment paper. Place in a preheated oven for 12–15 minutes or until fish is done.
2. Lift fish with a slotted spoon to a bowl. If the dish is to be served soon, keep warm on a warming tray. Pour the cooking juices into an 8-inch skillet.
3. Mash together the butter and flour in a cup. Slowly whisk the *beurre manie* (flour and butter) into the cooking juices over medium heat, until smooth and thick. Whisk in the cream. Season with sherry and nutmeg. Taste for salt and pepper. Fold 3/4 of the

sauce into the cooked fish. This may be refrigerated up to one hour before serving.

4. Divide the fish mixture among the crepes and roll loosely. Spray a baking dish, just large enough to hold the crepes, with cooking spray. Place the crepes, seam side down, in the dish. Pour the remaining sauce over top. Broil until bubbly and browned if ingredients are still warm or heat in a preheated 350-degree oven until warmed through, about 15 to 20 minutes, and then broil to brown top. Garnish with the parsley.

Yield: 4 servings

Calories per serving: 300

Protein per serving: 36g

Fat per serving: 10g

Carbohydrates per serving: 16g

Sodium per serving: 568mg

Fillets of Sole
with Basil and Tomato

You may prepare the sauce for this dish early in the day, or even 24 hours ahead, and finish the cooking in about 10 minutes on top of the stove. A few steamed mussels or clams in their shells would be a welcome addition to the sauce; add them the last 5 minutes of cooking. Complete the meal with a simple tossed salad and parsleyed rice.

6 tomatoes or 3 tomatoes plus a 10½-ounce can
   tomatoes
1 shallot, minced
1 clove garlic, minced
½ teaspoon fresh thyme or ¼ teaspoon dried thyme
1 teaspoon fresh tarragon or ½ teaspoon dried
   tarragon

1/4 teaspoon fennel seed
6–8 leaves basil or oil-cured basil or 1 teaspoon
    dried basil
1 bay leaf
1 teaspoon sugar
1 teaspoon salt (1/2 teaspoon if using canned
    tomatoes)
freshly ground pepper to taste
grated zest of 1 orange
2 tablespoons orange juice (half an orange,
    squeezed)
2 pounds sole or other firm-fleshed white fish fillets
half a lemon
6 ounces mushrooms, sliced
1 tablespoon lemon juice
1/4 cup chicken broth or bottled clam juice
1 tablespoon minced fresh parsley

1. Blanch the tomatoes by bringing a 2 1/2-quart saucepan 3/4 full of water to a boil. Immerse tomatoes, 30 seconds for very ripe ones, up to 1 minute for others. Drain and cool under running water. Spear the tomatoes on a fork, peel, and discard skins. Pull tomatoes in half. Put a strainer over a bowl. Squeeze the tomatoes over the strainer to remove seeds. Press the seeds with the back of a wooden spoon so juice drips into bowl. Discard the seeds, add squeezed tomatoes to juice. (Canned tomatoes are generally peeled; seed them as described here if desired.)

2. In a 12-inch skillet, combine the tomatoes with their juice, shallot, garlic, thyme, tarragon, fennel, basil, bay leaf, sugar, salt, pepper, zest, and orange juice. Bring to a boil. Reduce to a simmer, cover, and cook for 40–50 minutes. (On occasion you may need to add 1/4 cup red wine or chicken stock if the tomatoes boil dry.)

3. Meanwhile, prepare the fish. Place the fillets on a sheet of wax paper or aluminum foil with what was the skin side facing up. Cover with another sheet of wax paper and pound lightly with a

cleaver or flat-bottomed heavy pan. Remove the paper, sprinkle fish with a few drops lemon juice. Roll the fillets loosely with what was the skin side facing inward. Set aside or refrigerate until ready to cook. (May be held, chilled, up to 6 hours.)

4. Remove and discard the bay leaf from the simmering sauce. Puree the tomato sauce in a food processor or food mill. Strain back into the skillet. Discard dry pulp that remains in strainer. (Straining may be omitted if you prefer the sauce chunky.) Set sauce aside.

5. "Saute" the mushrooms in the lemon juice and stock in an 8-inch skillet, about 5 minutes or until softened.

6. Add the mushrooms to the simmering sauce. Refrigerate, if desired, until you're ready to complete the dish.

7. Bring the sauce back to a simmer. Lay the rolled fish fillets on top. Spoon a bit of sauce over. Cover pan. Cook 5 minutes per inch thickness of fish, about 12–15 minutes in total, at medium heat. The sauce should just simmer, not boil. Spoon the hot sauce over fish once or twice. When done, remove fish with a slotted spoon to a platter. Cover with a towel.

8. Raise heat under tomato sauce to reduce the juices the fish gave off during cooking. When reduced to about 2 cups, pour the sauce over fish, garnish with the parsley.

Yield: 6 servings
Calories per serving: 158
Protein per serving: 29g

Fat per serving: 1g
Carbohydrates per serving: 8g
Sodium per serving: 455mg

Fish Fillets
with Sauce Rouge

❖

A perfect weekday dinner, these poached fish fillets with their accompanying sauce may be done in about half an hour. With the possible exception of a single red pepper (or you may use a tomato) and a perfectly fresh fillet of fish, it's likely you'll have most of the ingredients on hand. Don't attempt this without a food processor, however, unless you leave the vegetables chunky rather than pureed into the thick, flavorful sauce as it is done here. If you're serving 2, just use half the amount of fish, the extra sauce may be refrigerated for up to 5 days.

> 1 bottle (8 ounces) clam juice
> 1 small onion, diced
> 1 medium carrot, diced
> 1 rib celery, diced
> 1 red bell pepper, seeded and diced
> 3–4 leaves spinach (use sorrel if you have it)
> 1 tablespoon minced fresh parsley
> 1 1/2 pounds thick white-fleshed fish fillets such as
>   haddock or halibut
> 1/2 teaspoon salt
> freshly ground pepper to taste
> 3/4 cup dry or semi-dry white wine
> 2 tablespoons crème blanc, page 37

1. Heat the clam juice in a 10-inch skillet until just bubbling. Add the onion, carrot, and celery. Bring back to a boil, reduce heat to medium, and simmer 10–12 minutes, or until the vegetables are limp and the clam juice reduced by about half.
2. Add the red pepper, simmer 5 more minutes.

3. Stack spinach or sorrel leaves. Roll tightly in jellyroll fashion. Slice, crosswise, into thin strips (known as *chiffonade*). See the drawing on page 201. Add to the vegetables with the parsley, turn heat to high, and stir until greens are wilted, about 30 seconds.

4. Place the fish fillets on the vegetables. If the fish has a thin tail, turn under to even thickness. Season with salt and pepper. Add wine, cover, and bring to a boil. Reduce the heat, barely simmer 10-12 minutes or just until fish is opaque. Remove the fish to a warmed serving platter just before it flakes easily with a fork.

5. Cover the fish with a towel to keep warm while finishing the sauce. Pour the vegetables and wine into a food processor. Puree, adding the crème blanc just before serving. Pour the sauce over fish fillets.

Note: The vegetables and wine could be pureed in a food mill as desired or left as is. Stir in crème blanc after sauce has cooled about 1 minute; if it is too hot the crème blanc will curdle.

Yield: 4 servings
Calories per serving: 164
Protein per serving: 34g

Fat per serving: trace
Carbohydrates per serving: 8g
Sodium per serving: 654mg

TO CHIFFONADE

1. Stack the lettuce, or other item, to be cut, then roll it up tightly, jellyroll fashion.

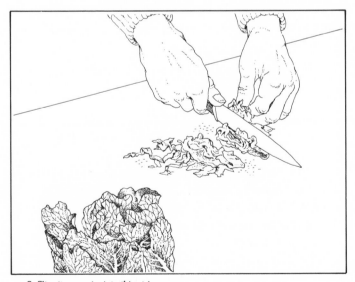

2. Slice it crosswise into thin strips.

Fillets of Fish Martini

❖

Steaming fish helps to retain its fresh, clean flavor better than any other cooking technique. This quickly done dinner is easily accomplished with a Chinese steamer and wok but you may fashion a steaming arrangement with a cake rack set on custard cups inside a deep electric frying pan.

> 1 1/4 pounds fillets of fish; haddock, cod, or other
>   thick white-fleshed fish
> freshly ground pepper to taste
> 2 cups broccoli flowerets and stems
> 2 carrots, peeled and julienned
> 4–5 strips lemon peel
> 2 cups fish stock or 2 8-ounce bottles clam juice
> 1/4 cup dry white vermouth
> 3 juniper berries, crushed (optional)
> 1 tablespoon minced fresh parsley
> 2 tablespoons gin
> 2 egg yolks
> 1 teaspoon cornstarch or potato starch
> 1 tablespoon butter

1. Place the fish on the rack of a Chinese bamboo steamer. Season with pepper (add salt only if using homemade fish stock, the commercial clam juice is salty).
2. Place broccoli flowerets on one side of fish. To prepare the stems, peel the tough outer skin with a knife or vegetable peeler. Slice the peeled stem thinly on the diagonal; add to the flowerets. Arrange the carrots on the other side of the fish. Arrange the lemon strips decoratively on top of fish.
3. In the bottom of a wok or deep electric skillet, combine the fish stock (reserving 2 tablespoons for Step 7), vermouth, juniper

berries, and half the parsley. Place the bamboo steamer or rack over the wok, cover, and bring to a boil over high heat. Begin timing when the liquid boils; steam 5–6 minutes.

4. Lift the steamer or rack from wok. Boil the fish stock, uncovered, until reduced to 1 cup.

5. Meanwhile, heat the gin in a long-handled, small saucepan, preferably one with a lip, until bubbles just appear at the edge. Ignite the gin and pour it over fish (still in steamer, placed over a plate). After the flames die out, cover with a towel while completing the sauce or keep warm in a turned-off oven.

6. Beat the egg yolks in a small bowl or measuring cup with a fork. Dribble ¼ cup of the reduced fish stock into the yolks, while stirring with the fork. Whisk the yolk-fish stock mixture into the remaining fish stock in wok over very low heat. Adjusting the heat as necessary, whisk until the sauce becomes opaque and foamy.

7. Dissolve the cornstarch in the 2 tablespoons reserved fish stock. Whisk this into the yolk-fish stock mixture over medium-low heat until thickened. Whisk in butter. Garnish fish with the remaining parsley. Serve fish right from the bamboo steamer with the sauce passed at the table.

Yield: 4 servings
Calories per serving: 240
Protein per serving: 32g

Fat per serving: 6g
Carbohydrates per serving: 14g
Sodium per serving: 596mg

❖ PARSLEY ❖

Fresh parsley is to dried parsley flakes as Wimbledon's grass courts are to Astroturf. Fresh parsley is readily available, inexpensive, and easy to use, if you have a good knife for mincing it. Store parsley, stem ends down, in a large glass of water in the refrigerator. Make a little tepee out of a plastic bag and cover the parsley. This will help keep it fresh for a few days longer.

Broiled Fish Fillets

❖

The success of this "nonrecipe" recipe lies in the freshness of the fish, for if it is not absolutely pristine it's best to use it in another recipe where stronger flavors can carry it.

> 3/4 to 1   pound white-fleshed fish fillets such as sole
> 1/4   teaspoon salt
> freshly ground pepper to taste
> a few drops lemon juice
> 3   tablespoons dry white wine, more or less
> 1   teaspoon butter
> 1   small clove garlic, minced (optional)
> 2   tablespoons dried bread crumbs
> 1   tablespoon minced fresh parsley

1. Lay the fish fillet in a baking dish. Fold the thin tail under to even the thickness of the fish. Season with salt, pepper, and lemon juice. Add just enough wine to film the bottom of the pan. Place the fish under the heated broiler while preparing the bread crumbs.

2. Melt the butter in an 8-inch skillet over medium-high heat. When foamy, stir the garlic over medium heat about 30 seconds, without browning. Add the bread crumbs, stir until just lightly golden. Remove from heat and stir in the parsley.

3. When the fish has turned opaque and flakes easily with a poke of the knife tip, about 5 minutes, spread the bread crumbs over the fish. Return to broiler until crumbs are lightly browned. Serve with the cooking juices poured over the fish.

Yield: 2 servings
Calories per serving: 195
Protein per serving: 42g

Fat per serving: 2g
Carbohydrates per serving: 3g
Sodium per serving: 420mg

Fillets of Sole
with Salmon Mousse

❖

You may vary the presentation of this dish by lining a ring mold with the fish fillets and filling with the salmon mousse mixture. Unmolded and with the center filled with a fresh green vegetable, it makes a pretty party dish. Although canned salmon may be used, it is a pale substitute for fresh. Serve with Hollandaise drizzled over the fish, and Nutted Braised Celery (page 244).

> 4 fillets of sole, each about 1/4 to 1/3 pound (1 pound total)
> 1/2 pound fresh salmon
> 2 tablespoons light cream
> 1/2 teaspoon salt
> freshly ground pepper to taste
> 1 teaspoon fresh tarragon or 1/2 teaspoon dried tarragon
> 1 tablespoon minced fresh parsley
> 2 egg whites, lightly beaten
> 1/4 cup dry white wine
> Hollandaise Sauce (page 21)

1. Place the fish fillets between sheets of wax paper and flatten slightly with a cleaver or heavy flat-bottomed saucepan. Set aside. (If using a ring mold, lay the fillets, cutting as necessary, in an oiled mold with what was the skin side facing in.)
2. Steam the salmon in a rack over 3 inches of water until it flakes easily with a fork, about 5 minutes per inch thickness. Cool and pick over the salmon to remove bits of skin, gristle, and fat. Flake it into a bowl or food processor.
3. Blend in the cream, salt, pepper, tarragon, half the parsley, and egg whites. Process or beat until fairly smooth.

4. Preheat oven to 350 degrees. Place sole fillets on work surface with what was the skin side facing up. Divide the salmon mixture over the fillets, roll loosely. (Or pack into a fish-lined ring mold, and bang the mold on a kitchen counter to remove air bubbles.) Place fillets in a baking dish with wine in the bottom. (If using a ring mold, place mold in a baking dish with 1 inch water on bottom.) Bake 20 minutes for fillets, 25-30 for a ring mold. Serve with Hollandaise Sauce, and garnish with the remaining parsley.

Note: If you wish, make the Hollandaise after the fish has baked, using the juices in the bottom of the pan to replace some of the chicken broth called for in the original recipe.

Yield: 4 servings
Calories per serving: 230
Protein per serving: 35g

Fat per serving: 9g
Carbohydrates per serving: 1g
Sodium per serving: 469mg

Broiled Fish Steaks
with Basil-Walnut Sauce

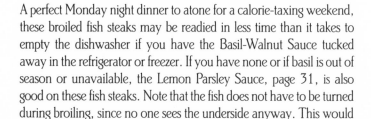

A perfect Monday night dinner to atone for a calorie-taxing weekend, these broiled fish steaks may be readied in less time than it takes to empty the dishwasher if you have the Basil-Walnut Sauce tucked away in the refrigerator or freezer. If you have none or if basil is out of season or unavailable, the Lemon Parsley Sauce, page 31, is also good on these fish steaks. Note that the fish does not have to be turned during broiling, since no one sees the underside anyway. This would be very nice with Fettuccine with Cepes, page 248, and a tossed salad.

> *1 1/4 pounds to 1 1/2 pounds fish steaks or fillets such*
> *as cod, haddock, or halibut, about 1-inch thick*
> *1/2 teaspoon salt*
> *freshly ground pepper to taste*
> *1 tablespoon butter, at room temperature*
> *juice of half a lemon*
> *1/4 cup dry white wine*
> *1/4 cup Basil-Walnut Sauce (page 32)*

1. Lay the fish in a broiling pan or roasting dish. Measure it at its thickest part. Season fish with salt and pepper and smear with butter. Squeeze a few drops lemon juice over fish. Pour the wine into pan (it should just cover the bottom, add more or less as needed). Broil 4 minutes, cover the top of fish with Basil-Walnut Sauce, and broil an additional 1–2 minutes, allowing about 5 minutes per inch thickness.

Note: For juicy fish, err on the side of undercooking.

Yield: 4 servings
Calories per serving: 190
Protein per serving: 32g

Fat per serving: 6g
Carbohydrates per serving: 2g
Sodium per serving: 382mg

Lemon-Lime Fillets
in Parchment Paper Hearts

❖

Cooking in parchment paper locks in natural juices and flavors and makes serving a snap. The paper hearts may be readied up to 3 hours ahead, but no longer or the paper will become soggy. If desired, top each of the fillets with a few scallops or shrimp. Serve with Bourbon Squash Souffle (page 280) and a salad.

>   1   lime and 1 lemon
>   2   cups water
>   2   tablespoons softened butter
>   2   tablespoons lemon juice
>   1   tablespoon lime juice
>   1   teaspoon minced ginger root
>   1 1/4   pounds white-fleshed fish fillets such as sole,
>   cod, or haddock cut into 4 serving-size pieces
>   1/4   teaspoon salt
>   freshly ground pepper to taste
>   1   tablespoon minced fresh parsley

1. With a vegetable peeler, remove the rind of both the lemon and the lime, taking care to remove only the colored skin and none of the white, which tends to be bitter. Julienne the peels into strips nearly as fine as pine needles.
2. Bring the water to a boil, immerse the julienned peels, and boil 2 minutes. Drain.
3. Mash the julienned peel in with the butter, half the lemon juice, all the lime juice, and the ginger root.
4. Preheat oven to 425 degrees. Cut four parchment paper hearts, place a fish fillet on each. (You may use a double thickness of wax paper if parchment paper is unavailable.) Season the fish with salt,

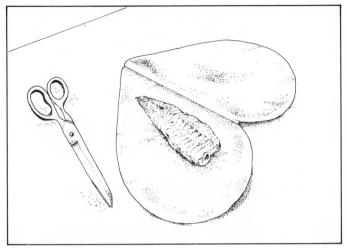

COOKING IN PARCHMENT PAPER HEARTS

1. Lay the fish fillet, or other food, on half the paper heart, then fold the paper over it.

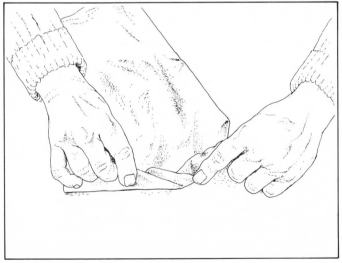

2. Pleat the paper tightly, securing the pleat with your fingertips as you move along the perimeter of the heart. Each pleat is made by making ¼-inch folds at 1½-inch intervals.

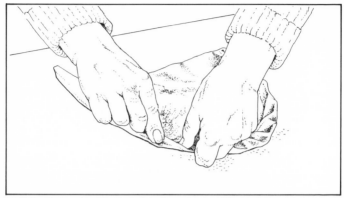

3. Continue making the pleats along the perimeter of the heart.

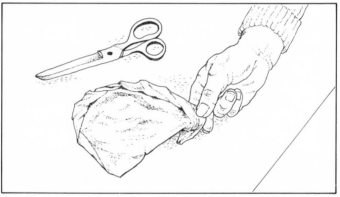

4. Secure the end by tucking the tip of paper under the package.

pepper, and remaining lemon juice. Divide the lemon-lime butter over it. Garnish with parsley. Fold as shown in the illustration above, pleating the edge and turning the tip under. Place on a baking sheet and bake 8 minutes in a preheated 425-degree oven. Let each diner open his/her own package and enjoy the aroma.

Yield: 4 servings
Calories per serving: 165
Protein per serving: 26g

Fat per serving: 6g
Carbohydrates per serving: 1g
Sodium per serving: 89mg

Sauteed Scallops

❖

This is an example of the "less is more" culinary school of thought, which believes food is best enhanced by simple rather than complicated cooking techniques. Its most basic tenet, "nothing but the best and the freshest," keeps the simply prepared fare from being nothing more than a bare bones offering. For this dish it is imperative the scallops be sweet and never frozen. Serve with Lemon Glazed Carrots (page 241) and Fire and Ice Salad (page 102). Ingredients may be doubled or tripled to accommodate more diners.

¾ to 1 pound scallops
2 tablespoons flour
freshly ground pepper to taste
1 tablespoon butter
2 tablespoons dry white wine or for a sweeter touch,
    sherry

1. Dredge the scallops in the flour, season with pepper.
2. Melt the butter in a 10-inch skillet. When foamy, add the scallops and saute over high heat, turning often, until opaque, about 5–7 minutes.
3. Add the wine to pan and stir until reduced to a syrupy glaze. Divide scallops and sauce between two baking shells and serve.

Yield: 2 servings
Calories per serving: 325
Protein per serving: 54g

Fat per serving: 9g
Carbohydrates per serving: 6g
Sodium per serving: 601mg

Grilled Shrimp
with Leeks and Fennel

❖

Grilling fish or shellfish over the feathery leaves of fennel is an old French technique. The greens protect the fish from tearing on the grilling rack while imparting a lovely, faintly sweet flavor to the flesh. If you don't have a grill, see the instructions in step 8 for broiling. This not only makes a nice meal for the calorie conscious but a delicious first course for a dinner party. Fennel bulbs are available in the fall, winter, and early spring.

1 to 1 1/4 pounds large, uncooked shrimp
1 tablespoon olive oil
1 tablespoon lemon juice
3 tablespoons fish stock, chicken broth, or clam broth
1 bay leaf
freshly ground pepper to taste
2 red bell peppers
2 fennel bulbs, with stalks
4 leeks
1 cup (or less) chicken broth
1/2 teaspoon salt
freshly ground pepper to taste
1 teaspoon oil
4 thin lemon slices

1. Shell and devein the shrimp. Marinate them 4 hours or overnight in the oil, lemon juice, fish stock, bay leaf, and pepper. Drain, discard bay leaf, and reserve the marinade.
2. Cut the red peppers in half and flatten them with the heel of your hand. (See illustration, page 260.) Place on a baking sheet, skin

side up, and broil, turning pan from time to time, until the skin is blackened and charred, about 8 minutes. Remove to a paper or plastic bag, roll tightly closed, and let rest until peppers are cool enough to handle.

3. Meanwhile, separate the feathery stalks from the fennel bulbs. Pare the tough, outer leaves from the fennel bulbs. Slice the bulbs on the diagonal. Rinse. Reserve the stalks.

4. Cut the leeks where the green turns to white. Discard the tops, cut white part in half the long way, and rinse.

5. Place the leeks and fennel bulb in a 10-inch skillet with enough chicken broth to half cover, season with salt, pepper, and oil. Cover and simmer 15-20 minutes or until tender. Remove cover and boil until liquid is reduced to a glaze. Set aside.

6. Meanwhile, remove peppers from the bag. Peel and discard the charred skin. Set peppers aside.

7. To grill: Place the fennel stalks directly on a hot grill. Place the shrimp on top of the stalks. Grill, turning shrimp once until cooked through, about 8 to 10 minutes. During the last 5 minutes of cooking, place peeled peppers directly on grill. Turn them after 2½ minutes. Baste shrimp and peppers occasionally with reserved marinade during cooking.

8. To broil: Place shrimp and peppers on the grid of a broiling pan. Broil, 3 inches from the coils, 2-3 minutes to a side, turning once, basting with the reserved marinade. Remove peppers if they are burning. Place fennel stalks in the bottom of broiler pan placed on a heatproof surface. Ignite the fennel stalks with a long match. *Note:* If broiling shrimp instead of grilling, it's a good idea to dry the fennel stalks, making it easier to ignite them. To dry the fennel stalks, remove the bulb for use in recipe. Cut thick stalks in half the long way. Place in a 200-degree oven on a baking sheet, turning often until dried. Place broiler grid with shrimp and peppers over burning stalks to ''smoke'' the food. When the flames die out, continue with recipe.

9. Divide the braised fennel from step 5 among 4 luncheon-size plates. Place the shrimp in a circle on top. Place the peppers in the

center of the circle. Place the leek halves on either side of shrimp. Garnish with lemon slices, cut in half, twisted, and placed flat side down on shrimp.

Yield: 4 servings
Calories per serving: 260
Protein per serving: 37g

Fat per serving: 6g
Carbohydrates per serving: 13g
Sodium per serving: 640mg

❖ THE NEW AMERICAN GRILL ❖

Grilling is hot. The day when barbecue meant hamburgers, steaks, and the occasional sausage is past. America's imaginative chefs are grilling everything from shrimp to squab and accompanying dishes with sauces that would leave Grandma gasping. From barbecue Hollandaise to Spicy Plum, from Burgundy Cherry to Mustard Mousse, today's concoctions make ketchup sound about as appealing as a plastic tomato. The innovations don't stop with the food and sauces, either. Where once charcoal would do, mesquite, applewood, hickory, cabernet grapevine cuttings, and cords of other woods now smoke. And all of this on equipment that makes the backyard $19.98 grill look about as current as a Model T. Gas and electric grills, covered models, water smokers, and 55-gallon tin drums are among the grill chef's options, making what was once the first and simplest of cooking techniques one where only the most sophisticated take charge. One note: While all the data is not yet in, it is suspected that browned parts of meat cooked at high temperatures by grilling, broiling, and frying may be carcinogenic.

Lobster Flamed with Drambuie

❖

This is an occasion sort of dish, the kind of dinner to commemorate a birthday, anniversary, or perhaps Christmas Eve dinner. The same proportions divided among 6 diners rather than 4 would also make a flamboyant beginning to a formal meal. Begin preparations the day before or at least early in the day as making the lobster stock requires some time. Freeze the remaining lobster glaze for up to a year for another dish. This recipe also makes an excellent sauce for pasta.

> 4 lobsters, about 1 1/2 pounds each
> 1 small rib celery, diced
> 2 shallots, diced
> 1 carrot, diced
> 2 cups dry white wine
> 2 sprigs parsley
> 1 clove garlic
> 3 tablespoons dry white wine
> 1 teaspoon mild paprika
> 4 ounces mushrooms, sliced
> 3 ounces pea pods, blanched 1 minute
> 1 leek, white part only, julienned
> 2 tablespoons Drambuie
> 6 tablespoons light cream
> 1 tablespoon minced fresh parsley

1. Early in the day or the day before serving, bring a lobster pot or a 10-quart saucepan 3/4 full of water to a boil. Immerse the lobster, boil for 3 minutes. Turn off heat, let rest 5 minutes, drain and cool in cold water. Remove meat from shells, cut into chunks, reserve shells and legs. Chill meat.
2. Place lobster shells and legs in a nonaluminum saucepan with the celery, shallots, carrot, wine, parsley, and garlic. Add water to

cover, bring to a boil, and immediately reduce to a simmer. Simmer 2 hours.

3. Strain the lobster stock, discarding vegetables and shells. Return to high heat, boil rapidly until reduced to about 2 cups, about 35–40 minutes. Watch closely for the last 10 minutes as the glaze will quickly evaporate and burn. The lobster glaze will be very dark and salty to taste. Glaze may be refrigerated now or the recipe continued.

4. Heat ¾ cup lobster glaze with the wine and paprika in a 10-inch skillet over medium heat. Freeze the remaining glaze. Add the mushrooms, pea pods, leek, and lobster meat. Stir until warmed through, about 3 minutes.

5. Heat the Drambuie in a long-handled small saucepan, preferably with a spout. When bubbles appear at the edge of the pan, ignite the liquor and pour it on the lobster and vegetables. Stir until flames die out. Stir in cream.

6. To serve, ladle sauce and lobster onto large salad or luncheon-size plates. Garnish with the parsley. Serve with a dinner-size liner plate underneath.

Yield: 4 servings
Calories per serving: 310
Protein per serving: 48g

Fat per serving: 9g
Carbohydrates per serving: 8g
Sodium per serving: 520 + mg

Poached Salmon with Reduced-Calorie Béarnaise

Poached salmon may be offered hot or cold, unadorned or complemented by any number of sauces. You may use a bit of the cooking liquid to replace some of the chicken broth when making the Reduced-Calorie Béarnaise sauce if desired. Accompany with asparagus spears or fresh peas if in season and begin with a Pear and Gouda Salad, page 107.

For the Court Bouillon

2 *quarts water*
½ *cup white wine vinegar*
1 *onion, sliced*
3–4 *sprigs fresh parlsey*
1 *teaspoon whole peppercorns*
1 *bay leaf*

The Fish

2 *pounds salmon roast (the midsection of the fish,
      with skin and bone intact) or 2 pounds salmon
      steaks*
1 *recipe Béarnaise Sauce, page 24*
6–8 *lemon slices (optional)*
minced fresh parsley (optional)

1. Combine all the court bouillon ingredients in a 4-quart saucepan. Bring to a boil, immediately reduce to a simmer.
2. Meanwhile, wrap the fish in cheesecloth (2 layers is sufficient) or an old, thin kitchen towel. Measure the fish at its thickest part.
3. Lower the fish into the simmering court bouillon, cover, and cook 5 minutes per inch thickness. Remove fish from court bouillon and unwrap it if serving immediately. Cool first if desired.
4. Scrape off skin. Slice roast in half horizontally at the backbone and remove bones. Serve with Reduced-Calorie Béarnaise and garnish with lemon slices rimmed in minced parsley if desired.

Yield: 6-8 servings
Calories per serving: 215
Protein per serving: 17g

Fat per serving: 15g
Carbohydrates per serving: trace
Sodium per serving: 90mg

Monkfish à L'Americaine

❖

Monkfish, also known as monkey fish or lotte, is called poor man's lobster in France for its firm-fleshed texture. Here, much like mussels, it's been regarded as a junk fish and used as bait or sometimes exported to France, where it is in demand. More recently it's become available in our fish markets, and the price has risen as has interest in it. Ask your fish merchant for it if he does not now carry this mild-flavored fish. The origin of the culinary term L'Americaine is obscure. Whether it was a term attached to a seafood dish prepared with tomatoes and olive oil in commemoration of an American customer by a French restaurateur or a dish brought to America by a French chef then re-exported to France isn't known—but it is decidedly Provençal in its origin, rich in onion, garlic, parsley, and oil. You know what's been left out here.

4   tomatoes or a 14-ounce can of tomatoes
2   leeks, white part only, thinly sliced
3   tablespoons chicken broth
½   teaspoon salt
freshly ground pepper to taste
2–3   tablespoons flour
1½   pounds monkfish, skinned and boned or other
      firm-fleshed whitefish, at least 2 inches thick
3   tablespoons Pernod
⅔   cup dry white wine
1   clove garlic, minced
3–4   tablespoons tomato paste
1   teaspoon fresh tarragon leaves or ½ dried tarragon
1   tablespoon minced fresh parsley

1. Core the tomatoes and cut a cross in each one's bottom. Bring a 2½-quart saucepan ¾ full of water to a boil. Blanch the toma-

toes 30 seconds to 1 minute, depending on ripeness. Drain and cool under running water. Spear on a fork and peel off the skins. Halve the tomatoes, extract seeds with your thumb or a spoon into a strainer held over a bowl. Dice the pulp. Press the seeds with the back of a wooden spoon to extract the juices. Discard the seeds. Add the juices to pulp. Set aside. Canned tomatoes may be used as is or seeded if desired.

2. "Saute" the leeks in the broth over medium-high heat, covered, until limp, about 5 minutes.

3. Mix the salt and pepper with the flour. Dredge the fish. Spray a 12-inch skillet with cooking spray. Place the skillet over high heat. Sear the fish for about 1 minute on each side to brown. Adjust heat as needed.

4. Add the Pernod and ignite it. When flames die out add the wine, leeks, broth, garlic, tomatoes, tomato paste, and tarragon.

5. Cover and simmer 10 minutes until the fish is cooked through, plan on about 5 minutes per inch thickness. *Note:* If monkfish fillets are over 4 inches thick, you may cut them into rounds 2-inches thick to hasten the cooking.

6. Remove the fish to a platter, cover to keep warm. If sauce is too thin, reduce it by boiling until it reaches desired consistency. Spoon over fish and garnish with the parsley.

Yield: 4 servings
Calories per serving: 200
Protein per serving: 28g

Fat per serving: 2g
Carbohydrates per serving: 17g
Sodium per serving: 510mg

Mussels in White Wine and Saffron

❖

Mussels, long enjoyed on the continent, are coming into such favor here that we can now buy a cultivated breed. These bivalves are much cleaner than naturally occurring mussels, making light work of a once time-consuming chore. Be wary when purchasing any mussels, though. The shellfish should be kept on ice, be as fresh as possible (ask the vendor when they came in, pass over any more than two days old), and the shells should be closed. This is not a do-ahead meal, but it is very quickly cooked. The mussels may be enjoyed as a first course, light dinner, or served on a bed of pasta for heartier fare.

> 3–4 pounds mussels
> 1 shallot, minced
> 2 cloves garlic, minced
> a few threads saffron
> a few parsley stems
> 1 sprig thyme
> 1 bay leaf
> 1 cup white wine
> 1 tablespoon butter, softened
> 1 tablespoon flour
> ½ teaspoon turmeric (optional, for color)
> 2 tablespoons light cream
> 1 tablespoon minced fresh parsley

1. To clean the mussels: Scrub each mussel with a brush and remove the "beard" with a sharp knife. Drop them into cold water and soak 1 to 2 hours. Some cooks add a handful of cornmeal or flour on the theory that it is ingested, thus plumping and cleansing the mussels. Lift the mussels from the soaking water and rinse again.

2. In a saucepan large enough to hold the mussels, put the shallot, garlic, saffron, parsley stems, thyme, bay leaf, and wine. Add the mussels, cover, and bring to a boil, shaking the pan frequently. When the shells open, about 5 minutes, remove from heat.
3. Pour the mussels and cooking liquid into a strainer set over a bowl. Discard the bay leaf, parsley stems, and thyme sprig. Pour cooking liquid back into saucepan (but not the grit at the bottom) and boil over high heat until reduced by a third.
4. Mash the butter and flour together. Whisk it into the simmering stock in two parts over medium-low heat. Stir in turmeric and cream.
5. To prepare the mussels for serving, discard one half of each shell. Arrange the mussels on a platter neatly. Pour the sauce over mussels and garnish with the parsley.

Yield: 4 servings
Calories per serving: 195
Protein per serving: 20g

Fat per serving: 8g
Carbohydrates per serving: 12g
Sodium per serving: 390mg

❖ **SAFFRON** ❖

The world's most expensive spice is the dried stigma of a crocus. There are only three such threads in each flower, and they must be picked by hand. Since it takes 225,000 stigmas to make a pound of saffron, small wonder it is so costly. Saffron is the signature spice of paella, a Spanish rice dish. It is also used in breads, pilafs, and with some shellfish. It comes in powdered and dried form.

Warm Seafood Salad
with Chinese Noodles

❖

This fragrant toss of seafood and noodles is a meal all by itself. Although presented here as a warm dish, it is very good served at room temperature as well. (Do not serve it chilled, because chilling shrouds some of the flavor.) To serve at room temperature, prepare the salad in advance, tossing the seafood, vegetables and noodles with the dressing to prevent the latter from becoming gummy. Or prepare the seafood and vegetables, marinating them in the dressing for several hours but cooking the noodles at the last minute. All the Oriental ingredients listed here are available at specialty food stores. The noodles are increasingly available in produce sections of larger supermarkets.

For the Court Bouillon

2 quarts water
1/2 cup rice wine vinegar or white wine vinegar
1 onion, sliced
3–4 sprigs parsley
1/2 teaspoon salt
1 teaspoon whole peppercorns
1 bay leaf

For the Seafood Salad

1/2 pound firm-fleshed whitefish such as cod,
    haddock, or halibut
1/2 pound medium raw shrimp, shelled and deveined
1/4 pound scallops
2 stalks broccoli

For the Dressing

6 *tablespoons light soy sauce*

1 *tablespoon sesame oil*

1 *tablespoon vegetable oil*

2 *tablespoons rice wine, Chinese cooking wine, or sherry*

2 *teaspoons minced scallion*

2 *teaspoons finely minced ginger root*

6 *tablespoons reduced court bouillon*

½ *pound fresh Chinese noodles*

10–12 *cherry tomatoes, halved*

1. Make a court bouillon by combining the water, vinegar, onion, parsley, salt, peppercorns, and bay leaf in a 4-quart saucepan. Bring to a rolling boil.
2. Wrap the fish and shellfish, individually, in double thicknesses of cheesecloth. Lower the fish into the court bouillon first, remove from heat, cover, and let it rest 30 seconds. Then add the scallops and shrimp, cover, and let them rest 5–6 minutes. Lift the fish and shellfish from the liquid and set aside to cool. Boil the court bouillon at high heat, uncovered, until reduced to about 1 cup, about 30 minutes.
3. Meanwhile, cut the stems from the broccoli flowerets. Slice the flowerets. Peel the stems and slice thinly on the diagonal. Bring a 2 quart saucepan ¾ full of water to a boil, blanch the broccoli 4 minutes, drain, and rinse under cool water.
4. Combine all the dressing ingredients in a screw-top jar and shake heartily to combine. Set aside.
5. Cook the Chinese noodles by immersing them in 2 quarts of boiling water for 2–4 minutes. Drain and rinse under cool water.
6. Heat the dressing in a wok or large skillet over high heat. Remove and discard the cheesecloth from the fish, scallops, and shrimp. Toss the seafood with the broccoli and cherry tomatoes in the warm dressing to heat through.

7. Place drained noodles in shallow, wide soup bowls (reheat if needed by dousing with a kettle of boiling water), and add the seafood salad.

Note: Noodles may be cooked as much as 30 minutes in advance, but rinse well under running water after cooking. Reheat noodles by dousing with at least 2 quarts of boiling water.

Yield: 4 servings
Calories per serving: 495
Protein per serving: 42g

Fat per serving: 9g
Carbohydrates per serving: 60g
Sodium per serving: 1910mg

Sole, Scallop, and Pea Pod Salad

❖

This salad may be prepared early in the day and served several hours later. Be sure to remove it from the refrigerator at least 30 minutes before dining as it is better closer to room temperature than chilled. Serve with crusty bread and offer a refreshing fruit sherbert for dessert.

For the Court Bouillon

1 *quart water*
2 *cups dry white wine*
1/4 *cup tarragon vinegar*
3–4 *stems parsley*
1 *bay leaf*
8 *peppercorns*
1/2 *teaspoon salt*

For the Salad

1 1/2 pounds sole
3/4 pound scallops
pieces of cheesecloth
3/4 pound pea pods, strings removed
15 walnut halves, roughly chopped

For the Dressing

4 1/2 tablespoons reduced court bouillon
3 tablespoons vegetable oil
1 tablespoon fresh lemon juice
3 tablespoons tarragon vinegar
1 tablespoon freshly chopped basil or 1/2 teaspoon
   dried basil
1 garlic clove, speared on a toothpick
1/2 teaspoon salt
a few grindings fresh pepper

1. Combine all the ingredients for the court bouillon in a 3-quart nonaluminum saucepan and bring to a boil. Reduce heat and simmer for 45 minutes.
2. Wrap the fish and scallops in a double thickness of cheesecloth. Bring court bouillon back to a boil. Lower the fish and scallops into bouillon, cover, and remove from the heat. Let it rest 5 minutes. Lift the fish and scallops from liquid and rinse under cold running water to stop the cooking. Chill.
3. Put 1 cup court bouillon in a saucepan over high heat. Boil until reduced to 4 1/2 tablespoons. Set aside.
4. Bring a 2 1/2-quart saucepan 3/4 full of water to a boil. Immerse the pea pods, remove from heat, and let them sit for 4 minutes. Drain and rinse under cold running water until peas are at room temperature.
5. Combine all the dressing ingredients in a jar, shake well, and let dressing rest 1 hour. Remove the garlic just before serving.
6. The salad may be assembled as much as 4 hours before serving

but is best done no more than an hour before. Flake the fish into a serving bowl, add the scallops, pea pods, and walnut halves. Toss with enough dressing to coat lightly. Serve on lettuce cups or in hollowed navel oranges, lined with lettuce.

Yield: 6 servings
Calories per serving: 254
Protein per serving: 32g

Fat per serving: 10g
Carbohydrates per serving: 9g
Sodium per serving: less than 580mg

Swordfish with Mustard Tarragon Sauce

❖

Here's a wonderfully satisfying meal that cheats on nothing but time, going from the refrigerator to table in about 15 minutes flat. Accompany with a simple rice pilaf and a Dilled Zucchini and Carrot Salad (page 104). The Mustard Tarragon Sauce may be kept in the refrigerator up to 1 week. The fish may be broiled rather than grilled. If the fish has any odor, soak it in 3 cups water mixed with 2 tablespoons bottled or fresh lemon juice for 10 minutes. Pat it dry before grilling.

1 1/4 pounds swordfish or thick fish steak such as tuna
half a fresh lemon
2 tablespoons mayonnaise
4 tablespoons plain yogurt
1 tablespoon plus 1 teaspoon stone-ground or
*   Dijon-style mustard*
1 teaspoon lemon juice

> 1 tablespoon fresh tarragon, snipped, or 1 teaspoon
> dried tarragon
> ½ teaspoon capers (optional)

1. Heat a broiler or grill. When hot, cook the fish on one side for about 4 minutes. Squeeze 1 teaspoon fresh lemon juice over.
2. While the fish cooks, combine all the remaining ingredients, except the capers. Mix well.
3. Flip the fish. On a grill, cover cooked surface of fish with the sauce. Under a broiler, cook the fish 1 minute on second side before covering with the sauce. Continue to cook until the fish is no longer soft when pressed with a finger, about 4 minutes more, 8 minutes in all. Sprinkle the capers over fish the last 2 minutes of cooking.

Yield: 4 servings
Calories per serving: 245
Protein per serving: 30g

Fat per serving: 12g
Carbohydrates per serving: 2g
Sodium per serving: 120mg

❖   **YOGURT**   ❖

Yogurt is a fermented milk product that has long been used in the Middle East but has only been used here since the 1940's. Widely regarded as a health food, it should be noted that it supplies no more nutrients than a glass of partially skimmed milk, although it does aid in digestion. Yogurt, like its roly-poly cousin, sour cream, must be cooked at low temperatures or it will curdle. Fruit-flavored yogurts are comparatively high in calories, one cup supplying about 260–300 calories.

Chapter 9

PRODUCE
PROPER

Vegetables

❖

Vegetables in this health-aware era have come into their own. Who wants the good old days when the 1941 edition of the *Fannie Farmer Cookbook* instructed Grandma to boil the green beans for 20 minutes! The vegetable is no longer an obligatory token item on the plate. Today we herald crisp but tender garden-fresh vegetables, prepared in an almost infinite variety.

Vegetables are predominantly carbohydrates, supplying us with fuel for energy. They also are sources of incomplete proteins, meaning they can't supply all the eight essential amino acids that must be gotten through foods. These amino acids—proteins—are used to build blood and other body cells. However, when whole grains, such as rice are consumed at the same meal with legumes such as dried beans, their proteins complement each other and are complete.

Most vegetables also contain fat, although in minute quantities. Some are an excellent source of vitamin A for healthy skin, teeth, and bones, and vitamin C, to aid in resisting infection. One cup of broccoli, for example, supplies three-quarters of your daily requirement of vitamin A and more than twice your vitamin C quotient. Some vegetables also supply several important minerals, particularly calcium and iron.

Making the most of these nutrients requires a bit of consumer knowledge. To that end there is a brief introduction before each of the vegetables with advice on selection, storage, and cooking methods.

Here you will find dishes suitable for both the weekday's restraint and also for the weekend's indulgences. As with all the recipes in this book, some can be accomplished with microwave speed, others require the old-fashioned investment of time. Some are truly sidekicks, others demand—and receive—the spotlight. All trade on their upbringing, nothing but the freshest and the best.

Asparagus

❖

Royalty has its privilege—Louis XIV had a gardener who provided the palace kitchen with asparagus year round. It's still a class act, though we commoners must content ourselves with a five-month season, stretching from February to June, peaking in April and May.

When purchasing asparagus, look for tightly closed heads and smooth, unwrinkled stalks. A pound of medium-size stalks holds between 16–20 spears, feeding 2–4 people depending on the menu. Asparagus's strong suit is vitamin A as well as appreciable amounts of vitamin C, potassium, and phosphorus. To protect those nutrients, store asparagus in the refrigerator crisper in a closed plastic bag or standing in an inch or so of water.

To prepare asparagus for cooking, cut or snap the stalks where the white turns to green. If the spears are more than a half inch in diameter, or if you're using white asparagus, peel to remove the stringy fibers, rendering the whole stalk edible. To peel, lay an asparagus flat on the work surface, tip facing you. Starting an inch or two beneath the tip, pull a vegetable peeler down the stalk, turning the spear after each stroke until you've peeled the circumference. Trimmings may be frozen for use in an asparagus soup.

Asparagus may be boiled or steamed. Because green vegetables tend to turn drab olive green when cooked with covers in place (see page 246 for more explanation), boiling will better retain the emerald green hue. To boil, fill a 12-inch or larger skillet ¾ full of water. Add ½ teaspoon salt. Bring to a boil. Immerse asparagus and boil for 6–8 minutes; the spears should be softened but still have some bite. Remove asparagus spears by lifting them with a slotted spoon or spatula. If you pour the water and all into a colander, they may break at the tip.

If you prefer to steam the asparagus, tie the stalks into a bundle with kitchen twine. Place an inch of water in the bottom of an asparagus steamer, stand asparagus upright, cover, and cook at high heat about 8 minutes or until somewhat softened but still crunchy. You may also fashion a steamer from any deep saucepan. Cover it with an inverted bowl or a double-boiler insert.

Asparagus looks wondrous laid upon a white linen napkin, with no more garnish than a lemon twist at the base. Pass *Gourmet Light* Hollandaise at the table, or try any of the simple variations that follow. Asparagus is so elegant a vegetable it may be served as a first course, but it also makes a first-rate casual supper alongside softly scrambled eggs.

Asparagus Mimosa

The crumb topping may be prepared far in advance and gently re-heated just before serving.

> 1 pound asparagus, peeled
> 1 teaspoon butter
> 2 tablespoons dried bread crumbs
> 1 hard-cooked egg yolk
> 1 tablespoon butter
> a few drops lemon juice
> ⅛ teaspoon salt
> freshly ground pepper to taste

1. Prepare the asparagus for cooking by following instructions as outlined in the introduction. While bringing the water to a boil, prepare the topping.
2. Spray an 8-inch skillet with cooking spray. Place it over medium-low heat, add the butter and when it's foamy, add the bread crumbs, stirring occasionally until lightly browned. Remove the skillet from the heat, and sieve the hard-cooked egg yolk into the

bread crumbs. Stir to combine. Scrape onto a piece of wax paper.
3. Boil or steam the asparagus, and drain it when tender but still crunchy. Lay the asparagus on a serving platter.
4. Melt the butter with the lemon juice in the now-empty skillet. Pour it over the asparagus, season with salt and pepper, and sprinkle the bread crumb mixture over the top.

Yield: 4 servings
Calories per serving: 65
Protein per serving: 3g

Fat per serving: 5g
Carbohydrates per serving: 5g
Sodium per serving: 80mg

Asparagus Maltaise

A subtle change from the ever-popular Hollandaise, Maltaise sauce is a similar emulsion spiked with orange instead of lemon juice. Serve this dish with poultry or duck. Should you have any leftover spears, serve them cold with chilled Maltaise sauce for lunch or snacks. The sauce may be prepared in advance and gently reheated over hot (only 130 degrees), not boiling water. Whisk it continuously.

> 1 pound asparagus, peeled
> 5 egg yolks
> 1/4 teaspoon salt, omit if using canned consomme
> 3/4 cup chicken stock or canned consomme
> 5 tablespoons orange juice, freshly squeezed
>   preferred
> 1 teaspoon lemon juice
> 2 tablespoons butter, melted
> salt to taste
> freshly ground pepper to taste
> grated zest of 1 orange

1. Prepare the asparagus for cooking and cook it by following the instructions in the introduction. While it cooks, prepare the sauce.
2. Place the egg yolks and ¼ teaspoon salt in a blender or food processor and process for 30 seconds.
3. Meanwhile, boil the stock with the orange juice and lemon juice until it's reduced to ½ cup.
4. Dribble the hot liquid into the egg yolks while the machine runs.
5. Transfer the mixture to a 1-quart heavy-bottomed saucepan over medium-low heat and whisk constantly until thickened, about 3 minutes.
6. Remove the sauce from heat and whisk in the butter.
7. Drain the hot asparagus, lay on a serving platter, and sprinkle with salt and pepper. Pour the sauce over the midsection of asparagus, garnish with orange zest.

Yield: 4 servings with 4 tablespoons of sauce
Calories per serving: 165
Protein per serving: 7g

Fat per serving: 13g
Carbohydrates per serving: 7g
Sodium per serving: 220mg

Beets

While beets are generally boiled, they are delicious baked as well. Choose medium-size smooth, firm beets for baking. Those that look shriveled or very large are apt to be too woody. The tops may be cooked like spinach, and served with a few drops of fruity vinegar. Beets are a good source of potassium, calcium, phosphorus, and magnesium and contain about 35 calories in a ½ cup.

Baked Beets

❖

1 1/4 pounds beets, stems removed
2 teaspoons butter, melted
juice of one orange
1/8 teaspoon salt
freshly ground pepper to taste
grated zest of 1 orange

1. Prick the beets in several places with a fork. Put them in a baking dish in a 350-degree oven. Bake beets until easily pierced with a fork, about an hour, maybe a little longer.
2. Peel and discard the skins. Slice the beets and place on a serving platter.
3. Combine the butter and orange juice in a 1-quart saucepan, and boil for 30 seconds. Pour the sauce over the sliced beets, season with salt and pepper, and garnish with the zest.

VARIATION: Baked or boiled beets are also delicious mashed or pureed in a food processor. Peel after cooking, mash, and add the seasonings described above.

Yield: 4 servings
Calories per serving: 95
Protein per serving: 2g

Fat per serving: 2g
Carbohydrates per serving: 18g
Sodium per serving: 150mg

❖ **THINKING THIN TIP** ❖

Ice water is far more appealing with a slice of lemon or orange.

Broccoli

❖

Another year-round vegetable, broccoli is the health addict's dream. One large cooked stalk fulfills your vitamin C requirement by half as much again, provides half your need of vitamin A, and supplies goodly amounts of riboflavin, iron, calcium, and potassium.

When purchasing broccoli, look for unopened buds that are dark green, not yellow. The butt end of the stalk should be neither brown nor slimy. Store broccoli in a plastic bag in the refrigerator or in the vegetable crisper for not more than four days; 1 ½ to 2 pounds will serve 4.

Peeling and slicing the broccoli stalks is a wonderful way to get full value from this vegetable. Cut the stalks an inch below the buds. Separate the flower stems. Remove the leaves and if they look fresh, plan to cook them for they are rich in vitamin A. Cut the branches from the stalks and peel the stalks using a vegetable peeler or a small, sharp knife. Slice the stalks into rounds on the diagonal.

Boil or steam broccoli as you would green beans (see page

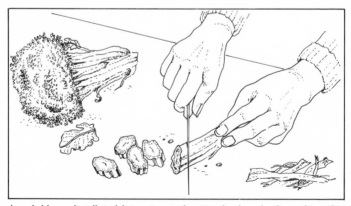

A peeled broccoli stalk is delicious to eat when it is sliced on the diagonal into thin rounds.

245), 6–8 minutes is about right for crisp broccoli. This vegetable also takes well to stir-frying, but watch that oil!

Very good hot with just a touch of butter and lemon (see the Lemon Butter Sauce, page 33), broccoli also takes well to dressing up with a cloak of Hollandaise or Cheese Sauce, both in the Primer. Don't overlook it as a cold salad tossed with a light vinaigrette.

Sesame Broccoli

This recipe is a nice change from the norm. Cook the broccoli ahead and reheat in the sesame oil at serving time if desired.

> *1 ½ pounds broccoli (1 bunch of 2 to 3 stalks)*
> *1 tablespoon sesame oil, available at specialty or*
>   *Oriental food shops*
> *2 tablespoons sesame seeds*
> *1 tablespoon soy sauce*

1. Prepare the broccoli for cooking. Boil or steam the broccoli, and drain it.
2. Heat the sesame oil in a skillet or wok for 15 seconds over high heat. Add the sesame seeds and the broccoli. Stir-fry until heated through. Remove from the pan to a serving dish, and pour soy sauce over.

Yield: 4-6 servings
Calories per serving: 115
Protein per serving: 7g

Fat per serving: 6g
Carbohydrates per serving: 11g
Sodium per serving: 160mg

Broccoli and Walnut Terrine

❖

An eminently portable package, this terrine makes a fine picnic lunch with, say, a side of Counter Slaw (page 106). It's also an interesting vegetable for an otherwise simple menu. It is good both hot and at room temperature. Don't be misled by the yeast in this skinny pastry, it merely lightens the dough without entailing tedious risings or kneadings. This pastry would also make any other *Gourmet Light* vegetable tarts good company and could be pressed into service for a reduced-calorie quiche. It represents a savings of more than 700 calories over a traditional flour-butter pastry dough.

For the Pastry

2 teaspoons dry granular yeast
1 1/2 tablespoons warm (105–115-degree) water
1 egg, lightly beaten
1 teaspoon olive oil
1/2 teaspoon salt
5 tablespoons each whole wheat flour and
    all-purpose flour

For the Broccoli Terrine

1 1/2 pounds (about 2 bunches) broccoli
3 eggs
2 ounces cheese (grated hard cheese such as Swiss is
    recommended)
3 ounces cottage cheese
1 onion, diced
2 sprigs fresh thyme or 1/2 teaspoon dried thyme
1 ounce (about 1/4 cup) walnuts

To Prepare the Pastry

1. Dissolve the yeast in the warm water in a small cup.
2. In a small bowl, beat together the egg, oil, and salt. When the yeast is dissolved, beat it in too.
3. In another bowl, combine the two flours. Make a well in the center and add the liquid, stirring well.
4. Flour a pastry cloth, board, or a kitchen counter. Turn the dough onto the floured surface. Knead about 15 times, adding a bit more flour if necessary. Form dough into a ball, place it in the now-empty flour bowl, and cover with plastic wrap or a kitchen towel. Let the dough rest in a warm spot about 20 minutes, or until lightened.
5. Flour the work surface again. Roll the dough out into a rectangle about 7 inches by 15 inches. The dough will be very thin. If it rips, simply patch it.
6. Spray a 9-inch by 5-inch loaf pan with cooking spray. Lay the dough gently into the pan. Set it aside while preparing the terrine filling.

To Prepare the Terrine

1. Preheat the oven to 400 degrees. Bring a 2 1/2-quart saucepan 2/3 full of water to a boil. Cut the stalks from the broccoli flowerets. Roughly chop the flowerets. With either a vegetable peeler or a knife, peel the broccoli stalks. Don't discard the leaves if they look fresh. Chop the stalks. When the water boils, immerse the broccoli and leaves, cook until crisp-tender, about 4 minutes if very fresh. Drain and cool under running water.
2. While the broccoli cooks, prepare the filling. In a food processor or bowl, beat the eggs. Add the cheeses, onion, and thyme. Mix well. If using a processor, add the broccoli and process until a chunky puree is achieved. By hand, chop the broccoli quite fine, add to egg-cheese mixture, and beat with a rotary beater. Stir in the nuts in either case.
3. Pour the mixture into the prepared pan. Make it smooth. Trim and discard any pastry that drapes over the short ends of the pan.

Drape excess pastry from long sides of pan over terrine. Place in the bottom third of the oven. Bake for 15 minutes at 400 degrees, then reduce heat to 350 degrees for the last 35 minutes. The terrine is done when the filling no longer shakes; however, a knife inserted in the center will show some moisture. Run a flexible-bladed metal spatula around the rim of the pan, invert, and cool 10 minutes before slicing.

Yield: 8 servings

Calories per serving: 200

Protein per serving: 12g

Fat per serving: 9g

Carbohydrates per serving: 18g

Sodium per serving: 240mg

Carrots

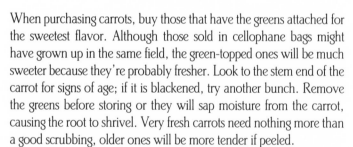

When purchasing carrots, buy those that have the greens attached for the sweetest flavor. Although those sold in cellophane bags might have grown up in the same field, the green-topped ones will be much sweeter because they're probably fresher. Look to the stem end of the carrot for signs of age; if it is blackened, try another bunch. Remove the greens before storing or they will sap moisture from the carrot, causing the root to shrivel. Very fresh carrots need nothing more than a good scrubbing, older ones will be more tender if peeled.

One carrot supplies you with more than the recommended daily requirement of vitamin A. There is debate among experts about the nutritive value of cooked versus raw carrots. Some feel carrots must be cooked for the human digestive tract to fully extract all the nutrients, others disagree.

The following recipes are uncommon ways for the common carrot.

Lemon Glazed Carrots

❖

This vegetable is easily reheated.

> 1 pound carrots
> juice of one lemon
> ½ teaspoon grated ginger root
> 1 teaspoon honey
> 1 tablespoon butter
> freshly grated nutmeg
> ⅛ teaspoon salt
> freshly ground pepper to taste
> 1 tablespoon minced fresh parsley

1. Prepare the carrots for cooking by peeling if desired. Bring a 2½-quart saucepan ¾ full of water to a boil. Meanwhile, slice the carrots thinly into rounds or like matchsticks. Immerse the carrots and boil until tender, which will depend on how they are cut. Remove one every minute after five to test. When tender, drain.
2. In the carrot saucepan, combine the lemon juice, ginger, honey, and butter. Heat and stir until mixed. Add the carrots and cook over high heat, shaking the pan all the while for 1 minute.
3. Turn onto a serving platter. Season with nutmeg, salt, and pepper. Garnish with the parsley.

Yield: 4 servings
Calories per serving: 85
Protein per serving: 2g

Fat per serving: 3g
Carbohydrates per serving: 14g
Sodium per serving: 120mg

Orange-Carrot Puree

❖

Nouvelle cuisine made purees fashionable once again. This combination of carrot and orange is an example. It is very nice with lamb and excellent for parties because it easily reheats in a double boiler.

> 1 pound carrots
> juice of 2 oranges
> grated zest of 1 orange
> 1 teaspoon sugar
> 1 tablespoon butter
> ½ teaspoon salt
> freshly ground pepper to taste
> a few gratings fresh nutmeg

1. Scrape or peel the carrots as you desire. Roughly chop them.
2. Bring a 2½-quart saucepan ¾ full of water to a boil. Immerse the carrots, cover the pan, and boil until carrots are easily pierced with a fork, about 10 minutes.
3. Put the cooked carrots in a food processor or in a food mill and puree. Add the orange juice, zest, sugar, butter, salt, pepper, and nutmeg. Mix well.

Yield: 4-6 servings
Calories per serving: 95
Protein per serving: 2g

Fat per serving: 3g
Carbohydrates per serving: 16g
Sodium per serving: 320mg

Carrot and Squash Puree

❖

This may also be made ahead and reheated in a double boiler. Delicious with turkey or other poultry. To vary, add a few tablespoons crème blanc (page 37) with the other seasonings.

> 1 small butternut squash, peeled and chopped
> 1 pound carrots, scrubbed, peeled, and roughly
>   chopped
> 1 tablespoon butter
> 2 teaspoons dark rum
> a few gratings fresh nutmeg
> 1/4 teaspoon salt
> freshly ground pepper to taste

1. Bring a 4-quart saucepan half full of water to a boil. Add the squash, cover, and cook 8 minutes. Add the carrots, cover, and cook until both are tender, about 12 minutes more.
2. Drain and mash the vegetables either in a food mill, food processor, or by hand. Add the butter, rum, and nutmeg. Season to taste with salt and pepper.

Yield: 6-8 servings
Calories per serving: 80
Protein per serving: 2g

Fat per serving: 2g
Carbohydrates per serving: 15g
Sodium per serving: 130mg

Celery

Celery is more than mere rabbit food. Cooked, it takes on a whole new personality, but with little alteration to its naturally skinny self.

One rib of this member of the parsley family (sometimes called a stalk, although technically the whole bunch is one stalk) supplies just 7 calories. It is a good source of potassium, and supplies vitamin A and C as well as fiber.

When purchasing celery, avoid stalks that appear to be pithy, woody, or have limp and yellowing leaves. It needs to be kept both cold and moist to maintain its crispy snap and to protect it from becoming a limp throwaway.

Nutted Braised Celery

Try this recipe to disperse the ho-hums.

>   8 large ribs celery, strings pared
>   ³⁄₄ cup chicken stock or canned consomme
>   ¹⁄₃ cup dry white wine
>   freshly ground pepper to taste
>   1 teaspoon butter
>   2 tablespoons finely chopped shallots
>   1 ¹⁄₂ tablespoons chopped walnuts or sliced water
>   chestnuts

1. Slice the celery thinly on the diagonal, or julienne it. Place it in a 9-inch baking dish with at least 1-inch sides (a quiche dish is appropriate).

2. Pour the stock and wine over the celery. Season with the pepper. Put the butter on top and add shallots. Cover the dish with a lid or aluminum foil, and place it in a 400-degree oven. Bake for 15 minutes, remove the cover, and stir.
3. Bake the celery, uncovered, another 20 minutes, add the walnuts, and stir. Continue to bake another 10-15 minutes, or until the liquid has been reduced to about ½ cup of semi-syrupy liquid. Serve with liquid poured over celery.

Yield: 4 servings
Calories per serving: 60
Protein per serving: 2g

Fat per serving: 3g
Carbohydrates per serving: 7g
Sodium per serving: 110mg

Green Beans

❖

Thanks to modern horticulture, the string in string beans has been permanently pulled. No longer do we have those pesky strings to contend with! And thanks to modern transportation methods, fresh green beans are available almost year-round. They are an excellent source of vitamin A and supply a fair amount of calcium, too, for their very little 31 calories a cup.

When selecting green beans, look for those that are pliant and smooth, not coarse and tough. Frequently, when harvested by mechanical means, the bean is snapped from the stem exposing the meat, leaving a spot prone to rapid decay. Avoid these beans if given a choice. One pound of beans serves 4. Store the beans in the refrigerator crisper in a plastic bag; use within three days of purchase or they will be tough.

Prepare beans a handful at a time. Align the ends and cut across. Turn beans around, realign, and cut again.

Beans may be boiled or steamed. To boil, bring 6 cups of water to a rapid boil, with or without salt. Immerse beans and boil, uncovered, about 8 minutes, sometimes more, sometimes less. Time is a variable that is dependent on your heat source, the size and maturity of beans, and so on. Count on inconsistency because what works this time may not work next. During cooking, remove a bean and bite into it or pierce it with a fork, it should be crunchy but not raw. If holding the beans for later use, as much as five hours, undercook them a bit then cool under running water.

To steam beans, prepare as above, place in a steamer over 2 inches of boiling water, cover, and cook until tender, about 8 minutes. Again, check during cooking for tenderness.

To steam or to boil? Is one superior, healthwise? Consider the facts:

Fact 1: Some B and C vitamins are water soluble, and will be lost if subjected to extended water contact. But if the vegetable is put in a large amount of rapidly boiling water, taking less time to come back to a boil and thus less time to cook, the vitamin loss is minimized. With steaming, the vitamin loss is minimized because the bean doesn't come in contact with the water at all.

Fact 2: Covered green vegetables turn drab olive green because acids, present in the vegetable, combine with heat and denature the chlorophyll. If these acids are allowed to escape in the form of steam in an uncovered pot, they simply dissipate, causing no damage. If not allowed to escape, the vegetable turns an unappetizing yellow green. If you wish to steam beans, you may somewhat circumvent this discoloration by keeping the cooking time as short as possible and uncovering the pan immediately after cooking. Or you may boil vegetables, uncovered, in *large* amounts of water—maintaining color and minimizing vitamin loss.

The Lemon Butter Sauce (page 33) is very good on either boiled or steamed beans. For a change, consider the following recipe.

Green Beans with Tomato Nuggets

❖

Prepare the beans early in the day by partially cooking them. Drain and cover them with plastic wrap. Place the beans on a counter or in the refrigerator if you're holding them for more than 2 hours. The butter sauce may also be made ahead, both elements heated and tossed together at serving time.

> 1 pound green beans
> 1 tomato, blanched, peeled, and seeded
> juice of half a lemon
> 1 small garlic clove, minced
> 1 tablespoon butter, melted
> 1/8 teaspoon salt
> freshly ground pepper to taste

1. Cook the beans according to preceding instructions. Set them aside.
2. Dice the tomato.
3. Add the lemon juice and garlic to the butter. Cook over medium heat for 30 seconds. Add the cooked beans and toss them in the pan until heated through. Add the tomato, stir just to heat through, and season with salt and pepper.

Yield: 4 servings
Calories per serving: 65
Protein per serving: 3g

Fat per serving: 3g
Carbohydrates per serving: 9g
Sodium per serving: 280mg

Mushrooms

❖

There's more to mushrooms than the bland, pale specimens commonly available. A whole new world of exotic mushrooms is coming to market, with flavors that whisper of earth and woods. Some are dried and imported such as cepes (rhymes with step), chanterelles, and morels, others are being cultivated and marketed fresh such as shitake and enoki—all are expensive but worth a pretty penny for those special occasions when you'd like to treat your guests, or yourself. The dried mushrooms are available at specialty food stores.

Although one would have to eat a lot of mushrooms to benefit from them, they are higher in minerals such as iron and copper than many other vegetables, and contain about 20 calories a cup. And few foods add such a touch of class for such little caloric expense.

Because of an already high water content and their porosity, it's better to wipe mushrooms clean rather than washing them. This is particularly true if they are coupled with a sauce that would be diluted by excess moisture.

The recipes that follow use both the readily available supermarket mushroom and the very in vogue cepe.

Fettuccine with Cepes

This wonderful pasta dish makes a great first course for a dinner party or a delicious main dish for a casual supper. The sauce may be easily made ahead and reheated just before tossing with freshly cooked fettuccine.

1 ounce dried cepes, also called porcini, *or other*
    dried mushrooms
boiling water
4 thin strips bacon
2 tablespoons minced shallots
1 clove garlic, minced
1 ½ cups beef stock or canned beef broth
1 cup tomato sauce (see page 36)
lots of freshly ground pepper to taste
8 ounces fresh fettuccine noodles
1 tablespoon butter, at room temperature
1 tablespoon minced fresh parsley
freshly grated Parmesan cheese

1. Cover the dried mushrooms with boiling water and soak for 20 minutes.
2. Meanwhile, fry the bacon in a 10- or 12-inch skillet. Discard the fat. Spray the skillet with cooking spray and "saute" the shallots over medium-low heat until limp. Add the garlic and cook another 30 seconds.
3. Add the beef stock and boil over high heat until reduced to 1 cup. Add the tomato sauce and boil until reduced to 1 ½ cups.
4. Drain the mushrooms and chop them. The juice may only be used if strained twice through a piece of double-thick washed cheesecloth. Add mushrooms to sauce base. Stir to combine. Season with freshly ground pepper.
5. Cook the fettuccine noodles according to package instructions. Drain the noodles and toss with the butter. Toss the fettuccine with cepe sauce. Sprinkle minced parsley on top. Pass cheese at the table.

Yield: 4 servings
Calories per serving: 345
Protein per serving: 12g

Fat per serving: 9g
Carbohydrates per serving: 54g
Sodium per serving: 430mg

Sherried Mushrooms

❖

This recipe is very nice with beef dishes and a treat when you add half an ounce to an ounce of dried mushrooms such as cepes. Soak the dried mushrooms for 20 minutes, drain and rinse, adding them at the end of Step 2. If made ahead, reheat the dish over very low heat or the crème blanc will curdle.

12 ounces mushrooms
2 teaspoons butter
2 tablespoons sherry or Madeira
3 tablespoons crème blanc (page 37) or plain yogurt
a few fresh gratings nutmeg
1/8 teaspoon salt
freshly ground pepper to taste
1 tablespoon minced fresh parsley

1. Wipe the mushrooms clean and slice them, removing a sliver off the stem end if hardened.
2. Melt the butter in a 10-inch or a 12-inch skillet. When the foaming subsides, add the mushrooms and cook over medium-high heat, shaking the pan often until the mushrooms are lightly browned and all their moisture has evaporated.
3. Add the sherry, and shake the pan while the wine evaporates. Remove the pan from heat and let it cool for 2 minutes.
4. Stir in the crème blanc, and season with nutmeg, salt, and pepper. To serve, garnish with the parsley.

Yield: 4 servings
Calories per serving: 50
Protein per serving: 3g

Fat per serving: 2g
Carbohydrates per serving: 5g
Sodium per serving: 110mg

Onions

❖

Onions are as basic to the larder as shoes are to the wardrobe. While not exactly nutritional powerhouses, they do contribute lots of flavor for a minimal calorie cost.

Members of the onion family that you are likely to use include:

"Yellow" Onions: The yellow onion is the most common variety of onions. Actually brown-skinned, they are available year-round and are dried before being brought to market. They are generally sold in fishnet bags.

Spanish, Bermuda, and Red Onions: With skins ranging from yellow to red, these milder varieties of onions are often eaten raw.

Pearl Onions: These small onions with white skins are often served boiled as a vegetable side course. The slightly larger variety is called a boiling onion.

Scallions: Also called spring onions or green onions, these pencil-shaped onions are generally used raw.

Leeks: Leeks are to the French what a yellow cooking onion is to us—an all purpose flavor enhancer. In this country, however, leeks are expensive, probably a compensation for low sales volume and spoilage. This is unfortunate because leeks are more subtle than the onion. Their mild flavor is prized for soups, stews, and vegetable side courses. They look like overgrown scallions.

Shallots: Looking like pearl onions, but with brown skins, shallots taste like a cross between garlic and onion. They are much used in French cooking.

Chives: A variety of onion in which the top rather than the bulb is used, chives look like thick grass. If chives are unavailable, use the minced green of scallions.

Dry onions (the all-purpose cooking onions, Spanish, Bermuda, and red onions, pearl onions, and shallots) should be stored in a cool, dry place where they are fine until they sprout (about 3 to 4 weeks). Never store onions near potatoes, because they will sprout quickly because of the moisture the potato gives off. Leeks and scallions will keep up to 3 weeks if closed in a plastic bag in the refrigerator.

Scotch Onions

❖

This deliciously simple vegetable goes very well with roasted poultry or a beef dish. It may be made as much as a day ahead and gently reheated.

> 1 pound pearl or small white boiling onions
> 1 cup homemade chicken broth or canned
> ½ cup water
> ½ teaspoon salt
> freshly ground pepper to taste
> 2 teaspoons butter
> 2 tablespoons Scotch
> 1 tablespoon minced fresh parsley (optional)

1. Slice the ends from the onions and put a cross in the root end to prevent them from exploding.
2. Cover the onions with water in a 2½-quart heavy-bottomed saucepan and bring to a boil. Boil onions for 2 minutes, drain, and cool under running water. Slip and discard skins from the onions.
3. Return onions to the saucepan with the broth, water, salt, pepper, and butter. Cover, boil gently until the liquid is almost absorbed and the onions are tender. Onions that are 1½ inch in diameter will be done in about 12 minutes. If the onions are easily pierced with a fork before the liquid is absorbed, lift them from the pot

with a slotted spoon and boil liquid at high heat uncovered until only 2–3 tablespoons remain. Alternately, add more broth or water and extend cooking time if needed.
4. Remove the cover from the pan. Add Scotch with heat turned high. Boil uncovered until a semi-syrupy liquid remains. To serve, dribble a spoonful of sauce over onions. Sprinkle with the parsley if desired.

Yield: 4 servings
Calories per serving: 70
Protein per serving: 2g

Fat per serving: 2g
Carbohydrates per serving: 11g
Sodium per serving: 280mg

Pea and Leek Puree

Leeks are very low in calories and are a good source of potassium and a fair source of vitamin C. Here they are perfectly paired with peas for a do-ahead dinner party dish worthy of the most sophisticated occasion.

Although "fresh" is today's culinary password, here I feel frozen peas will pass the test. Frozen peas, however, are higher in sodium than fresh peas; the sodium content for this recipe is for fresh peas.

> 1 bunch leeks (about 3 stalks)
> 3/4 cup homemade or canned chicken broth
> 1 cup fresh or frozen peas
> 1/3 cup homemade or canned chicken broth
> 1 teaspoon butter
> 1 teaspoon freshly snipped tarragon leaves or 1/2
>   teaspoon dried tarragon
> 1/4 teaspoon salt
> lots of freshly ground black pepper to taste

1. Cut and discard the green stalks from the leeks. Slice the white of leek in half the long way, then dice. Rinse very thoroughly in a colander.
2. Put the leeks and the broth in a 1-quart saucepan. Cover and cook over high heat until tender, about 20 minutes. When the liquid is evaporated and the leeks are limp, empty into a food processor.
3. Put the peas and the broth into the now-empty saucepan. Cover and cook for 2 minutes at high heat (a little longer for fresh peas). Empty into the food processor, unevaporated liquid and all.
4. Add the butter, tarragon, salt, and pepper. Puree. The vegetable is ready to eat or may be reheated in a double boiler before serving time.

Note: Without a food processor, you may puree the vegetables in a food mill, or in batches by hand, but you will have some difficulty pureeing it in a blender.

Yield: 4 servings
Calories per serving: 60
Protein per serving: 3g

Fat per serving: 1g
Carbohydrates per serving: 9g
Sodium per serving: 140mg

Leek Quiche with a Cornmeal Sage Crepe Crust

❖

The quiche, a luncheon favorite for the last decade or so, has been responsible for a lot of spread. A typical pastry crust for one pie tallies up a whopping 1,000 calories, and that's just the bottom of things. Add to that a heavy dose of cream, bacon, and cheese, and one little slice of quiche weighs in at about 350 calories, with a very high percentage of fat. This leek quiche, with its crepe crust and milk instead of cream, is considerably lighter and very delicious. Although the quiche may be made ahead and reheated, you'd do better to make the crepe crust and the filling beforehand, then assemble at the last minute and bake. The crepe could be prepared 24 hours in advance, the filling, 4–5 hours.

For the Crepe Crust

3 tablespoons all-purpose flour
3 tablespoons yellow cornmeal
1/2 teaspoon salt
4 or 5 leaves fresh sage, snipped, or 1/2 teaspoon
    dried sage
1 egg
1 egg white
4 tablespoons milk
3 tablespoons chicken stock or canned consomme

For the Quiche

1 pound sliced white of leek (about 31/2 cups from 2
    or 3 bunches)
1/2 cup chicken stock or canned consomme
3 eggs
11/2 cups milk
freshly grated nutmeg
1/2 teaspoon salt
freshly ground pepper to taste
1/2 teaspoon Dijon-style mustard
2 ounces Swiss cheese, grated

To Prepare the Crepe

1. Preheat the oven to 325 degrees. Spray a 12-inch round pizza pan (or a rectangular 11-inch by 14-inch shallow baking sheet) that has 1/2-inch sides with cooking spray.

2. Sift the flour, cornmeal, and salt together in a small bowl. Mix in the sage.
3. Beat the egg, egg white, milk, and stock together in a measuring cup. Pour into the flour mixture and stir to combine.
4. Pour into the prepared pizza pan (just cover the bottom, you may not use all the batter) and bake in the oven for 15–18 minutes. Remove the pan from oven and prick a fork into any bubbles that have risen. Set the crepe aside while preparing the filling. Adjust oven temperature to 375 degrees.

For the Quiche

1. Wash the sliced leeks well. Place them in a 12-inch skillet with the stock, cover, and simmer until tender, 15–20 minutes. Remove from heat and set aside.
2. In a bowl or food processor, mix together the eggs, milk, nutmeg, salt and pepper.
3. Spray a 9½-inch quiche pan with cooking spray. Lay the crepe in it. Trim any excess pastry.
4. With a pastry brush, spread the mustard over the crepe.
5. Spread cooked leeks over bottom, cover leeks with grated cheese, and pour filling over. Set in the lower third of the hot oven and bake until puffed and golden, 30 to 35 minutes. Let the quiche rest for 10 minutes before slicing.

Yield: 6 servings
Calories per serving: 170
Protein per serving: 12g

Fat per serving: 7g
Carbohydrates per serving: 15g
Sodium per serving: 473mg

❖ **THINKING THIN TIP** ❖

Make dinner an occasion by setting the table and eating by candlelight.

Potatoes

❖

Shopping for a plain old potato poses a surprisingly large amount of choices. There are many varieties, from round white to long russet, from new potatoes to old (mature). There are waxy spuds and mealy ones, some sold loose and others in bags. What's a body to do? Short of memorizing every variety and its particular use, let this be a simple guide. Purchase new potatoes, those that look like they're suffering from bad sunburn with chafed and peeling skin, for salads, boiling, and steaming. New potatoes are less likely to break in tossing because their high-moisture/low-starch ratio means they absorb less of the cooking liquid. Happily, new potatoes will absorb less of the dressing, too. Choose the old (mature) potatoes for mashing and baking. Their low-moisture content make for fluffier mashed and baked potatoes.

Purchase only as many potatoes as you can use within 2 weeks, and don't store them in the refrigerator, if possible. Excessive cold converts the potato's starch to sugar, affecting the flavor. Store potatoes in a cool, dark spot. At room temperature they should keep 2–3 weeks. If kept in the light, green spots develop that give the tuber a bitter taste.

As has been widely reported, a plain baked potato has about the same number of calories as a banana. I can't speak for everyone, but while I would certainly eat a banana out of hand, I'd have to be awfully hungry to eat a plain baked potato. Yet nutritionally and economically the humble potato is an excellent buy. It's high in energy-sustaining carbohydrates, yet low in fat. With a good amount of iron and potassium, some calcium, phosphorus, and vitamins B1, C, and niacin, it seems sensible to enjoy potatoes. The trick is to enhance the flavor without inflating the calorie count. The following recipe is such an attempt.

Red Bliss Potato Salad

❖

Red Bliss potatoes are sometimes simply called red-skinned potatoes. This salad is quick to prepare because the potatoes don't need to be peeled. It is very good with a simple grilled fish or the Parchment Chicken with Tomato Vinaigrette on page 165.

1 pound Red Bliss potatoes
3 tablespoons sherry vinegar or red wine vinegar
1 teaspoon sugar
5 tablespoons plain yogurt
4 tablespoons mayonnaise
2 tablespoons freshly chopped dill
1/2 teaspoon Dijon-style mustard
1/2 teaspoon salt
freshly ground pepper to taste
1/2 teaspoon capers, drained

1. Cover the potatoes with water by a generous inch and boil them until easily pierced with a fork, about 25 minutes. Drain, cool under running water, and let potatoes rest 10–15 minutes before slicing.
2. Pour the vinegar over sliced potatoes, and sprinkle with sugar. Set aside while mixing sauce.
3. Combine yogurt, mayonnaise, dill, mustard, salt, and pepper in a bowl. Mix. Toss the sauce gently with potatoes. Taste for seasoning adjustment. Serve just slightly chilled with capers sprinkled over.

Yield: 6 servings
Calories per serving: 125
Protein per serving: 2g

Fat per serving: 8g
Carbohydrates per serving: 12g
Sodium per serving: 260mg

Red Peppers

❖

About a dozen years ago, French chefs began experimenting with roasting red peppers, turning them into wonderful sauces or delicious salads, or combining them with herbs such as basil to create subtle but distinctive compound butters. Today it's almost impossible to open any cooking magazine without seeing at least one recipe using roasted red peppers.

Roasting a pepper, red or green, is actually to broil it, then allow it to cool in a tightly closed bag. The steam loosens the charred skin, which then pulls off as easily as old paint—if you've broiled it sufficiently but not overdone it. The broiling process cooks the flesh, turning it yet a deeper scarlet. It has a mild, sweet taste quite unsurpassed by other vegetables. It may then be marinated and served at room temperature as a salad; sauteed with any combination of vegetables; or pureed with herbs, oils, and a touch of vinegar or, if this were not a waist-conscious book, cream. As a sauce it is delicious over other vegetables such as green beans, broccoli, and the like, or over fish or even poultry. It is wonderful on spinach fettuccine as a fine first course or a casual dinner.

A red pepper is nothing more than a green pepper allowed to mature and ripen on the vine. Yet because most peppers are harvested when green, red peppers are somewhat scarce and often expensive. Although you can sometimes ripen a green pepper that has begun to blush by putting it with a cut apple in a paper bag for a day or two, it is likely to decay before becoming scarlet. When they are available, take advantage of their high vitamin A and C content by making up the following puree and freezing it.

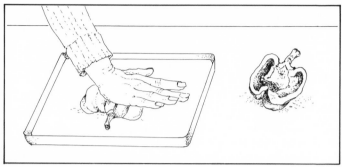

TO ROAST PEPPERS

1. Place a seeded, halved pepper, skin side up, on a flat surface. Flatten pepper with the heel of your hand.

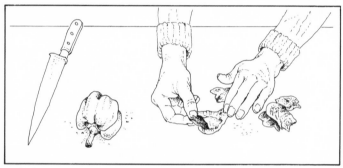

2. Broil pepper until it is completely blackened, cool, then peel away the charred skin and discard.

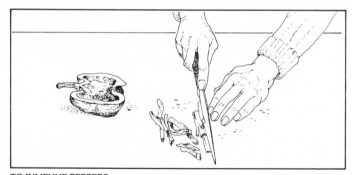

TO JULIENNE PEPPERS

A roasted or raw pepper is often sliced into julienned strips for use in cooking.

Red Pepper Puree
with Prosciutto

❖

This delicious sauce may be made ahead and reheated at serving time. When used as a sauce for vegetables, the prosciutto may be omitted.

> 4 large red bell peppers
> 1 tablespoon extra-virgin olive oil
> 2 tablespoons minced fresh parsley
> 8–10 fresh basil leaves, snipped, or 1 teaspoon
>   dried basil
> 1 clove garlic, minced
> 2 ounces prosciutto, cut into thin strips
> 1/2 teaspoon salt
> freshly ground pepper to taste

1. Cut the peppers in half. Remove and discard the seeds and inner membranes. Flatten a pepper with the heel of your hand and place it, skin side up, on a baking sheet. Repeat. Broil the peppers until they're completely blackened and charred. The skin will not peel off easily unless it's burned, so don't be shy about doing so. Don't let the peppers dry out, however. Remove the burned peppers to a plastic or paper bag, roll the bag tightly closed, and place it in the freezer until the peppers are cool enough to handle, about 10 minutes.

2. With your fingers, peel and discard the loosened skin from the peppers. Rinse the flesh under running water.

3. Roughly chop the peppers and combine them with the oil, parsley, basil, and garlic in a food processor. Puree. If using a food mill or blender, puree the vegetables first, then combine it with the other ingredients.

4. Spray an 8-inch skillet with cooking spray. "Saute" the pro-

sciutto over high heat, just to heat through.

5. Stir the meat into the red pepper puree, add salt and pepper, and taste for seasoning adjustment.

Yield with prosciutto: 6 servings   Fat per serving: 6g
Calories per serving: 95   Carbohydrates per serving: 8g
Protein per serving: 3g   Sodium per serving: 370mg

Yield without prosciutto: 6 servings Fat per serving: 3g
Calories per serving: 60   Carbohydrates per serving: 8g
Protein per serving: 1g   Sodium per serving: 190mg

Pasta with Prosciutto and Red Pepper Puree

Use the above recipe to coat 12 ounces fresh linguine. Cook and drain noodles according to package instructions. Toss with 1 table-spoon butter and the puree. Delicious as a side dish with lamb or as a first course for a dinner party. Remember to heat the plates when serving pasta. Pass grated cheese at the table if desired. Serves 4–6.

Green Beans with Red Pepper Puree

Use the above puree, without the prosciutto, to sauce 1 pound cooked green beans tossed with 1 tablespoon butter. Serves 6.

Marinated Roasted Peppers

❖

Roasted red peppers are also delicious when marinated in oil (tiny amounts, of course!), vinegar, and herbs and served at room temperature as a vegetable side dish. This dish is best made a day ahead.

> 2 red bell peppers
> 2 green bell peppers
> 1 tablespoon oil, walnut oil recommended
> 1 tablespoon balsamic or malt vinegar, available at specialty food stores
> 2 tablespoons beef stock or canned consomme
> 1 clove garlic, minced
> 8 fresh basil leaves, snipped, or 1 teaspoon dried basil
> 1/8 teaspoon salt
> freshly ground pepper to taste
> 1 tablespoon minced fresh parsley

1. Cut the peppers in half. Discard the seeds and inner membranes. Place the peppers, skin side up, on a baking sheet. Broil them until they're blackened and charred. Put the peppers in a plastic or paper bag, roll bag tightly closed and chill them until cool enough to handle.
2. Peel and discard the skin. Lay the peppers in a glass or ceramic dish.
3. Combine the oil, vinegar, stock, garlic, and basil. Pour the mixture over peppers. Sprinkle the peppers with salt, pepper, and parsley just before serving.

Yield: 4 servings
Calories per serving: 70
Protein per serving: 2g

Fat per serving: 4g
Carbohydrates per serving: 9g
Sodium per serving: 80mg

Wok Saute
of Peppers and Broccoli

❖

This is a basic method for sauteing any combination of vegetables with roasted red peppers. Likely combinations are sliced Chinese celery, pea pods, zucchini, and so forth. Strips of cooked ham or prosciutto are very good, too, when served with vegetable dinners. The use of a wok cuts down on the amount of fat needed, and also allows you to push the quicker-cooking vegetables up on the rim out of heat's way. If you're using a traditional flat skillet, just add the slowest-cooking vegetable first. These vegetables may be readied for cooking ahead of time, but stir-fry them at the last moment. Their freshness will be compromised if reheated.

> 4 tablespoons chicken stock or canned consomme
> 1 small clove garlic, minced
> 1 cup broccoli flowerets sliced, and stems, peeled and julienned (see page 45)
> 1 teaspoon oil, possibly more if using a skillet instead of a wok
> 1 cup mushrooms, sliced
> 3 red bell peppers, roasted, peeled (see Steps 1 and 2, page 261), and julienned
> 1/4 teaspoon salt
> freshly ground pepper to taste
> 1 tablespoon minced fresh parsley

1. Heat the wok over high heat. Add the stock and garlic and cook, stirring constantly, for 30 seconds.
2. Add the broccoli and cook over high heat, stirring until crisp-tender, about 1 minute. Push the broccoli up onto the sides of wok (or remove from the wok and keep warm).
3. Add the oil and mushrooms. Cook, stirring over high heat, about

1 minute. Push the mushrooms up onto the sides of wok.
4. Add the red peppers. Cook over high heat, stirring constantly until heated through, about 30 seconds longer.
5. Push all the vegetables down to the bottom of wok to heat through. Season with salt and pepper. Sprinkle with parsley and serve.

Yield: 4 servings
Calories per serving: 70
Protein per serving: 3g

Fat per serving: 2g
Carbohydrates per serving: 12g
Sodium per serving: 20mg

Spinach

❖

This versatile vegetable might not have made Popeye's muscles bulge, but certainly contributed to his general well-being. A mere half-cup of cooked spinach supplies an adult with twice the daily requirement of vitamin A, half the vitamin C, and one-fifth the RDA of iron. It is also a good source of folic acid, a B vitamin. All this for just 28 calories! You might have also heard that it is rich in calcium, but because of the presence of oxalic acid, the calcium is not available to the body.

When purchasing spinach, avoid spinach with yellowing or mushy leaves. Spinach sold in bulk (that is, by the pound) requires very thorough washing to remove the inevitable sand and grit. You'll also want to strip off the stems as they are both tough and slightly bitter. After stemming, soak the leaves in a sinkful of tepid water for a few minutes. Lift the leaves from the water, drain, rinse the sand from the sink, and repeat, this time with cold water.

Spinach sold in cellophane bags is generally sand-free, but you still may wish to remove the stems and backbones and rinse the leaves in cold water, especially if serving them raw in a salad.

Stored in a plastic bag in the refrigerator, spinach will keep 4 to 5 days.

Spinach-Ricotta Tart

❖

This simply made tart is quick to put together, easy to trek to a picnic, and a treat to eat hot or at room temperature. It makes a nice lunch, light dinner, or out-of-the ordinary vegetable side dish. Alternate slices of summer squash with the tomato for a colorful change. Make as much as a day in advance, but for best results, do not freeze. Phyllo is available in the frozen food section of most supermarkets. Leftover phyllo dough will keep in the refrigerator up to 4 weeks; if refrozen it tends to get crumbly.

> 2 pounds fresh or frozen spinach
> 1 16-ounce container part-skim ricotta cheese
> 1 onion, diced
> 3 eggs
> 10 fresh basil leaves, snipped, or 1 teaspoon dried basil
> 1 teaspoon salt
> freshly ground pepper
> a few gratings nutmeg
> 2 sheets phyllo dough
> 2–3 medium tomatoes
> black olive (optional)
> 2 tablespoons crumbled blue cheese, or grated Parmesan cheese

1. Wash the spinach very thoroughly. Pack it into a 2-½ quart saucepan with the water that clings to its leaves. Cover, and cook over high heat until the leaves are wilted, about 30 seconds to one minute. Drain in a colander, pressing the spinach with the pan bottom to extract as much water as possible. If using frozen spinach, simply thaw and squeeze to remove excess moisture.
2. Put the spinach in a food processor (or chop finely and place in a

bowl), add the cheese, onion, eggs, basil, salt, lots of pepper, and nutmeg. Mix well.

3. In a 9-inch quiche pan, crisscross the two sheets of phyllo. Pour in the spinach-cheese mixture. Trim the corners of the phyllo so just 2 inches remain, and roll the edges in to create a rim of pastry. Don't be alarmed when the dough tears, that will make it appear flaky when cooked.

4. Preheat oven to 400 degrees.

5. Slice the tomatoes. Cut each slice in half. Arrange slices to resemble a flower by overlapping them in a circle on top of the tart. Put a black olive at center if desired. Season with more pepper. Spray the edges of the pastry with cooking spray.

6. Bake the tart in the lower third of the preheated oven. Sprinkle the cheese over the top after 25 minutes. Cook about 15 minutes more. The tart is done when the center no longer shakes when wiggled, and a knife inserted slightly off center comes out cleanly. Let the tart rest 10 minutes before slicing.

Yield: 6-8 servings
Calories per serving: 245
Protein per serving: 19g

Fat per serving: 11g
Carbohydrates per serving: 19g
Sodium per serving: 640mg

❖ **THINKING THIN TIP** ❖

You can enjoy cheese, just choose those made from milk instead of cream.

Summer Squash

❖

Soft-shelled summer squash (though many varieties are available year round) is a good supplier of vitamins A and C with a virtually free calorie count—about 15 calories in a half cup. And—joy of joys!—they taste good, too.

A rundown on the most popular varieties:

Zucchini and cocozelle: both pale green, best harvested about 5 inches long and 2–3 inches in diameter.

Yellow crookneck and straightneck: pale yellow that deepens as the squash reaches maturity, sometimes has bumpy skin. Best harvested when about 6 inches in length and 3–4 inches in diameter.

Scallop, pattypan, or cymling: dish-shaped squash with a scalloped edge, pale green changing to white as the vegetable matures. Best 3–4 inches across.

Purchase summer squash when the skin is soft enough not to need peeling. Refrigerate it for up to a week. If you garden or have ever been the dubious recipient of those baseball bat-sized zucchini, don't give it to your kids for batting practice. Peeled and seeded, just as you would a cucumber, it makes a fine soup (page 82). You also may prepare it as outlined here with the addition of a little chopped onion and a sprinkling of dried bread crumbs, then freeze it. Bake it in a 350-degree oven until heated through.

Zucchini Saute

❖

This recipe works well with any of the summer squash. While it may be readied for cooking in advance, saute it just before serving. Don't be put off by the amount of salt (it's washed out).

> 3 *small zucchini*
> 2 *teaspoons salt*
> 1 *tablespoon butter*
> 1 *whole clove garlic, peeled*
> *a few gratings fresh nutmeg*
> *lots of freshly ground pepper to taste*

1. Cut the ends from the zucchini and grate either by hand or in a food processor. Place the squash in a sieve and toss with the salt. Let the vegetable rest at least 20 minutes. The salt draws excess moisture from the vegetable.
2. Rinse the salted zucchini very thoroughly under running water, tossing and squeezing the vegetable in your fingers to rinse out the salt. Squeeze the zucchini against the sieve to remove the water. Taste to be sure the salt is removed.
3. Melt the butter in a 10-inch skillet over medium-high heat. Spear the garlic clove on a toothpick and add it to the butter. When butter is foamy, add the squeezed zucchini and saute, stirring constantly until just heated through, about 2 minutes. Season with nutmeg and pepper. Remove the garlic.

Yield: 4 servings
Calories per serving: 50
Protein per serving: 2g

Fat per serving: 3g
Carbohydrates per serving: 4g
Sodium per serving: 130mg

Zucchini Boats
with Eggplant Caviar

—————————————❖—————————————

Make the eggplant caviar for this dish a day or two before serving, and prepare and assemble the boats early in the day. Bake or reheat at dinnertime. Or pile the eggplant caviar into hollowed, salted, and drained tomatoes for cool dining on sun-sweltering days. Leftover eggplant caviar can have another life as an hors d'oeuvre mounded on cucumber slices, stuffed in blanched mushroom caps for broiling, or spread on *croustades* and sprinkled with cheese.

For the Eggplant Caviar

1 *medium eggplant, a little over a pound*
1 *tomato, blanched, peeled, seeded, and chopped*
1 *clove garlic, minced*
1 *tablespoon red wine or raspberry vinegar*
1 *tablespoon extra-virgin olive oil*
1 *tablespoon minced fresh parsley*
2 *tablespoons pine nuts (or blanched almonds)*
a few drops hot pepper sauce
1/2 *teaspoon salt*
freshly ground pepper to taste

For the Zucchini Boats

3 *small zucchini or 1 overgrown one*
1/2 *teaspoon salt*
2 *tablespoons grated cheese such as Swiss, or dried*
    bread crumbs

To Prepare the Eggplant Caviar

1. Preheat oven to 400 degrees. Cut off the ends of the eggplant and pierce it in several places with a fork. Bake eggplant until soft, about 30 minutes. Cool slightly.
2. Skin the eggplant, cut it into quarters, and scoop out seeds. Put the pulp in a food processor or blender.
3. Add the tomato, garlic, vinegar, oil, parsley, pine nuts, pepper sauce, salt, and pepper. Blend but leave the mixture chunky. Taste for seasoning.
4. Refrigerate the eggplant caviar at least 2 hours to marry flavors. May be frozen without flavor loss up to 2 months.

For the Zucchini Boats

1. Cut the zucchini in half the long way. Scoop out a hollow with a teaspoon. Repeat. Seed and cut each half in thirds if using 1 overgrown squash.
2. Bring a 2½-quart saucepan half full of water to a boil. Add the halved zucchini and blanch 3 minutes (10 minutes if using a very large one). Drain.
3. Preheat oven to 350 degrees. Place the zucchini boats in an oven-tempered serving dish just large enough to hold them. Season with salt. Mound 3 tablespoons of eggplant caviar into each small half, or divide the mixture to fill the larger zucchini boats. Sprinkle with cheese or bread crumbs. Bake in the 350-degree oven about 30 minutes or until bubbly and cheese is browned.

Note: Boats may be held for several hours, even a day, before cooking.

Yield: 6 servings
Calories per serving: 90
Protein per serving: 4g

Fat per serving: 5g
Carbohydrates per serving: 8g
Sodium per serving: 420mg

Ratatouille

❖

Ratatouille is a medley of eggplant, zucchini, onions, peppers, and tomatoes heady with the perfume of sweet basil. It takes a bit of time to prepare, but is best made a day ahead. It also freezes well. Make it when summer's produce is at its peak and serve beside a cold poached salmon or a simple roasted chicken. All by itself it makes for a most satisfying lunch.

1 small eggplant, about ½ pound
3 teaspoons extra-virgin olive oil
1 medium zucchini
4 tablespoons chicken stock or canned consomme
2 green peppers, diced
2 medium onions, about 1¾ cups, diced
1 clove garlic, minced
1 pound tomatoes, blanched, peeled, and seeded
10 fresh basil leaves, snipped, or 1 teaspoon dried
    basil
1 teaspoon salt
freshly ground pepper to taste
1 tablespoon minced fresh parsley

1. Cut the ends from the eggplant and slice it into rounds ½-inch thick. Stack the slices and cut the rounds into 6 or 8 wedges.
2. With cooking spray, spray a skillet large enough to hold the eggplant in one layer. Add 2 teaspoons of the oil and turn the heat to high. When hot, add the eggplant and cook over high heat until tender and lightly browned, about 8 minutes. Lower heat if eggplant starts to burn. Shake pan vigorously by the handle during cooking to keep the eggplant from sticking, and to turn it. Remove to a casserole.
3. While the eggplant cooks, cut the ends from the zucchini, slice it

into rounds, stack the slices, and cut them into wedges.

4. Spray the skillet again, add the rest of the oil, along with the zucchini, and cook over high heat until lightly browned. Shake the pan often during cooking. Remove zucchini to the casserole with the eggplant.

5. Add the stock to the now-empty skillet, add the peppers, onions, and garlic, cover the skillet, and cook over medium-low heat until the vegetables are limp. If there is visible liquid after cooking, raise the heat to high to evaporate. Add these to the eggplant mixture.

6. Bring a 2½-quart saucepan half full of water to a boil. Core the tomatoes and make a cross in each one's bottom. Immerse in the boiling water until the skins loosen, about 40 seconds. Cool under running water. Skin the tomatoes. Holding a tomato over a strainer within a bowl, squeeze the seeds from each one. Chop the pulp and add it to the eggplant-onion mixture. Hold the strainer over the casserole. Press the seeds with a wooden spoon to extract the juice. Discard the seeds.

7. Snip the basil over the eggplant-tomato mixture. Season with salt and lots of freshly ground pepper. Toss to mix well. Sprinkle parsley over.

8. Casserole may be baked, covered, at 350 degrees for about 35 minutes or until heated through, or cooked over low heat, covered, on top of the stove. Be careful the vegetables don't burn on the bottom! Serve warm, at room temperature, or cold.

Yield: 6 servings
Calories per serving: 65
Protein per serving: 2g

Fat per serving: 3g
Carbohydrates per serving: 7g
Sodium per serving: 370mg

Tomatoes

❖

The only good tomato is a local tomato. It doesn't matter where "local" is—though New Jerseyites will disagree—it only matters that the tomato be allowed to ripen on the vine to develop peak flavor. Don't be misled by the "vine-ripened" label. Vine ripened does mean the fruit was picked at maturity, but possibly while still green. The reddening is accomplished by spraying the shipment with ethylene gas. Other vine-ripened tomatoes are picked when just pink. These need no booster of ethylene gas, but they do need, in my opinion, Mother Nature to raise them right. Only the sun can impart the sweet, rich flavor of a truly vine-ripened tomato, the sort you buy at a local farmstand.

Another tomato you may have seen is the greenhouse or hydroponic tomato. This is grown in water and is amazingly good, though quite expensive.

Although tomatoes, or a not so reasonable facsimile, can be purchased all year long, the season for most local tomatoes is from May to September, depending on your location. "Seconds," bruised or misshapen tomatoes, are perfect for many uses at about half the price of the perfect specimens.

An uncooked tomato supplies a little over half an adult's daily need of vitamin C, for a meager 35 calories.

The recipes that follow are for those sun-dappled months when local tomatoes abound.

Cheese Frosted Tomatoes

❖

Select small- to medium-size local tomatoes for this quick vegetable dish. To cook on a covered grill, place them on a sheet of aluminum foil. Tomatoes may be prepared for cooking hours before baking.

> 6 ripe tomatoes
> ¼ teaspoon salt
> freshly ground pepper to taste
> 2 tablespoons olive oil
> 6 teaspoons Basil-Walnut Sauce, page 32, or 15
>   leaves fresh basil, snipped, or 3 teaspoons dried
>   basil
> 6 tablespoons grated cheese, such as Jarlsberg

1. Core the tomatoes and make a cross on each one's bottom. Bring a 4-quart saucepan half full of water to a boil. Immerse the tomatoes for 30 seconds, or just long enough to loosen the skins. Remove them, cool under running water, and peel off the skins.
2. With a melon baller, make a well where the core was. Place the tomatoes in a baking dish.
3. Preheat oven to 325 degrees. Season tomatoes with salt and pepper. Drizzle with oil. Place a teaspoon of Basil-Walnut Sauce or the basil in each tomato well. Divide the cheese over the top and bake in a 325-degree oven for 20 minutes. If desired, broil until the cheese is lightly browned.

Yield: 6 servings
Calories per serving: 90
Protein per serving: 2g

Fat per serving: 7g
Carbohydrates per serving: 5g
Sodium per serving: 110mg

Tomato and Chèvre Tart

❖

Tomatoes and cheese, a standard coupling of age-proven compatability, are updated here with the introduction of chèvre. The production of chèvre, essentially a cottage industry, has caught on in this country, although most chèvre is imported. Although the import of chèvre has increased as much as 137 percent in the last 2 years, it still accounts for less than 1 percent of all cheese consumed in America. For your pleasure, here's a tart that travels well and, like most vegetable tarts, is as tempting at room temperature as it is hot from the oven.

> 3 pounds tomatoes
> 3 tablespoons homemade or canned chicken broth
> 2 medium onions, chopped (preferably mild)
> 1 clove garlic, minced
> 8–10 fresh basil leaves, snipped, or 1 teaspoon
>   dried basil
> 1/8 teaspoon fennel seed
> 1 teaspoon sugar
> 1/2 teaspoon salt
> freshly ground pepper to taste
> 3 eggs
> 1/2 cup crème blanc (page 37) or sour cream
>   substitute
> a few gratings fresh nutmeg
> 2 ounces chèvre cheese, such as Montrachet or
>   Banon (if a milder taste is preferred)
> 2 sheets phyllo dough

1. Bring a 4-quart saucepan ¾ full of water to a boil. Blanch the tomatoes, peel the skins, and seed the tomatoes into a strainer supported over a bowl. Press the seeds with a spoon to extract the juices,

discard seeds. Chop the tomatoes roughly and set aside with reserved juices.

2. Put the broth in a 10-inch skillet over high heat. Add the onion, cover, and cook over medium-high heat until limp, about 6–8 minutes. Add the garlic the last few minutes of cooking.

3. Add the reserved juice, tomatoes, basil, fennel seed, sugar, salt, and pepper. Cook over medium-low heat, stirring occasionally, for 5 minutes. If there is more than 1/4 cup liquid left, raise the heat to high to evaporate. Set the mixture aside.

4. In a bowl or a food processor, beat together the eggs, crème blanc, and nutmeg. Set it aside.

5. Crisscross the 2 sheets of phyllo in a 9-inch removable-bottom tart ring or in a 9-inch quiche pan. Trim the overhanging pastry with scissors to 1 1/2 inches.

6. Preheat oven to 350 degrees. Pour the tomato-onion mixture into the pan. Pour the egg mixture over. Crumble the chèvre on top. Roll and crumple the pastry edges in to create a rim. Don't worry if the pastry tears. Spray the pastry edge with cooking spray to help it brown. Place in the bottom third of the preheated 350-degree oven and bake 45 minutes or until the center no longer wiggles when shaken. Let it rest 10 minutes before slicing.

Note: Never spray cooking spray into the oven; an explosive fire could result.

Yield: 6 servings
Calories per serving: 155
Protein per serving: 10g

Fat per serving: 6g
Carbohydrates per serving: 16g
Sodium per serving: 330mg

Winter Squash

❖

Hard-shelled squash, commonly called winter squash, is available much of the year. Some varieties such as Acorn and Buttercup are marketed throughout the year.

Squash was indigenous to the New World and unknown in Europe until explorers returned home with the new vegetable. When North American Indians introduced the English settlers to "askoota-squash," meaning eaten raw, the Europeans shortened the name to squash and proceeded to cook it. Cooking is still the norm.

The common varieties include:

Acorn: ribbed dark-green skin.

Buttercup: dark green with stripes of gray; blossom end is turban shaped.

Butternut: smooth buff-colored skin with a bulbous end.

Hubbard: warty skin with maybe blue-gray, green, or an orange tint.

Turban: two-toned with the top knot blue-gray, and the remainder an orange with stripes.

Spaghetti squash: a recently popular hard-shelled squash. It is a gourd of Oriental origin that is becoming increasingly available. When cooked, its bland but pleasantly crunchy strands resemble thin spaghetti, but with far fewer calories.

Most varieties of winter squash provide a tasty source of vitamin A, along with significant amounts of riboflavin and iron. They supply from approximately 35 to 70 calories a half-cup.

Winter squashes are long-keeping vegetables. They do best in a cool, dry, well-ventilated spot where they will keep one to four weeks.

Spaghetti Squash Primavera

❖

Spaghetti squash may be tossed with just a hint of butter and seasoned with salt and pepper, or you can gussy it up, as it is here. It is delicious with either the Basil-Walnut Sauce (page 32), or the Lemon Parsley Sauce (page 31). Though it may be baked, boiled, or steamed, I find baking the simplest.

This casserole will satisfy some appetites as a complete meal, though others may want a little something else. It may be assembled early in the day or at the last minute.

> 1 2-pound spaghetti squash
> 1 tablespoon butter, at room temperature
> 2 ounces grated Italian cheese, Fontina
>   recommended
> 1/2 bunch broccoli flowerets, sliced
> 1 cup shelled fresh peas (about 1 pound in the pod)
> 1 small zucchini, julienned
> 3 ounces cooked ham, cut into strips
> 3/4 cup sliced mushrooms
> 1 teaspoon salt
> freshly ground pepper to taste
> 2 ounces bacon, about 4 slices, fried and drained
> butter

1. Cut the squash in half the short way. Place it, cut side down, in a baking dish just large enough to hold it, with 1 inch of water.
2. Bake at 350 degrees until the shell is easily pierced with a fork and the flesh shreds when pulled with a fork, about 45 minutes. Cool, scoop out, and discard the seeds. Pull the strands from the squash into a bowl. Discard the tough skin. Toss the squash strands with the butter and the cheese.
3. While the squash is baking, prepare the vegetables. Bring a 2 1/2-

quart saucepan ¾ full of water to a boil. Add the broccoli, boil 1 minute, add the peas, cook 1 minute more, add the zucchini, and cook 30 seconds more. Drain and cool all the vegetables under running water. Set vegetables aside.

4. Spray an 8-inch skillet with cooking spray, add the ham strips, and stir-fry them until they're lightly browned. Remove strips from the pan to a paper towel.

5. In the same pan, spraying again if necessary, stir-fry the mushrooms until lightly browned.

6. In a large bowl, combine the cooked spaghetti squash, the drained, blanched vegetables, the mushrooms, and the ham. Season with salt and pepper and toss well to combine. Spoon into a casserole. Crumble bacon on top. Casserole is ready to eat, or set aside. Reheat, covered, in a 350-degree oven for 30–35 minutes with a small dab of butter on top. Uncover the last 10 minutes of cooking.

Yield: 4-6 servings
Calories per serving: 185
Protein per serving: 11g

Fat per serving: 10g
Carbohydrates per serving: 13g
Sodium per serving: 490mg

Bourbon Squash Souffle

A puffy presentation of pureed butternut squash combined with bourbon and a hint of maple syrup, this souffle is just the thing when you want a vegetable dish of distinction. Everything except beating the egg whites may be readied far in advance of the actual cooking, making this an easy to make dinner party dish. If you prefer, you can make the souffle in its entirety and freeze it, uncooked. Turn the freezer to its coldest setting. Cover the souffle with aluminum foil or plastic wrap and freeze solidly. If the souffle was frozen in a freezer-to-oven dish, bake it frozen, and double the cooking time. In a more fragile dish, thaw for 30 minutes, then bake, again doubling cooking time. Some of the dramatic puff is sacrificed in this method, but it is convenient.

1 medium butternut squash, about 1 ¼ pounds
2 tablespoons bourbon
3 tablespoons maple syrup
½ teaspoon salt
freshly ground pepper to taste
a few gratings nutmeg
3 tablespoons cornstarch
1 ½ cups milk
2 egg yolks, lightly beaten
1 tablespoon grated Parmesan cheese or dried bread
        crumbs
4 egg whites
a pinch cream of tartar

1. Preheat the oven to 400 degrees. Peel the squash, chop into eighths, and discard the seeds. Bring a 2 ½-quart saucepan ⅔ full of water to a boil, immerse the squash, and cook it until tender, about 20 minutes. Drain.
2. Mash the squash with the bourbon, maple syrup, salt, pepper, and nutmeg. Set the mixture aside.
3. Dissolve the cornstarch in the milk. Set it over medium-high heat and whisk until thickened, about 3 minutes. Set aside.
4. In a food processor or a bowl with a hand-held mixer, beat the egg yolks into the squash puree. Beat in the thickened milk. Set aside or refrigerate.
5. Spray a 1-quart souffle dish or other straight-sided baking dish (preferably with a 6-inch diameter) with cooking spray. Sprinkle in cheese or bread crumbs. Shake the dish to evenly distribute. Make a collar for the dish by folding a length of aluminum foil, long enough to encircle the dish with a 2-inch overlap, into thirds.

Spray the nonseamed side of the foil with cooking spray, or butter it heavily. Wrap this collar seam side out, tightly around the dish, secure it with a straight pin or paper clip.

6. When you're ready to complete this souffle, beat the egg whites until foamy. Add the cream of tartar. Beat until soft peaks form. Scoop the egg whites on top of the squash mixture. Fold them in gently. Ladle (pouring can deflate the whites) the souffle mixture into the souffle dish.

7. Put 1 inch water in an 8-inch square baking dish. Put the souffle dish in the baking dish on top of the stove. Turn heat to high, simmer for 5 minutes. Baking pan and all, slide souffle into the bottom third of a preheated oven. Check the souffle after 35 minutes, if the top is browning too fast, cover loosely with foil. Cook 15 to 25 minutes more. Souffle is done when a skewer inserted slightly off center comes out dry. Remove collar and serve immediately.

Yield: 6 servings
Calories per serving: 105
Protein per serving: 6g

Fat per serving: 2g
Carbohydrates per serving: 16g
Sodium per serving: 250mg

Chapter 10

SWEETS AND TREATS

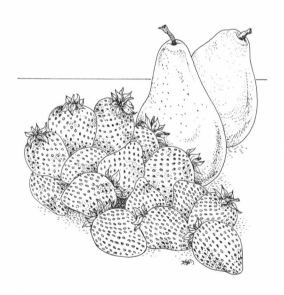

Sweets and Treats

❖

Because the premise of *Gourmet Light* rests on fine foods skillfully prepared, there is no room for ersatz, make-do ingredients. This restriction (but certainly no limitation) excludes the use of sacharrin or other artificial sweeteners. Thus most of the desserts here capitalize on the naturally occurring sugars (fructose) in fruits and/or rely on reduced amounts of cane sugar. Most desserts are based, in some combination, on sugar, flour, and fat, either butter and/or cream. These key ingredients are among the most caloric of all foods, while contributing few nutrients. Sugar, white or brown, contains about 873 calories a cup. White sugar is virtually nutrient empty while 3 ½ ounces of brown sugar supplies almost as much potassium as does a banana and a small amount of calcium—but at a terrific calorie toll. The second key ingredient in sweets is cream at 838 calories a cup. And flour is another 800 calories a cup, to say nothing of butter at 1,600 calories a cup, an important component of the dessert cart, however in hidden form. The body tallies these calories more accurately than the bank does your checks—not a one is ever forgotten or overlooked. This small collection of dessert recipes, in keeping the *Gourmet Light* theme, limits the use of sugar, fats, and flours. But by its mere existence this section acknowledges that one cannot live by fish and green beans alone, nor even the ideal dessert of unadorned fresh fruit. It is hoped, particularly if weight loss rather than maintenance is your goal, that portion sizes are closely watched.

Berries and Almond Cream

❖

Fresh strawberries, blueberries, or raspberries smothered in cream—
sweet heaven that can be yours given the *Gourmet Light* touch. This
custard sauce, with the texture of heavy cream and the fragrance of
vanilla or almond, is wonderful over fresh, ripe fruits or as a dipping
sauce for a fruit fondue. It is also delightful spooned over slices of
Almond Angel Cake, page 309. If you prefer a thicker custard sauce,
try Crème Anglaise, on page 286.

For the Almond Cream

1 ½ cups milk
2 eggs
3 tablespoons sugar
a few drops almond extract or ½ teaspoon pure
vanilla extract

For the Berries

3 to 4 cups fresh strawberries or other berries,
stemmed and rinsed
1 tablespoon sugar

1. Scald the milk in a 1-quart saucepan. Set aside.
2. Meanwhile, beat the eggs and sugar together in the top part of a
   double boiler with a hand-held electric mixer until the eggs thicken
   and turn very pale in color, about 2 to 3 minutes.
3. Put 1 inch of water into the bottom part of the double boiler, set
   over high heat until it comes to a simmer. Put eggs in top part of
   double boiler over hot water, adjusting heat as necessary to keep
   water just simmering. Beat the eggs until the mixture doubles in
   volume and feels tepid to the touch. Beat in scalded milk, pour
   into a heavy-bottomed 2 ½-quart saucepan, and stir constantly
   with a wooden spoon over medium heat until the custard sauce

thickens slightly. Insert a thermometer at the side of the pan if you wish. Stir constantly over medium heat until the thermometer registers 175. The custard sauce should not exceed 175 degrees. Without a thermometer, cook the custard sauce, stirring constantly, until it coats a metal spoon lightly and sauce is thickened, about 8 minutes.

4. Strain into a bowl, stir in extract, and chill or serve warm.
5. Clean the berries; cut strawberries in half if desired. Toss with sugar. Divide berries among serving dishes, spoon almond cream over.

Note: Some French chefs like to toss fresh strawberries with just a touch of black pepper on the premise that it heightens their flavor.

Yield: 4 servings
Calories per serving: 175
Protein per serving: 7g

Fat per serving: 4g
Carbohydrates per serving: 142g
Sodium per serving: 80mg

Burgundy Poached Pears with Crème Anglaise

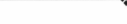

For this variation on a classic dessert, poached pears perched atop a puddle of custard sauce are gently broiled until lightly browned. The components of the dish may be readied a day before, then assembled up to 4 hours before serving. The poaching liquid may be frozen and reused over and over again.

> 4 pears, peeled, halved, and cored
> 2 tablespoons lemon juice

For the Poaching Liquid

1 liter burgundy wine
1/2 cup sugar
1 vanilla bean
juice of half a lemon
a cinnamon stick
3 whole cloves

For the Crème Anglaise

4 egg yolks
3 tablespoons sugar
1/4 teaspoon salt
1 cup milk, scalded
1 teaspoon vanilla extract

To Prepare the Pears

1. As you peel the pears, slip them into a bowl with the lemon juice to keep them from turning brown.
2. Bring the poaching ingredients to a boil in a 4-quart saucepan. Reduce to a simmer, immerse the pears, cover, and poach until a skewer easily pierces the fruit. Turn the pears during cooking as they will not be completely covered. Do not cook until mushy. The cooking time will depend entirely on the ripeness of the fruit, anywhere from 10-25 minutes or even longer.
3. Drain the pears when tender on a rack over a sheet of wax paper (to collect drippings). Freeze liquid for future poachings (you may leave the spices in the wine).

To Prepare the Crème Anglaise

1. In a heavy 2½-quart saucepan, beat together the egg yolks, sugar, and salt. Do not ribbon the mixture.
2. Slowly add the scalded milk, whisking all the while.
3. Insert a thermometer at the side of the pan if you like. Stirring with a wooden spoon over medium heat, notice the changes that oc-

cur. At 140 degrees, steam rises from the custard. At 155 degrees, the foam starts getting lighter, and at 165 degrees, the surface is smooth and the custard is ready. You may heat the custard to 180 degrees, but not higher, or the yolks will curdle. Without a thermometer, stir the custard over medium heat until it is thick enough to coat a metal spoon, about 3–4 minutes.

4. Strain the custard into a bowl, stir in vanilla extract.

To Finish the Dessert

1. Preheat broiler. Spread the custard sauce on an ovenproof serving dish such as a quiche dish, or on 4 ovenproof serving dishes such as baking shells.

2. Place a poached pear half, flat side down, on a cutting surface. Cut into 5–6 segments, but leave stem end uncut so the pear becomes "fanned." Repeat with remaining pears. Place the pear fan on the custard sauce and broil until heated through.

Note: A few drops of red food coloring added to the poaching liquid will heighten the color of the poached pears.

Yield: 4 servings
Calories per serving: 220 +
Protein per serving: 6g

Fat per serving: 6g
Carbohydrates per serving: 38g
Sodium per serving: 180mg

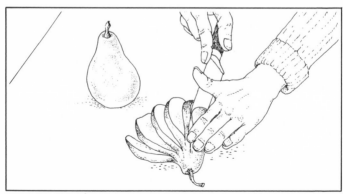

MAKING A PEAR FAN

Place a poached pear half, flat side down, on a flat surface. Cut it into five or six segments, leaving them attached at the stem end.

Candied Oranges with Melba Sauce

❖

The simplicity of this classic dessert I find very appealing—juicy seedless oranges enhanced with a sugar syrup and drizzled with ruby red raspberry sauce. It may be prepared a day in advance.

> 8 small navel oranges
> 3/4 cup sugar
> 1 1/2 cups water
> juice of 1/2 lemon
> 2 kiwis
> 2 tablespoons orange-flavored liqueur such as Triple
>   Sec or Grand Marnier
> a 10-ounce package frozen raspberries, thawed

1. With a vegetable peeler, remove the rind (colored part only, no white) from 2 of the oranges. Julienne the rind and set aside.
2. In a heavy 2 1/2-quart saucepan, dissolve the sugar in 1/2 cup of the water over very low heat. The solution must not boil until the sugar is thoroughly dissolved or it will crystallize. Do not stir the sugar as it dissolves, but swirl the pan by its handle.
3. When all the sugar is dissolved add the remaining cup of water, the lemon juice, and julienned orange peel. Bring to a boil for 30 seconds, lower the heat so solution simmers. Cover and simmer 1 hour.
4. Meanwhile, peel the oranges over a bowl to catch the juices. Peel the kiwis. Slice both the oranges and kiwis thinly horizontally. Reshape the oranges into their original form, interspersing the kiwi slices between the orange slices. Hold together with toothpicks. Pile into a deep glass bowl and chill until serving time.
5. Remove the sugar syrup from heat. Stir in the orange-flavored liqueur. Pour it over the oranges.

6. Place the berries in a food processor or blender and puree. Force the puree through a strainer. Discard the seeds. Stir in orange juice from peeling the oranges in Step 4. Drizzle half of the sauce over oranges, pass remaining sauce at the table.

Note: The oranges may be sauced with the sugar syrup and held at room temperature up to 6 hours before serving.

Yield: 8 servings

Calories per serving: 195

Protein per serving: 2g

Fat per serving: trace

Carbohydrates per serving: 48g

Sodium per serving: trace

Grand Marnier Mousse

This cool, cloudlike mousse literally melts in the mouth. It needs at least 2 hours chilling time to set before serving, yet it should be served within 24 hours as the egg whites break down with time.

> 1 envelope unflavored gelatin
> ¼ cup cold water
> ½ cup sugar
> ½ cup cold water
> 4 eggs
> ¼ teaspoon salt
> ⅔ cup freshly squeezed orange juice
> zest of 1 orange
> 3 tablespoons orange-flavored liqueur such as Grand Marnier or Triple Sec
> 2 tablespoons rum
> 2 tablespoons sugar

1. Soften the gelatin in the ¼ cup water in a glass measuring cup for about 2 minutes. Place the cup in a small saucepan ⅓ full of water and warm over medium heat stirring occasionally until gelatin is dissolved and clear, about 3 minutes. Set aside.
2. Meanwhile, combine the sugar with ½ cup water in a 1-quart saucepan. Dissolve the sugar over very low heat, swirling the pan by the handle. Do not stir with a spoon. When the solution is clear, turn the heat to high and boil 1 minute. Do not let sugar syrup begin to brown. Set it aside.
3. Separate the eggs. Break the egg yolks into the top part of a double boiler, the whites into a glass, ceramic, or copper bowl. Set the bottom of the double boiler with 1 inch of water over high heat. Insert the top half of double boiler. Beat the yolks over the simmering water until thickened and very pale in color, about 2 minutes. Regulating heat so the water just simmers, continue beating while dribbling in the hot sugar syrup from Step 2. Beat until the mixture doubles in volume, thickens, and feels warm to the touch, about 6–8 minutes. Remove from heat and continue beating until mixture ribbons (falls from beaters in a wide band that lies on top of the mass for a moment before sinking in).
4. Stir the dissolved gelatin, salt, orange juice, zest, orange liqueur, and rum into the yolks.
5. Wash the beaters thoroughly and beat the egg whites until stiff. Gradually beat in the sugar.
6. Fold the whites into gelatin-yolk mixture.
7. Pour the mousse into individual glasses or a 6-cup mold sprayed with cooking spray and chill at least 2 hours to set. Unmold if desired.

Yield: 8 servings
Calories per serving: 140
Protein per serving: 4g

Fat per serving: 3g
Carbohydrates per serving: 21g
Sodium per serving: 100mg

Crepes Suzette

❖

Crepes Suzette were invented by the Franco-American cook Henri Charpentier. Quite by accident the butter sauce he was preparing caught on fire, with results that thousands of cooks have since plagiarized. Here is my reduced-calorie version. The crepes and sauce may be readied early in the day, then assembled and flamed before serving to appreciative guests.

For the Crepes

1 egg
1 egg yolk
¾ cup milk
6 tablespoons flour
pinch salt
1 tablespoon butter

For the Sauce

1½ tablespoons butter
2 tablespoons sugar
2 tablespoons orange marmalade
1 tablespoon each orange and lemon zest
juice and pulp of 3 fresh oranges (reserve 2
        tablespoons for dissolving cornstarch)
2 teaspoons cornstarch
1 tablespoon orange-flavored liqueur such as Grand
        Marnier, Curaçao, or Triple Sec
1 tablespoon kirsch (or use 2 tablespoons orange
        liqueur)

To Prepare the Crepes
(May be done as much as 1 day in advance.)

1. Beat the egg, egg yolk, and milk together, add the flour sifted with the salt, and stir just to combine. Chill 2 hours.
2. Melt ½ teaspoon of the butter in a nonstick 8-inch skillet until foamy. Ladle just enough batter into the pan to film bottom. Pour excess batter back into bowl when bottom sets. Cook a crepe over medium-high heat until browned on one side. Flip, cook on underside just to firm (this will be the inside, unseen part), and slide onto a plate. Continue cooking, adding butter as necessary and placing a sheet of wax paper between the crepes. Crepes may now be used or chilled up to 12 hours or frozen until needed. The recipe makes ten to twelve 12-inch crepes.

To Prepare the Sauce

1. Combine butter, sugar, marmalade, orange and lemon zest, and juice and pulp of oranges in a 1-quart saucepan over medium heat until heated through.
2. Dissolve the cornstarch in the reserved juice. Stir into the hot orange sauce and stir over medium heat until thickened, about 4 minutes.

To Assemble the Crepes and Serve

1. Fold the crepes in triangle shapes with the unbrowned side facing in, by folding first in halves and then into quarters. Arrange on a flameproof serving dish that has sides such as a quiche dish or a chafing dish. Overlap the crepes by ½ inch. If preparing early in the day, cover with aluminum foil. Before serving sprinkle very lightly with water and heat in a 350-degree oven for about 15 minutes, covered, until warmed through.
2. Pour the warmed sauce over the heated crepes. Keep them warm in the oven or over hot water in a chafing dish while preparing the liqueur for flaming.
3. Heat the liqueurs in a long-handled butter warmer, one with a lip

is preferred. When bubbles appear at the pan's edge, remove from the heat. Place dish of warmed crepes on the table. Ignite liqueur with a fireplace match or other long taper. Pour the flaming liqueur over the crepes. Use a spoon to lift sauce as it flames. Serve when flames die out.

Yield: 6 servings
Calories per serving: 160
Protein per serving: 5g

Fat per serving: 7g
Carbohydrates per serving: 22g
Sodium per serving: 50mg

❖ **FLAMING** ❖

Recipes frequently call for igniting liquor, sometimes for effect, sometimes to mellow the sharp alcohol taste. For success with flaming liquors, remember the following tips.
• the liquor must be heated just to the point where small bubbles appear at the edge of the pan
• if it boils longer than about 10—20 seconds, add more liquor
• add a pinch of sugar to ensure long burning
• select a long-handled, small pot, preferably with a spout, to heat the liquor. Butter warmers are ideal.

Cheesecake with Orange Zest

❖

This cheesecake with its light, refreshing hint of orange makes a pleasant finish to a meal. To reduce the calories even further, make it without the graham cracker crust.

For the Crust

3 1/2 ounces (about 8 2 1/2-inch by 5-inch) graham crackers
2 tablespoons orange juice

For the Cheesecake

1 pound cottage cheese
1 pound part-skim ricotta cheese
1/2 cup sugar
1 tablespoon flour
1 teaspoon vanilla extract
grated zest of 1 orange
1/2 teaspoon salt
2 egg yolks
1 egg
2 tablespoons sliced almonds

1. Preheat oven to 350 degrees. Pulverize the graham crackers in a food processor or blender. Moisten the crumbs with orange juice and press into the bottom of a 9 1/2-inch pie or quiche dish "buttered" with cooking spray. Place in the preheated 350-degree oven for 12 minutes.
2. Beat together or puree in a food processor all the remaining ingredients except the almonds.
3. Pour into the graham cracker crust. Sprinkle almonds on top. Bake for 1 hour at 350 degrees. Reduce the heat to 300 degrees and bake an additional 20 or 25 minutes or until the middle is firm when wiggled. Cool and chill 2 hours.

Yield: 8 servings
Calories per serving: 275
Protein per serving: 17g

Fat per serving: 10g
Carbohydrates per serving: 29g
Sodium per serving: 540mg

Port Wine Sorbet

❖

A cool finish, perfect for a warm summer meal, this port wine sorbet is ideal with melon. To serve, fill a fluted champagne glass two-thirds full of melon balls that have been marinated in a bit of port wine and top with a scoop of this sorbet. A tiny dollop would also make a refreshing intermezzo for a formal meal. An ice cream maker is necessary to produce the needed texture. The ginger is available at specialty markets and some general food stores.

> 1/3 cup sugar
> 1/2 cup port wine
> 1 teaspoon minced crystallized ginger
> 1 cantaloupe
> juice of 1 lemon
> seedless red grapes, optional

1. Combine the sugar, wine, and ginger in a small saucepan over very low heat. Swirl handle until the sugar dissolves. Raise heat to high and boil 5 minutes, without stirring, remove from heat, and chill until cool to the touch.
2. Cut the cantaloupe in half and discard the seeds. Cut off and discard the rind. Puree the flesh in a food processor or food mill.
3. Combine the puree in the cream can of an ice cream maker with the chilled wine syrup and the lemon juice. Process according to manufacturer's instructions, then harden in the freezer.
4. Serve garnished with red grapes, if desired.

Yield: 4 servings
Calories per serving: 139
Protein per serving: 1g

Fat per serving: trace
Carbohydrates per serving: 124g
Sodium per serving: 16mg

Fruit Fondue

❖

This is more of an idea than an actual recipe, because proportions and ingredients are strictly up to the cook and the pantry. Assemble a variety of fruits. Cut them into bite-size pieces. Arrange them around a pot or chafing dish of raspberry dipping sauce. Include if you like a batch of Almond Cream (page 285) and squares of Almond Angel Cake (page 309). Diners can dip the fruits and cake into either the almond cream or the raspberry. If you prefer you may film the bottom of a small saucer with 2–3 tablespoons of raspberry sauce, place a skewer of fruit over the sauce, and drizzle almond cream on top—a light and pretty summertime dessert.

For the Raspberry Dipping Sauce

1   10-ounce package frozen raspberries or
     strawberries, thawed
1   tablespoon cornstarch
1   tablespoon orange-flavored liqueur such as Grand
     Marnier or Triple Sec
1   tablespoon kirsch (optional)

1. Puree the berries in a food processor or blender. Strain and discard the seeds.
2. Dissolve the cornstarch in the liqueurs.
3. Stir the dissolved cornstarch in the raspberry puree over medium-high heat in a 1-quart saucepan until slightly thickened. Serve hot or chilled.

Yield: Approximately 1 cup
Calories per tablespoon: 22
Protein per tablespoon: trace

Fat per tablespoon: trace
Carbohydrates per tablespoon: 5g
Sodium per tablespoon: trace

Hot Apple Tart

❖

Personally, I find any recipe that calls for a half cup of something from some other recipe immediately unappealing. After all, gearing up for one recipe doesn't mean I'm willing to make another. But I urge you to make an exception in this case, or you'll miss perhaps the best dessert in this modest collection. This thin apple tart, with its crust of phyllo and icing of Almond Cream (page 285) is best served hot. All components may be readied up to 4 hours in advance, then assembled and baked just prior to serving time. Poached pears may be used in addition to or to replace the apples. Leftovers may be gently reheated in a 300-degree oven for 10 minutes.

> $1/2$ ounce sliced or slivered almonds
> 2 tablespoons dried bread crumbs
> 1 tablespoon sugar
> dash cinammon
> 2 sheets phyllo dough
> 2 tablespoons butter, melted
> 1 apple, Granny Smith or Yellow Delicious
>   recommended
> 1 tablespoon brown sugar
> 4 tablespoons Almond Cream (page 285)

1. Spray a $7 1/2$-inch removable-bottom tart ring with cooking spray. You may use a slightly larger pan, but results won't be as pleasing.
2. In a food processor or blender, combine the almonds, bread crumbs, sugar, and cinnamon. Pulverize until they're fine crumbs. Set aside.
3. Lay a sheet of phyllo into the tart ring, vertically, overlapping it in the middle as you would a sheet of tissue paper in a box. Butter sparingly with a pastry brush dipped in the melted butter. Sprinkle with half the nut-crumb mixture.

4. Now lay another sheet in the pan, horizontally, also overlapping in the center. Butter very lightly and sprinkle with the remaining crumbs.
5. Fold the overhang inside the rim of the pan.
6. Slice the apple in half the long way, then into quarters. Core it. Slice the quarters very thinly. Arrange the apple slices over the tart ring in circles, with pieces of the apple resting on the phyllo dough rim. Brush all with the remaining butter. Sprinkle brown sugar over the apples. Set aside, if you wish.
7. When you're ready to complete the tart, preheat the oven to 425 degrees.
8. Place the tart in the lower third of a preheated oven for 20 minutes or until the apples are softened.
9. Spread almond cream over the apple tart and broil for 4–5 minutes until the almond cream is bubbly and golden. Let the tart rest 5 minutes and serve warm. It also can be held up to 1 hour on a serving tray.

Yield: 4 servings
Calories per serving: 145
Protein per serving: 3g

Fat per serving: 9g
Carbohydrates per serving: 17g
Sodium per serving: 20mg

❖ **THINKING THIN TIP** ❖

If you're trying to wean yourself from cream and/or sugar in coffee, try adding a 3-inch piece of vanilla bean or a cinnamon stick to the grounds when you make it. The added flavor will help.

Mimosa Sherbet

❖

Celebrate your success with this champagne-based sherbet. While it may be made without an ice cream freezer simply by hardening in a conventional freezer, it will have a smoother texture if processed in an ice cream freezer.

> 1 scant cup sugar
> 7/8 cup water
> juice of 1 orange
> 1 cup Brut champagne
> 1 tablespoon orange-flavored liqueur such as Triple
>   Sec or Grand Marnier
> 2 egg whites
> mint leaves (optional)

1. Combine sugar and water in a 2 1/2-quart saucepan. Swirl the pan by the handle over very low heat until the sugar is dissolved. Do not stir. When the solution is perfectly clear and sugar is dissolved, raise heat to high and boil without stirring for 7 minutes.
2. Remove the sugar water from heat, pour it into a bowl, and place in the freezer for 15 minutes.
3. Remove from freezer, stir in orange juice, champagne, and orange liqueur.
4. Beat egg whites until stiff, fold into champagne mixture. Freeze in an ice cream freezer according to manufacturer's instructions. Sherbet will be soft after processing. Ripen in freezer to harden. Garnish with a mint leaf if available.

Yield: 6 servings
Calories per serving: 180
Protein per serving: 1g

Fat per serving: 0
Carbohydrates per serving: 37g
Sodium per serving: 20mg

Mango Mousse

❖

This is a very light, refreshing dessert. Because its color is so pale you might like to garnish the serving dish or individual servings with a few slices of fresh, colorful fruit, more mango or perhaps oranges. Use only very ripe fruit for this mold.

> 1 ripe mango, peeled and pitted
> 1 envelope unflavored gelatin
> 1 tablespoon cold water
> juice of 2 limes
> 2 egg whites
> a tiny pinch salt
> 1/4 teaspoon cream of tartar
> 1/3 cup sugar or 4 tablespoons fructose

1. Peel and puree the mango in a food processor or blender.
2. Soften the gelatin in the cold water until it's spongy.
3. Heat the lime juice in a 1-quart saucepan. When steaming, stir in the gelatin, stir until dissolved, about 1–2 minutes, over medium-low heat.
4. Stir the dissolved gelatin into the fruit puree.
5. Beat the egg whites and salt until foamy. Add the cream of tartar and continue beating until soft peaks form. Gradually add the sugar while beating until stiff.
6. Gently fold the whites into the puree-gelatin mixture.
7. Spray a 2-cup mold with cooking spray. Spoon mousse into mold, tap on kitchen counter to knock out air bubbles, and chill for 4 hours. Unmold and garnish with fresh fruits before serving if desired.

Yield: 4 servings
Calories per serving: 115
Protein per serving: 4g

Fat per serving: trace
Carbohydrates per serving: 26g
Sodium per serving: 70mg

Mocha Parfait Pie

❖

Here's a do-ahead confection for mocha fanciers. If you prefer, make the flavor predominantly coffee by omitting the cocoa powder and substituting Tia Maria for the crème de cacao.

For the Crust

2 cups corn flakes
1 tablespoon butter, melted
2 teaspoons sugar

For the Pie

1 5⅓-ounce can evaporated milk
1 envelope unflavored gelatin
1 tablespoon water
¾ cup milk
1 tablespoon instant coffee powder
1 egg, separated
⅓ cup sugar
1 tablespoon unsweetened cocoa powder
1 tablespoon crème de cacao
2 tablespoons sliced almonds

To Prepare the Crust

1. Preheat oven to 350 degrees. Combine all the crust ingredients in a food processor or blender and combine until the corn flakes are crushed. Pour into an ungreased 8-inch pie pan and press onto bottom and sides with the help of a wooden spoon. Place in the bottom third of a preheated 350-degree oven for 5 minutes or until slightly crisped. Remove and chill.

To Prepare the Pie

1. About 2 hours before making the dessert, pour the evaporated milk into an ice cube tray and place in freezer.
2. Soften the gelatin in the cold water until spongy, about 2 minutes.
3. Heat the milk and coffee powder until steaming, add the softened gelatin, and stir over medium heat until dissolved. Set aside.
4. Beat the egg yolk. Slowly dribble it into the hot milk, and whisk over medium-low heat until mixture thickens. Remove from the heat and cool in the refrigerator until mixture is at room temperature.
5. Beat the egg white until soft peaks form. Gradually beat in the sugar and cocoa powder.
6. Fold the beaten egg white into the milk-yolk mixture, stir in the crème de cacao.
7. Beat the icy evaporated milk until it looks like softly whipped cream.
8. Fold the whipped evaporated milk into the mocha mixture. Gently pour into prepared crust, sprinkle almonds on top, and chill at least 2 hours.

Yield: 6–8 servings
Calories per serving: 185
Protein per serving: 7g

Fat per serving: 7g
Carbohydrates per serving: 25g
Sodium per serving: 130mg

❖   **THINKING THIN TIP**   ❖

There is no such thing as a forbidden food, only food that must be eaten in moderation.

Raspberry Crepes Souffle

❖

This showy dessert—a raspberry meringue folded inside a thin crepe, which is in turn doused with more raspberry—waits for no man, woman, or child. It needs to be served immediately from the oven or a slumped collection of crepes will be all you have to show for your efforts. However, the crepes and the meringue souffle mixture may be readied and assembled days in advance, frozen, and baked without thawing, making a light and lovely dessert that takes just 20 minutes from freezer to table.

For the Crepes

1 egg, beaten
½ cup milk
¼ cup flour
pinch salt
1 tablespoon sugar
1 tablespoon orange zest
1 tablespoon butter or less for frying the crepes

For the Souffle

a 10-ounce package frozen raspberries, thawed
    (fresh, of course, would be wonderful)
4 egg whites
½ teaspoon cream of tartar
4 tablespoons sugar (slightly more for fresh berries)
1 teaspoon cornstarch or arrowroot
1 tablespoon orange flavored liqueur such as Grand
    Marnier or Triple Sec

To Prepare the Crepes
(May be done as much as 1 day in advance.)

1. Beat the egg and milk together, add the flour (sifted with the pinch of salt) and remaining ingredients except the butter, stir just to

combine. Chill for 2 hours.

2. Melt ½ teaspoon of the butter in a nonstick 8-inch skillet until foamy. Ladle just enough batter into the pan to film bottom. Pour excess batter back into bowl after bottom has set. Cook crepe over medium-high heat until browned on one side. Flip, cook on underside just to firm (this will be the inside, unseen part of the crepe), slide onto a plate, and continue cooking, adding butter as necessary and placing a sheet of wax paper between the crepes. Crepes may now be used or chilled or frozen until needed. The recipe makes six to eight 6-inch crepes.

To Prepare the Souffle

1. Preheat oven to 350 degrees and spray an ovenproof serving dish large enough to hold 8 folded crepes with cooking spray.
2. Puree the raspberries in a food processor or blender. Strain and discard the seeds.
3. Measure ⅓ cup raspberry puree and set it aside.
4. Beat egg whites until foamy. Add cream of tartar, gradually beat in sugar, and beat until just shy of stiff peaks.
5. Fold the ⅓ cup raspberry puree into the beaten egg whites. Divide souffle mixture among the crepes, placing about 3 heaping tablespoons on the unbrowned side of each crepe. (Discard or cook separately any leftover souffle.) Fold crepe ends to middle. Place crepes seam side down, in prepared ovenproof dish. Crepes may now be frozen or they must be baked immediately. Bake unfrozen crepes souffles 12 to 15 minutes (bake frozen crepes souffles 15 to 20 minutes) or until puffed and golden. Serve with confectioner's sugar sifted over or the following sauce.
6. Combine the remaining raspberrry puree with cornstarch dissolved in the orange liqueur. Cook, whisking over medium-low heat until slightly thickened, about 2 minutes. Film serving plates with thickened raspberry puree, place puffed crepe souffle on top, or drizzle raspberry puree over the crepe souffle.

Yield: 6-8 servings
Calories per serving: 155
Protein per serving: 5g

Fat per serving: 3g
Carbohydrates per serving: 28g
Sodium per serving: 80mg

Vanilla Ice Milk

❖

This basic recipe is far better than any store-bought version you might buy. With additions this ice milk may become flavored with coffee, maple walnut, pumpkin rum, ginger, or any other concoction you might devise. It does require an ice cream maker to develop the proper texture, however.

> 4 cups low-fat milk
> 1 cup sugar
> 1 1/2 teaspoons good-quality vanilla extract
> 1/8 teaspoon salt

1. Pour the milk, sugar, vanilla, and salt directly into the cream can of the ice cream maker. Stir with a wooden spoon until sugar dissolves. Process in an ice cream maker according to manufacturer's instructions.

Yield: 12 1/2-cup servings
Calories per serving: 115
Protein per serving: 3g

Fat per serving: 2g
Carbohydrates per serving: 22g
Sodium per serving: 70mg

Coffee Ice Milk

Dissolve 4 tablespoons instant powdered coffee in the milk. Continue with the recipe.

Yield: 12 1/2-cup servings
Calories per serving: 120
Protein per serving: 4g

Fat per serving: 2g
Carbohydrates per serving: 23g
Sodium per serving: 70mg

Maple Walnut Ice Milk

Use ¾ cup sugar and ¼ cup maple syrup. Substitute 1 tablespoon maple extract for the vanilla extract. Fold in ⅓ cup nuts to the processed ice cream before hardening in freezer.

Yield: 12 ½-cup servings
Calories per serving: 140
Protein per serving: 4g

Fat per serving: 4g
Carbohydrates per serving: 22g
Sodium per serving: 70mg

Pumpkin Rum Ice Milk

Substitute 1 tablespoon rum for the vanilla extract. Add several gratings fresh nutmeg and ½ teaspoon ground cinnamon to the milk-sugar mixture. Stir in ½ cup canned or homemade unsweetened pumpkin puree to the ice milk after processing and before hardening in the freezer.

Yield: 12 ½-cup servings
Calories per serving: 150
Protein per serving: 4g

Fat per serving: 4g
Carbohydrates per serving: 23g
Sodium per serving: 70mg

Ginger Ice Milk

Simmer the milk with a 3-inch piece of peeled ginger root for 20 minutes. Discard the ginger. Cool. Stir 1 tablespoon finely minced crystallized ginger into the ice milk just before hardening in freezer.

Yield: 12 ½-cup servings
Calories per serving: 125
Protein per serving: 3g

Fat per serving: 2g
Carbohydrates per serving: 24g
Sodium per serving: 70mg

Raspberry Ice
with Cassis Sauce

❖

Tart raspberry tempered with a sweet sauce of vanilla and cassis—a seasonless dessert thanks to the year-round availability of frozen berries. An ice cream maker is necessary to produce the fine texture. Like most homemade ice creams and sherbets, this is best made no more than 24 hours before serving.

1/2 cup sugar
1/2 cup water
2 10-ounce packages frozen raspberries (in light
*   syrup) or 1 pint fresh raspberries*
1 teaspoon lemon juice
1 tablespoon crème de cassis

For the Sauce

3 tablespoons crème de cassis
1/2 cup vanilla ice cream, softened

To Prepare the Ice

1. Combine the sugar and water in a 1-quart saucepan over low heat. Swirl the pan by the handle until the sugar is dissolved. Do not stir. Raise heat to high, boil 5 minutes. Chill.
2. If using fresh berries add sugar, sparingly, to taste. Puree the berries in a food processor or blender. Strain and discard the seeds.
3. Combine chilled syrup with raspberry puree, lemon juice, and cassis. Freeze in ice cream maker according to manufacturer's instructions.

To Prepare the Sauce

1. Stir the crème de cassis into the softened ice cream. Serve 2 table-spoons over each serving.

Yield: 7 3-ounce servings
Calories per serving: 175
Protein per serving: 1g

Fat per serving: 1g
Carbohydrates per serving: 38g
Sodium per serving: 10mg

Almond Angel Food Cake

❖

This quickly made cake pairs the lightness of beaten egg whites with the crunch of almonds. Baked in a ring mold, it could be served with a mound of fresh sliced fruit in the center, and the whole napped with almond cream (page 285). It would also make a nice addition to a fruit fondue tray, and is very tempting all by itself.

> 1 ounce slivered or sliced almonds
> 1/2 cup sugar
> 6 tablespoons cake flour
> 1/2 cup egg whites (about 5–6)
> a pinch salt
> 1/2 teaspoon cream of tartar
> 1 teaspoon vanilla extract
> 1/2 teaspoon almond extract

1. Use a 4-cup ring mold, sprayed with cooking spray or buttered and floured. Preheat the oven to 300 degrees.
2. Pulverize the almonds in a food processor or blender. Do not allow them to get mushy. Set aside in a bowl.

3. Sift together the sugar and flour, mix with the almonds.
4. Beat the egg whites until foamy, add salt, and continue to beat until soft peaks form. Add the cream of tartar, and continue to beat until stiff but not dry.
5. Fold the flour-sugar-nut mixture into the egg whites along with the extracts. Do not overbeat. Spoon into the prepared ring mold and place in the bottom third of a preheated 300-degree oven. Turn heat off after 30 minutes but leave the cake in oven for another 10 minutes. Then cool, inverted on a rack for 30 minutes. Run a flexible-bladed spatula around the rim and center of the mold to release the cake. If it doesn't come free, let it cool a while longer.

Yield: 8 servings
Calories per serving: 95
Protein per serving: 3g

Fat per serving: 2g
Carbohydrates per serving: 18g
Sodium per serving: 40mg

❖ **VANILLA** ❖

Vanilla beans come from a variety of orchid. When fresh, the pods are green and oddly odorless, but when dried, they become incredibly fragrant. To make your own vanilla extract, split a vanilla bean in half and make a slit along its length to expose the minute tiny beans inside. Place the beans in a 2-ounce jar (an old vanilla extract bottle is perfect), fill it with vodka, cap the jar tightly, and let it rest 1 month in a cool, dark place. The resulting extract is wonderful in many desserts. Add 2 drops to the ground coffee beans in your next pot for a delicious cup of coffee. The bean may be reused.

GOURMET LIGHT MENUS

Entertaining Menus

Mushrooms à la Grecque
Duxelle Melba (with cocktails)
Two Mushroom Consomme
Breadsticks*
Roasted Tenderloin of Beef
Béarnaise Sauce
Scotch Onions
Green Beans with Red Pepper Puree
Crepes Suzette

Seviche
Grilled Duck Zinfandel
Wild Rice with Golden Raisins*
Sauteed Young Spinach*
Pea Pod and Water Chestnut Salad
Sherry Ginger Dressing
Raspberry Crepes Souffle

Chèvre-Stuffed Artichokes
Rolls*
Lobster Flamed with Drambuie
Bibb, Red Leaf, and Watercress Salad
Herbed French Vinaigrette
Burgundy Poached Pears
Crème Anglaise

Informal Dinner Menus

Fettuccine with Cepes
Veal Chops with Red Pepper Butter
Pea and Leek Puree
Japanese Dressing on Snow Peas
Candied Oranges with Melba Sauce

Pear and Gouda Salad
Poached Chicken Breasts with Mustard Hollandaise
Asparagus
Boiled New Potatoes with Parsley*
Mimosa Sherbet

Pasta with Basil-Walnut Sauce
Veal Roast with Sun-Dried Tomatoes
Julienned Summer Squash
Grand Marnier Mousse

Mussels in White Wine and Saffron
Basil-Walnut Chicken Paillards
Cheese Frosted Tomatoes
Green Beans*
Fresh Fruit Macerated in Champagne*

Grill Menus

Swordfish with Mustard Tarragon
Red Bliss Potato Salad
Zucchini Saute
Fresh Fruit in Season*

Clam and Sausage Appetizers
Grilled Shrimp with Leeks and Fennel
Confetti Rice Salad
Mango Mousse

Dinners for a Summer Evening

Chilled Tomato Soup
with Tarragon Ice
Sole, Scallop and Pea Pod Salad
Fruit Fondue

Chilled Potato and Sorrel Soup
Sesame Chicken Salad
Breadsticks*
Raspberry Ice with Cassis Sauce

Midweek Dinner Menus

Pork Cutlet in Cider Cream Sauce
Baked Beets
Dilled Zucchini and Carrot Salad

Chicken and Pork Skewers
Warm Seafood Salad with Chinese Noodles
Almond Angel Food Cake

Beef Paupiettes with Sausage and Zucchini
Brown Rice*
Lemon Glazed Carrots
Vanilla Ice Milk

Gingered Carrot Soup
Fillets of Fish Martini
Steamed Rice*

Scotch Chicken
Leek Quiche with a Cornmeal Sage Crepe Crust
Tossed Salad with Sesame Seed Dressing

Sunday Supper Menus

Bouillabaisse of Scallops
Rolls*
Caesar Salad
Mocha Parfait Pie

Pasta with Red Pepper Puree and Prosciutto
Fire and Ice Salad
Hot Apple Tart

Home from Vacation Pound-Chaser

Lemon-Lime Fish Fillets in Parchment Paper Hearts
Sesame Broccoli
Tossed Salad
Balsamic Walnut Oil Vinaigrette Dressing
Fresh Melon with Port Wine Sorbet

Picnics in the Park

Gazpacho
Bibb, Tuna, and Green Bean Salad
Whole Wheat Crackers*
Strawberries to dip in Almond Cream

Ratatouille
Broccoli and Pecan Terrine
Grapes in Brandied Crème Blanc*

Chinese Tea Smoked Turkey
Marinated Roasted Red Peppers with Chèvre
Wilted Cucumber Salad
Cheesecake with Orange Zest

*The asterisk means the recipe
is not in this cookbook.

Index

❖

A

B

Drambuie, lobster flamed with, 215
Duck, Zinfandel, grilled, 184
Duxelle melba, 52

E

Egg drop soup, Chinese, 76
Eggplant
    caviar, 270
    in ratatouille, 272
Eggs, and Hollandaise, 20

F

Fennel, with grilled shrimp and leeks,
    212
Fettucine with cepes, 248
Fillets of fish martini, 202
Fillets of sole with basil and tomato,
    196
Fire and ice salad, 102
Fish, 189-227
    about, 190-192
    in bouillabaisse of scallops, 69
    broiled steaks with basil-walnut
        sauce, 206
    broiled fillets, 204
    fillets of, martini, 202
    fillets with sauce rouge, 199
    and gribiche, 28
    grilled, and basil-walnut sauce,
        32
    grilled, and Béarnaise, 24
    grilled, and lemon parsley sauce,
        31
    and Hollandaise, 20
    lemon-lime fillets in parchment
        paper hearts, 208
    and mousseline, 23
    salad, and dill-mayonnaise, 28
    salad, and fresh herb vinaigrette,
        100
    seafood crepes in champagne
        sauce, 194
    in seviche, 62
    in sole and crab peppers, 60
    stock, 19
    warm seafood salad with Chinese
        noodles, 222

Flaming, about, 294
Flank steak in gingered beer sauce,
    124
Flour vs. cornstarch, 7
Fondue, fruit, 297
Fresh herb vinaigrette, 100
Fricassee, chicken, with leeks and
        carrots, 163
Fruit
    compote, curried, fall, 146
    fondue, 297

G

Game
    grilled duck Zinfandel, 184
    grilled quail, 187
Game hens, grilled, 187
Garlic, about, 55
Garnishes, about, 9
Gazpacho, 80
Ginger, about, 127
    ice milk, 307
Gingered beer sauce, for flank steak,
    124
Gingered carrot soup, 84
Gouda cheese, in pear and pine nut
        salad, 107
Graham cracker crust, 294
Grand Marnier mousse, 290
Green beans, see Beans, green
Gribiche sauce, 28
Grilled duck Zinfandel, 184
Grilled Quail, 187
Grilled shrimp with leeks and fennel,
    212
Grilling, about, 8, 214
    equipment, 10

H

Haddock
    in broiled fish steaks with
        basil-walnut sauce, 206
    in fillets of fish martini, 202
    in fish fillets with sauce rouge,
        199
    in lemon-lime fillets in parchment
        paper hearts, 208

in warm seafood salad, 222
Halibut
in broiled fish steaks with
basil-walnut sauce, 206
in fish fillets with sauce rouge,
199
in warm seafood salad, 222
Hamburgers, and mayonnaise, 28
Ham, in wok saute of peppers, 264
Herbed chicken breasts, 176
Herbed French vinaigrette, 95
Hollandaise
about, 20-21
blender or food processor
method, 22
direct heat method, 21
variations, 23
Horseradish Béarnaise, 26
Hot apple tart, 298

I

Ice cream maker, about, 10
Ice milk
coffee, 306
ginger, 307
maple walnut, 307
pumpkin rum, 307
vanilla, 306
Immersion blender, about, 10

J

Japanese dressing for snow peas, 101

L

Lamb
mock tenderloin, 147
and mustard Hollandaise, 20
Langoustine, with roasted tenderloin
of beef, 63
Leek(s)
about, 251
chicken fricassee with, and
carrots, 163
grilled shrimp with, and fennel,
212
and pea puree, 253

quiche, 254
Lemon butter sauce, 33
Lemon caper sauce, 142
Lemon glazed carrots, 241
Lemon-lime fillets in parchment paper
hearts, 208
Lemon parsley sauce, 31
Lemon vinaigrette, 96
Lettuce
about, 91-93
soup, "Cream" of, 77
Lobster flamed with Drambuie, 215

M

Maltaise sauce, 23, 233
Mango mousse, 301
Maple walnut ice milk, 307
Mayonnaise I, II, 26, 27
variations, 28
Marinade, for artichokes, 41
Marinated roasted peppers, 263
Meat(s), 115-149
about, 116-121
glaze, 15
and sauce Robert, 26
Melba sauce with candied oranges,
289
Menu planning, about, 9
Milk vs. cream, 6
Mimosa sherbet, 300
Mocha parfait pie, 302
Monkfish à l'Americaine, 218
Mousse
Grand Marnier, 290
mango, 301
salmon, 205
Mousseline sauce, 23
Mozzarella
and tomato pizza, 65
with veal scallops and prosciutto,
140
Mushroom(s), 248-250
about, 248
à la Grecque, 54
caps, 63
caps, with eggplant caviar, 270
in chicken saute with cepes, 162
consomme, two, 86

Salmon
  mousse with fillets of sole, 205
  poached, with Béarnaise, 216
Salt-encased cooking
  about, 8
  for beef tenderloin, 131
  for chicken, 178
  for veal roast, 134
Sauce
  acid-based, about, 33
  basil and tomato, 196
  basil-walnut, 32
  béarnaise, 24, 25
  black bean, 60
  cassis, 308
  champagne, 194
  cheese, 29
  for chicken salad, 160
  cider cream, 141
  cranberried apple, 180
  crème blanc, 37
  discolored, about, 35
  egg-based, about, 20
  flour-based, about, 28
  gingered beer, 124
  gribiche, 28
  herb-based, about, 31
  Hollandaise, 21, 22
  horseradish Béarnaise, 26
  lemon butter, 33
  lemon caper, 142
  lemon parsley, 31
  maltaise, 23
  mayonnaise, 26, 27, 28
  melba, 289
  mousseline, 23
  mustard Hollandaise, 174
  mustard tarragon, 226
  remoulade, 56
  Robert, 26
  rouge, 199
  tomato, 36
  velouté, 30
  verte, 50
  wine, 34
Sausage
  beef paupiettes with, and
    zucchini, 128
  and clam appetizers, 46

"Saute," about, 6
Sauteed Scallops, 211
Scallops
  bouillabaisse of, 69
  coquilles St. Jacques, 192
  sauteed, 211
  in seviche, 62
  sole and pea pod salad with, 224
  in warm seafood salad, 222
Scotch chicken, 175
Scotch onions, 252
Seafood (also see Fish)
  crepes in champagne sauce, 194
  warm salad with Chinese
    noodles, 222
Sesame broccoli, 237
Sesame chicken salad, 158
Sesame seed dressing, 99
Sesame seeds, how to toast, 159
Seviche, 62
Shellfish, 189-227
  about, 191-192
Sherbet, mimosa, 300
Sherried mushrooms, 250
Sherry ginger dressing, 113
Shrimp
  in confetti rice salad, 110
  grilled, with leeks and fennel, 212
  in mushrooms caps, 63
  in pasta and lemon parsley sauce,
    31
  in seafood crepes, 194
  in sole and peppers, 60
  in warm seafood salad, 222
Silverstone-coated pans, about, 10
Simply roasted chicken, 168
Smoking foods, about, 183
  turkey, 182
Snow peas, see Peas
Sole
  in broiled fish fillets, 204
  and crab peppers, 60
  fillets of, with basil and tomato,
    196
  fillets of, with salmon mousse,
    205
  in lemon-lime fillets with
    parchment paper hearts, 208
  scallop and pea pod salad, 224

Tuna
and Bibb, and green bean salad,
108
with mustard tarragon sauce,
226
Turkey
Chinese tea-smoked, 182
cutlet with cranberried apple
sauce, 180
Two mushroom consomme, 86

V

Vanilla, about, 310
Vanilla ice milk, 306
Veal
chops with red pepper butter,
136
paupiettes, 138
and pork croquettes, 142
roast with sun-dried tomatoes
roasted in salt, 134
scallops, 140
stock 16
Vegetables, 229-282
about, 230
and Béarnaise sauce, 24
and Hollandaise sauce, 20
pureeing, 9
raw, see Crudités
stir-fried chicken and, 172
Velouté sauce, 30
Vinaigrette
about, 93-94
balsamic-walnut oil, 97
fresh herb, 100
herbed French, 95

lemon, 96
tomato, 165
Vinegars, about, 96

W

Walnut oil and balsamic vinegar,
vinaigrette, 97
Water chestnut and pea pod salad,
with sherry ginger dressing,
113
Wilted cucumber salad, 105
Wine
sauce, 34
white, with mussels and saffron,
220
Winter squash, see Squash, winter
Wok saute of peppers and broccoli,
264

Y

Yogurt
about, 227
in crème blanc, 37
and mayonnaise dressing, 94

Z

Zinfandel, grilled duck, 184
Zucchini
in beef paupiettes, 128
boats with eggplant caviar, 270
dilled, and carrot salad, 104
in ratatouille, 272
saute, 269
soup, curried, 82
in wok saute of peppers, 264

About the Author

❖

For eight years **Greer Underwood** has been a cooking teacher specializing in reduced-calorie gourmet dishes. Her love of cooking was sparked by two years in Europe during which she was exposed to and fascinated by the foods of many countries. Being small in size, however, Greer had to learn ways to combine her love of fine food with her knowledge of calories and nutrition.

Besides teaching Greer markets a small line of specialty sauces under the name, Foodstuff. She is a member of Boston's Women's Culinary Guild, and lives in Hingham, Massachusetts, with her husband and two small children.

Greer's food articles have appeared in *The Boston Globe, The Christian Science Monitor, Early American Life, Self, Creative Ideas for Living,* and other national magazines.

Enjoy other fine cookbooks from Globe Pequot Press:

Bluefish Cookbook
Canning and Preserving without Sugar
Catch-of-the-Day
Catfish Cookbook
Enlightened Gourmet
Feast of Fishes
Fructose Cookbook
Salmon Cookbook
Seafood As We Like It
Substituting Ingredients
Sweets Without Guilt

Available at your bookstore or direct from the publisher. For a free catalogue or to place an order, call 1-800-243-0495 (in Connecticut, call 1-800-962-0973) or write to The Globe Pequot Press, 138 West Main Street, Chester, Connecticut 06412.